Bubby's Stories

Belarus to the Bronx

a biography

ROSLYN ROTHSTEIN

BUBBY'S STORIES is a biography, and as such a work of non-fiction. It is to the best of my ability and my family's memories, historically factual and accurate.

Roslyn Rothstein

ISBN-13: 978-1539591238

ISBN-10: 1539591239

ACKNOWLEDGMENTS

I want to thank all those who have helped with this book. In particular, my son Roger Rothstein; without his encouragement and guidance BUBBY'S STORIES would not have been finished or published. My heartfelt gratitude goes to my daughter, Sonnie Elahna for her love and wisdom, and to my niece Lesli Kalin Stolov for her beautiful smile and generosity of spirit. I also want to thank my friends Roberta Collins, Natalie Dornfest, Eleanor Fein, Janet Giewat, Linda Markowitz, Barbara Mair, Victoria Rosenstreich and Carole Siegel for their kindness and love and for being so smart. Additionally, my thanks for his help go to Stephen M. Samtur, publisher/editor of "Back In The Bronx Magazine".

I especially want to thank my very dear friend the Hon. Carole P. Levy for her patience and all her efforts in editing this book.

I am forever appreciative that my sister and brother-in-law, Bea and Morton Kalin and my brother and sister-in-law, Martin and Sandra Mann are older than me, because they have always been there for me. For this and for all they have done for me and for their generous love, I am grateful.

Finally, my deepest gratitude to everyone in my family for their patience with my questions and for opening their hearts and memories to tell me these stories.

Roslyn Mnuskin Rothstein

৯০ TABLE OF CONTENTS ଓ

DEDICATION

This book is dedicated to my parents, Frieda and Solomon Mnuskin, (the *bubby* and *zaidy* of Bubby's Stories). They were always there for me, my sister and brother, and our children. My parents taught us that we are remembered for what we do for those who have the least among us. My father, a very loving person, always gave everyone he met the benefit of the doubt and, in so doing, taught us to trust and love our fellow man. My mother always taught us, and still said this when she was 95, that if she and her sister could come across the world all by themselves when they were no more than little girls, we can do anything anyone else can do, and we can only succeed if we try. For these things, and for everything else they did for us, I am grateful to them and for them.

Roslyn Mnuskin Rothstein

Bubby's Stories

❧ *Not A Children's Book* ❧

$\mathcal{G}$oing back to nobody remembers when, my parents, their entire families, and all of our ancestors were all born in Belarus. My brother, sister and I, and most of our first cousins, are our family's first generation that were born in America.

This book started in my mom's kitchen in 1979, when my son, Roger, a ten-year-old little boy then, made fun of her Yiddish accent. I told Roger that we don't make fun of the way people speak, and if he came from somewhere else, he would speak differently chartoo. His response surprised my mother, father and me, when he asked what we were talking about, and didn't Bubby and Zaidy just come from right there on 94ᵗʰ Street? My mother, (Roger's bubby), started telling him about where she came from. Growing up, I had heard a lot of these stories many times. Some of them were new to me, but, as an adult, I was listening with new ears.

Roger always called my parents bubby and zaidy. We all called my parents that, starting with their first grandchild. The Yiddish words bubby and zaidy mean grandma and grandpa, and my parents accepted being called bubby and zaidy very proudly.

Bubby's Stories was originally meant to be a children's book composed of the stories that my mother had told Roger. The truth is that my mother had other stories and so did my father, but I had a hard time writing about them; some of the stories were unbearably painful and not suitable for children. Then every time I thought I was finished writing this book, somebody else in the family told me about another episode in this saga that just had to be included. My family's stories are incredible, but they are all true. You couldn't make this stuff up.

My parents were very wonderful people who were warm, generous and affectionate, and had been through a lot in their lives. They were both very witty, smart, and had a lot of common sense, even though my father used to say that common sense was not so common. I felt I had to write their stories. I felt compelled to write and share my family's history not because it is unique to my family, but because it isn't. *Bubby's Stories* is the story of a typical Jewish immigrant family that came and settled in America in the early part of the twentieth century.

It is strange but I seem to be writing using almost the same syntax as that of my mother's speech. I can hear her talking.   os

๙ *Bubby's Kitchen* ෫
(about 1979)

"Okay, boychick, it's time for lunch. Go get washed-up and come to the table. I have some of your favorites."

"All right Bubby," Roger answered his grandmother.

Roger's grandmother almost always called him *boychick*. *Boychick* means "little boy" in Yinglish.

Ten-year-old Roger was visiting my parents for the weekend. He loved being there. Roger thought that the little, overcrowded apartment on the Upper West Side of Manhattan, where his grandparents doted on him, and introduced him to things that were different from home, was the most wonderful place in the world.

There was something interesting to look at wherever you turned. Bubby and Zaidy's apartment was filled with their overstuffed furniture that was all covered in plastic slipcovers, even the lampshades. The furniture looked like it was still in the packaging, even though it was all bought a long time ago. In summer, the plastic slipcovers were uncomfortable to sit on because your skin would stick to the seats, and in the winter the seats were cold. But Bubby wanted to keep the furniture covered so it would stay clean and new because they could not afford to replace it easily. Every tabletop in the apartment was covered with papers, bills, letters, ads, solicitations of one kind or another. And everywhere were framed and unframed photographs of important people that Bubby and Zaidy admired, mainly Democratic politicians. Photographs of the family were there too, of course. There was all sorts of stuff from Israel and from years ago. The walls were covered with pictures and Jewish mementos, new Jewish and American calendars, and old New York City political posters.

The apartment was clean but not very neat. Housekeeping wasn't one of Bubby's favorite activities. There were always more important things that my mother felt she had to do that kept her from housekeeping. And neither of my parents ever threw anything out. Thrifty and not believing in waste, my father always used to say, "Save it, it may comes-to-needs." Meaning, whatever it was, may one day come in handy.

One of the many reasons Roger loved coming to visit them was because of the food. Bubby's kitchen always smelled so good. This time, it smelled of onions and beef frying in a pan. Bubby was making *kreplach* (krep' lock), pan fried beef and onion dumplings. They're the Jewish version of Chinese won tons, and Roger's favorite food in the world. She always made some special foods when he came. Sometimes you couldn't recognize what it was, and some of the names were hard to say, but it always tasted delicious.

Bubby loved to cook and almost nothing ever came out of a can when Bubby was cooking. She didn't believe in restaurants either. She thought they were a waste of good money when there was plenty of good food right there in the house. Bubby's cooking also tasted better than anything you could get in a restaurant. She would say that she didn't cook much anymore, because she usually had no one to cook for but Zaidy. Whether she had anyone to cook for or not, it seemed as though when she was home she spent all of her time in the kitchen cooking.

Zaidy was the only person who ever complained about Bubby's cooking. He was always saying it was either too lumpy or too hard - something was always wrong with it. It was mainly because of his false teeth. They made it hard for him to chew. He frequently took his dentures out because they were uncomfortable.

Whenever Roger was there, and he had to take his false teeth out, Zaidy would make the funniest faces. It made Roger laugh until Roger could barely stop.

During Roger's visits, unless it rained, Zaidy always took Roger for a walk. They would go to the little ice cream store on Broadway that sold raspberry ices. Zaidy always teased him about his not really wanting ices, but they both knew that it was a game.

The best part of the visit for Roger was always Bubby's stories. She knew so many good ones. Some of them were about Bubby when she was young. She always said that they were true, but Roger found it hard to picture his chubby bubby any differently than she was.

Zaidy, who was pretty chubby himself, would often say that when they met, Bubby was one of the prettiest girls in the city. Bubby would smile whenever he said it, and her cheeks would get almost as pink as Zaidy's always were.

Roger hurried to get washed. He knew he was in for a treat. His grandmother was always willing to tell him a story while he ate. She thought it made him eat more. Bubby thought that Roger never ate enough, and was always wishing that he wasn't so skinny. She would do anything to get him to eat more food.

"Are you ready to eat boychick?" she asked him. "Let me see your hands. Are they clean?"

"Yes, Bubby."

"Ok, so come sit down while the food is hot."

"Tell me about where you came from Bubby," Roger asked while sitting down at the table.

"Oh, you don't want to hear about that again, do you?"

"Yes, I do Bubby," Roger pleaded.

"All right, my little love. You eat, and I'll talk."

After Roger had finished his lunch, his zaidy was about to take him to get ices, when Roger begged his bubby to go with them to buy ices. "I want you to come, "Roger pleaded.

"I can't come now. I have to clean out the Frigidaire[1]. Something spilled in there and made an awful mess," his grandmother answered him.

"Come with us Fradal (frAy′ dal)." Zaidy called to his wife by her Jewish name. We will help you when we come back, and I promise to get you a double pistachio ice cream, in a sugar cone." Roger's grandpa said.

"Well, if you make promises like that, how can I refuse? All I need is an ice cream cone to add another few inches to my skinny, mini waist." Roger's chubby grandmother joked. "And the *Frigidaire* is going to walk away and hide in shame."

"Don't worry so much from the Frigidaire." his grandfather said, helping Bubby on with her coat. "If the Frigidaire is so stupid as to leave such a good home, where it's always kept full, in case someone should maybe come, then let it go. It will be a good excuse for the landlord to give us a new one." Zaidy answered her jokingly.

"Be careful *fa da* cars Roger." his grandmother warned as she always did when they walked down the crowded, Manhattan streets.

"I am not a baby, Bubby. I know how to cross the street." Roger told his grandmother.

"Yes, I know, I am just reminding you." Bubby said.

"How come you and Bubby don't have a car Zaidy?" Roger asked.

"Well to tell you the truth boychick, I don't see as well as I once did, and I can't hear so good *neader*." his zaidy answered him. "It would be hard for me to drive. But I'll tell you a secret, just between you and me and the lamppost, your bubby is still afraid *fa* cars. She's been here in this country almost 60 years already, she should live and be well, she still doesn't trust them."

---

[1] *Frigidaire* frid ge dare′ *n.-* the brand name of one of the first mass produced refrigerators for residential use. It became a generic word for all refrigerators.

"Okay, already you don't have to give away all of my secrets." Bubby told Zaidy. To Roger she said, "When we get home I will tell you about the first time I ever saw a car."

"Roger watch your step crossing the street. There is a car coming." Roger's bubby warned, as she tightened her hand on his. "There is the ice cream store on the next corner."

"Zaidy can I have a double too, like Bubby? And I want a spoon with it so I won't drop any."

"I thought we were only coming here to get some ice cream for Bubby and me. You want some too boychick?" *Zaidy* chuckled at his own joke.

Almost as soon as they came back into the apartment, Roger's bubby said, "Okay, you two. You promised to help clean out the Frigidaire, and I'm holding you to it. Come over here and take some of these things," she said, as she bent over the refrigerator shelves. "I should have stayed home and done this instead of going for pistachio ice cream, but I love pistachio ice cream. It's my weakness. I can't resist it and your zaidy knows it. He tempted me."

"Bubby, would you tell me about when you saw a car for the first time?" Roger asked. "Roger honey, you can't imagine how scared I was the first time I saw a one." Bubby said. "You know the world didn't always have cars. Some smart guy built one for the first time. He took a wagon and put a machine on it to make it go. Before that we used horses, oxen and other animals to ride on, and to pull the wagons. I'm still not sure that wasn't one hundred percent better. They didn't go so fast or make so much pollution. A person can't even cross the street today without taking his life in his hands; a car shouldn't knock him down. Who needs it! Feh! But I still wish I knew how to drive.

"You know Roger; I can't understand your mother, or what she sees in it. Museums, restaurants we got here, maybe even better ones. Your mommy is dying she should be able to go to Europe. We couldn't wait to get out from Europe and that's where she wants to go. She isn't the only one; lots of people want to go to Europe today. They call that a vacation yet! I ask you, what could be better than here? Well must be a new world. I guess next you'll want to go to Europe too...hey boychick? Me, I'll go to Miami, better."

With his pleading and my mother's own pleasure in sharing her stories, she would tell Roger about where she came from on the other side of the ocean.   ❧

ஃ *On the Other Side the Ocean* ௧

My mother, Fradal Valevelsky was born in a small village called Drohitchin (Dra' hit chin) in Yiddish and Drahichyn in Belarussian. It was a *shtetl²*, really a *dorf. Shtetl* is the Yiddish word for village. A *dorf* is a village that was even smaller than a shtetl. Drohitchin is in Belarus, in what used to be a part of the Russian Empire that was called The Pale of Settlement. The Pale as it was known, was where the Jews were allowed to live in Russia until the Russian Revolution. But there were Jews in Belarus long before the Russians stopped allowing the Jews to live anywhere they wanted to other than The Pale. There were Jews in Drohitchin for more than five hundred years.

Drohitchin is in the area known as the Paliessie. The Paliessie is a marshy lowland that spreads all along the banks of the Pripyat River from the Dnieper River on the western end all the way through the southern part of Belarus to the Bug River on the eastern end. The Paliessie area is very famous for its swamps and marshes. Drohitchin is in the middle of a particularly large marsh called the Vion.

Places near marshy areas are wet, damp and muddy. The Vion made Drohitchin very damp and the ground was always full of

---

² *shtetl* - shtet' el *n.* – Yiddish: a small Eastern European town or village with a predominantly Jewish population; *pl. n.* – *shtetlakch* shtet' lokh

puddles of mud. People covered the deep puddles with large wooden boards so that it was easier to walk down the street. Everybody wore galoshes and boots most of the time to keep their feet dry. In the winter, the puddles froze and turned to ice, making the ground very slippery. Where you have a marsh, you have bugs and frogs. The Vion had a lot of both. You could hear the frogs from the Vion croaking all during the spring and summer. Each spring, when the farmers heard the first frogs begin to croak, they knew that it was time to plant oats. The higher ground was dryer and very sandy. That is where the people who had more money lived. Not that many people had much money, but some had more than others.

The Vion didn't just have frogs and bugs; it also had small fish, crabs, snails, lizards, loaches and worms, turtles and small animals. The *goyim*[3] used to catch crabs and loaches and cook them. They said they made delicious dishes with these creatures, but Jews don't eat that kind of animal. My mother said that she never tasted that stuff; those animals aren't kosher. It didn't sound too tasty to her anyway.

---

[3] *goyim* go' yim *pl.n.*– Gentiles, non-Jews; *goy* goy - (rhymes w. boy)*sn.* - a Gentile, a man who is not Jewish; *goya* goy' a *n.*- a woman who is not Jewish; *goyish* or *goyishe* or *goyisher* goy' ish / goy' ish e / goy' ish er *adj.* - Gentile, not Jewish   These words are not pejorative. The words *goy, goyim, goyish*, etc. are neutral words that only mean Gentiles, non-Jews or non-Jewish. The words *goy, goyim* and *goyish* are similar in use to the words black and white when referring to African Americans and Caucasians. As the words black and white are not in themselves pejoratives, the words *goy, goyim* and *goyish* also depend on the intent of the speaker to know if their use is derogatory or not.

BELARUS

**[Map:]Belarus (aka White Russia) part of Imperial Russia
(Belarus is an independent country as of the collapse of
the Soviet Union in 1991)**

Sometimes in the fall and spring, after a lot of rain, the Vion would overflow and the water would flood Drohitchin. Sometimes, the water would reach the houses. In the winter, the Vion froze over. Winter time a lot of the kids played in the Vion. It was fun to go sledding there on the ice. You had to be careful that the ice wasn't too thin. In the summer, the Vion used to dry out somewhat.

Weeping willow trees, reeds and all sorts of grasses grew there. The kids used to go barefoot and run around in the marsh grasses. They played hide-and-seek; that was fun. They made whistles out of the reeds.

People had to be very careful walking near the Vion. When the ground felt too soft, you walked a different way, because you could fall into a mud hole that was literally up to your neck if you didn't watch where you were going, and then you would have a very hard time getting out. Before *Sukkot*[4], the Jews used to go to the Vion to get reeds and branches to use for their *sukkahs*[5].

Drohitchin was also situated right near a very deep forest. There were all sorts of animals in the forest: foxes, wolves, deer. There were beavers, raccoons, opossums, muskrats. And there were all kinds of little birds and big birds, like owls and hawks. People said there were bears in the woods, but Fradal never saw one there.

The house Fradal's family lived in when she was born was a little wooden house with only two rooms. It didn't have indoor plumbing with sinks and toilets. They kept a barrel for water that they filled from the outdoor well they shared with a lot of their neighbors. They used to take the buckets to the well to get water, and then had to shlep the very heavy buckets back. The people who could afford it used a paid water carrier, but Fradal's family didn't have money for that kind of extravagance. If they wanted hot water, they had to build a fire and heat the water in a kettle on the stove. The toilet was a little chamber pot. When they finished using it, they took the chamber pot outside to a hole that they dumped the contents in. They didn't have electricity and electric lights; nobody in Drohitchin did. Oil lamps and candles were used at night.

Drohitchin was very poor. Almost no one had anything much at all. There wasn't much money in the shtetl and there weren't

---

[4] *Sukkot* is the Feast of Tabernacles and is the Jewish harvest holiday similar to American's Thanksgiving Day

[5] Sukkahs are temporary little huts that Jewish people build to eat, sleep and spend time in during the week of Sukkot

enough jobs. Russia was at war, and things weren't well. From hunger they didn't starve, but plenty of times their bellies were empty. There were the pogroms and then the wars. In wartime, nobody had anything. It seemed like Russia was always at war, and every time they had a war, Belarus was where it all happened. Belarus was a battleground for more than six hundred years. It has the bad luck to be right in the middle between Poland, Ukraine, Russia and Germany. These countries have always wanted each other's land. So they were always fighting with each other. The Jews that lived in Belarus took no glory and no benefit from these wars. They were just on-lookers, in the way, and innocent victims.

By 1921, Drohitchin had been burned down and rebuilt three times, and lots of people lost everything. Fradal's family was lucky; in the last fire they lost their house, but they went and lived in a house where the people had run away. Those people were Gentiles. Fradal's family were afraid they would come back and kill them for moving into their house; but they never did come back. Sometimes the people of Drohitchin even had to go hide in the trenches. They were frequently afraid that their homes would be bombed or burn down. The trenches had been dug by the town's people years before during another war.

The Jews in Drohitchin were not rich. They were mainly tradesmen working from day to day, trying to scrape out a living. When the war was going on, people really couldn't get much work done. A lot of the men who didn't have jobs left their families and went looking for jobs elsewhere. One day, Fradal's father kissed his wife and three children and said goodbye. He said he was going to go to America to find a job in the "golden land." The children were Fradal, her brother Hunia (rhymes with bun' ia) and her sister Hasha. Fradal's papa said he would send for them when he got settled and got some money. He told them he had to try to make a better life for them than the one they could expect in Drohitchin. He told Hunia he would have to be strong and take care of the family, because he was the man now. Before they could say no, don't go, he was gone.

Their papa often sent them letters telling them how hard things were until he got to America and found a job, and how much he missed them. They couldn't wait for their papa's letters to come. They were frightened without him and missed him very much. When they were cold or hungry, they always took comfort from his singing. Their papa was always singing and telling stories, even when he was sad. It always made them feel better to hear their papa. After he left they couldn't even hear him singing. Then only the marsh frogs sang.

Fradal used to chase after her father's cousin, Gedaliah (Ge dal' ya). He was the mailman. After her father left, Fradal was always pestering Gedaliah for a letter from him. Whenever she saw Gedaliah she went shouting after him, asking, "*A brievele fun mine taten?*" (A letter from my father?). Gedaliah would bend down and kindly tell her, "Fradal, I'll bring it when it comes. You could be sure."

Once in a while, a letter would come from their father with a little bit of money. Fradal's mother's name was Chaiya Bailya. Chaiya Bailya used to take the money and buy food for them. Neither one of Fradal's parents knew how to write. They knew how to read a little Yiddish and the Hebrew *siddur* (sid' der - prayer book) but not much else. So their papa used to ask someone to write his letter for him. When the letters came, Chaiya Bailya would ask Gedaliah to sit down and wait for her to read it. And then Gedaliah would write an answer for her. They used to wear the paper out trying to read their papa's letters.

It wasn't like here in America, where everybody goes to school, like it or not. They were poor and their world seemed to always be at war. The men in the *shul* (synagogue) pushed for the smart boys like Hunia to go to school to learn the *Torah*. They even gave Hunia food and made him stay there when things were bad. But Fradal and Hasha couldn't go to school very much. It was often out of the question. They were poor; so they would have let them go for free, but they didn't have proper clothes or shoes to wear. They used to wear cut up rubber from old galoshes on their feet tied together with twine. Fradal's mother used to say that they had to learn to read and write and to know things; that they shouldn't be ignorant like her. She would say it is a sin not to be educated. But Hasha and Fradal were girls. People then thought girls didn't need to study like boys. It doesn't seem possible that they could have managed to learn anything because they would go to school one day and ten days not. But somehow, Hasha and Fradal tried hard to learn and they did learn to read and write in Yiddish. Yiddish is written in the Hebrew alphabet so the girls were able to read the Bible and the prayer books.

Sometimes they were able to go to the classes that Gedaliah taught. He, like his father, was very educated. Gedaliah used to say, "It is a Jewish tradition to study and gain as much knowledge as possible so they could be good Jews and good people. Almost nothing is more important to Jews than learning. Because in ignorance there is fear and fear is what makes people do stupid, evil things." Gedaliah used to say, "You should study and learn and teach the blessing of knowledge and study to your children and to your children's children."

When winter came, they had very little food and almost no warm clothing. Chaiya Bailya made coats for them from an old, army horse blanket a friend had given her. The blanket still had the Czar's army stamp on it and it itched like crazy but kept them warm. Fradal was very ashamed to wear that coat, but felt lucky to have it. When somebody would tease her by asking her which regiment she belonged to, she would tell them to go ask the horse. ❦

℘ *Hasha, She Was the Oldest* ℘

One day, Gedaliah brought a small package from Fradal's father with a letter. Gedaliah never brought them a package before, only the letters from their papa, and once in a great while, a letter from their mama's family in Pinsk. But there it was, on the table. Not just a letter, this time it was a package from America. It wasn't a large package but was obviously not just a letter. There was something more to this bundle. They were afraid to open it. They just starred at it. Then their mother very carefully opened it. Out rolled, almost falling on the floor, a *dudki*[6] - musical double pipes. Hunia's eyes lit up as he grabbed for it. He didn't even wait just put it in his mouth and started playing. It was made of two wooden pipes of different lengths. You blow into both pipes at the same time blowing out a song. I don't know how Hunia knew how to play the dudki the minute he put it in his mouth, but he did.

After they stopped watching Hunia dance around, making music with the dudki, they went back to looking at the rest of that little package. It had a surprise in it for each of them. For Hasha and Fradal and their mama, their papa had sent each of them a shining,

---

[6] dudki - parnyia dudki, also called "parniouka." "parnyaty." "hoosli." – wooden, musical double pipes,. One is longer than the other and they are attached by a cord. About a foot long, each pipe has a hole at the top and fingering holes at the bottom.

little gold locket. Their eyes nearly burst when they saw the jewelry. They put these precious little golden hearts on their necks; they could not believe that they had gotten such wondrous gifts. None of them had ever had anything so luxurious, so fancy before. They never expected to have anything like that. They were so proud. Their papa had sent them gold from the *golden land.*

**[Photo:] Belarusian man playing a *dudki*,
Belarus, (ca. 20th century)**
Photo courtesy of National Tourism Agency of Belarus

Chaiya Bailya picked up the letter and read it to them. It said that their papa had met a *landsman* (someone from the "old country") who made the dudki for him. In the letter their father also said that he was working hard and was saving the money to send for them so they could go to America.

Fradal's mother put the letter down and looked at Fradal and Hasha admiring the lockets around their necks. She held her own locket hanging from her own neck. She told her two daughters she was sorry, but they had to be careful. And that they should wear the lockets under their shirts and not say anything about them to anyone. She said that they should just enjoy the lockets privately and that nobody needs to know their business. She wasn't used to having such fancy things and it made her nervous to be wearing gold when they had so little else.

Chaiya Bailya asked Gedaliah if he knew anybody who needed help with their children. Gedaliah said yes. He had heard that there was a family on the other side of Drohitchin that needed help - the Torah scribe and his wife.

Their mama said that she thought that it would be better if Hasha would go to work for them, if they would have her. At least she would be warm and have food. Their mama also said that she was having trouble with her stomach, but when it stopped hurting she would also find a job, as a *dinst* (a maid). That was what she used to do in Pinsk, where she was from, before she married her husband and came to live in Drohitchin.

Hasha's full name was Hasha Devorah, but everyone just called her Hasha. She was five years older than Fradal. Hasha was the oldest and Fradal was the youngest. Fradal stayed home with her mama. You could see Hasha didn't want to go but she knew things would be better if she went. She would be able to help the family more if she went than if she stayed. So, when Gedaliah came back and said that he had spoken to the scribe and his wife, and that they wanted Hasha to come work for them, she went.

It was so many years ago, that, in telling me this story, my mother didn't remember that family's name. They had five children and lived near the bridge on Kobrin Street. Once she was there, she hated working for that family. Hasha said she liked the children, but the mother was mean. She said she thought it was because the woman was pregnant with her sixth child and was not doing well. She let out her pain on Hasha. The woman made Hasha work very hard doing a lot of the cleaning, cooking, getting wood for the stove, getting water from the well, not just taking care of the children. And worst of all, that woman never had a kind word to say. Hasha said that the husband, the scribe was a nice man. He was a very quiet, but a learned man. He had a lot of books, and he let Hasha read his books.

Besides making Torah scrolls, scribes make a living by also doing wedding certificates and other religious papers that have sacred writing, but they mainly spend their time making Torahs. It takes about a year to make a kosher Torah scroll and it must be perfect to be kosher. Machine printed Torahs or improperly written Torahs are not kosher. And if a Torah isn't kosher, you can't use it in prayer service in a synagogue. To be kosher, it cannot have even one letter wrong. So, the scribe spent most of his time in his studio at a table, bent over some parchment or another that he was inscribing. Concentrating on his work, the scribe didn't have time to see what was happening in the rest of his house, and he didn't see how mean his wife had become.

The scribe started allowing Hasha to read his books after one time, when he had heard his wife yell at Hasha without real reason. The scribe called Hasha into his study. He asked Hasha to please be patient with his wife, because she was having a hard time with this pregnancy and was in pain. He said she was not always like this. He told Hasha he knew it was hard, but he hoped she would not take it to heart. Hasha was standing next to his bookcase. He hadn't noticed till this time, the look of admiration she had on her face for his books. Books were very dear then. The scribe asked Hasha if she liked to read. She said yes, but that she didn't read well. He told her it took practice. You have to keep reading, and then you get to be able to read easily. The scribe said it is a sin to be ignorant. As a peace offering and an act of kindness, he offered to let Hasha read his books if she promised to be very careful with them. Whenever Hasha had time, she buried herself in one of his books. And whenever she could, she went home.

[Photo:] Dovid Elye, a Torah and sacred document scribe,
Annopol, Poland (ca. 1912)

The Torah is the Bible, the Five Books of Moses. It is believed to be the word of G_d as He told it to Moses. The Torah is sacred to the Jewish people and is the written Jewish law. Gentiles call the Five Books of Moses the Old Testament. The Torah is so sacred to Jews that they will run into a synagogue that is on fire to save the Torahs scrolls.

The Torah is read formally, out loud, during services in the synagogue on *Shabbat*[7] *(the Sabbath)*, holidays, Rosh Chodesh[8], Monday and Thursday mornings. It takes about a year to read the whole Torah. It is read starting at the beginning, reading every week a different part called a *parsha*. In this way, it is read straight through to the end. In synagogues all over the world, every year on

---

[7] *Shabbat* (Hebrew) or *Shabbos* (Yiddish) the Sabbath
[8] Rosh Chodesh – is the first day of each month on the Jewish calendar. It begins with a new moon and is a minor holiday.

Simchat Torah, the Torah holiday, about 23 days after Rosh Hashanah[9], they finish reading the Torah with the last two verses of Deuteronomy, and then start again with reading the first verses of Genesis. Jews have been reading the same part of the Torah, the same week of the year, all over the world, for thousands of years. And regardless of what country they live in, and what language they usually speak, on Shabbos, and the other designated days, in synagogues all over the world, Jews, whether wrapped in their prayer shawls, with their heads covered or not, all read the same part of the Torah, and say the same blessings.

The Torah scrolls, used in synagogues, are written on parchment. Parchment is made from animal skins, and every part of the Torah, from the skins for the parchment, to the sinews that bind the skins together, to the feather quills used to write, all must come from kosher animals. From the beginning, the parchment maker knows that the parchment is going to be used for a Torah and he has been trained to make parchment that is meant to be used to make sacred documents.

The skins are treated with salt, flour and gallnut water. They are scraped, dried, cured and stretched. Once, when the scribe was starting a new Torah, he sent Hasha to the parchment maker, to ask when the first skins he had ordered would be ready for him. He needed some of the parchment to be dried and ready in about a week. Hasha told Fradal that she was able to watch the parchment maker stretching the skin.

---

[9] Rosh Hashanah - a solemn Jewish feast day commemorating the beginning of the Jewish New Year and the creation of the world.

.

[Photo:] **parchment maker, Havant, England**
(ca. early 20th century)
Photo courtesy of the Havant Museum, Hampshire Cultural Trust, England

A kosher Torah scroll is a masterpiece. It is a lot of work to make one and to be a Torah scribe. The Torah scribe must be trained to do every part of it. Torahs are usually about two feet high and weigh about twenty to twenty-five pounds. They use between 62 and 84 sheets of parchment, and every part of the Torah must be made by Jews according to very exact rules, the same way that it has always been done. From beginning to end, it must be made and written the same way it was by Moses the first time, 5,000 years ago.

Besides, knowing how to write a kosher Torah, and how to put it together, the Torah scribe must learn more than 4,000 Judaic laws so that he can understand what he is writing.

Today, the Torah scribes buy the special ink. It is much easier now, because it is a job and a half to make the ink. Years ago, a scribe started getting ready to make a Torah by making the very black, non-erasable ink himself. He made the ink by boiling oils, tar and wax, and mixing them with tree sap, soot, and honey. He then dried that mixture out. Before he used it, he mixed it with gallnut juice and water. Gallnuts are not really nuts; they are the empty nests from gall wasps which are found on oak trees. Gallnuts have been used to make ink since the beginning of time.

The scribe only mixes about two teaspoons of ink at a time, so it won't get too dried out. Then he gets his feather or reed pens ready. The pens cannot be made of iron because weapons are made of iron, and it is a sin to touch a Torah with a weapon. Most scribes use a feather from a goose or a turkey as a pen. These animals are kosher and the pen that is used to write a Torah must also be completely kosher. The rabbis say that if a Torah is only 99% kosher, it is also 100% not kosher.

A Torah has exactly 304,805 letters. Each page has 42 lines that are written in perfect Hebrew calligraphy (and some Aramaic). If the scribe is right-handed, he can only write with his right hand, and if he is left-handed, he can only write with his left hand. It is forbidden to add any other decorations or drawings. One letter must never touch another letter and every word must be spelled exactly right. If even one letter is missing, or misshapen, it wouldn't be kosher, and that Torah cannot be used.

The scribe must also be very pious. Before the scribe begins, he enters an almost spiritual state of mind. He prays that he will be worthy to make a Torah. First he goes to the *mikvah*[10] for a ritual bathing of his spirit. Then, and each time he picks up his quill to write, and again each time he writes the name of G_d, he says the blessing, "For the sanctity of the Torah." Some scribes chant each letter as they are writing it.

The scribe may not rely on his memory. He copies the letters word for word from another kosher Torah. When he has finished, he and another pious, learned man read the new Torah three times. When they are certain it is perfect, the scribe sews all of the 80 or

---

[10] A *mikvah* is a ritual bath similar to a baptism. The *mikvah* is not for purposes of cleansing the body but a spiritual bathing in order to cleanse the soul.

so sheets of parchment together with thread called *gidden*. The *gidden* is made from the leg sinews of a kosher animal. The scribe attaches each end of the now very long parchment on to a wooden shaft that is used for handles to roll and unroll the Torah. Most Torahs are crowned in silver and covered in beautiful fabric mantles.

[Photo:] Torah scrolls wrapped in mantles and crowns
with breast plates and *yads* (pointers) hanging down.
Photo courtesy of the Ashkenazi Jewish Synagogue, Plymouth, England

When a Torah has become damaged by fire or flood or just torn and worn out, it can't be thrown away or burned. It must be ceremoniously buried in a Jewish cemetery on consecrated ground. Jews bury all holy books this way. This is because we can't and won't destroy anything that has the name of G_d written on it; not even a small scrap of paper. We consider it blasphemy. That is why Jews write the word G_d, on papers that are not sacred, by leaving out the o. This is so that it won't matter if that paper is soiled, thrown away or destroyed. Holy books don't just have the name of G_d, but they also have the word of G_d. We bury religious items and holy books with the utmost respect. Holy books, sacred papers, and any papers that have the name of G_d written on them, are sometimes buried with a Jewish person who has died.

When a scribe finishes a Torah that he is making for a synagogue, that synagogue's congregation celebrates. They will be dancing and singing in the street. The Torah will be joyously paraded through the street and carried into the synagogue under the blessings of a wedding canopy, just like a bride. The canopy is to symbolize that G_d is always above us and the Jewish people were wedded to G_d when he gave us the Torah. ⚕

**[Photo:] People dancing and celebrating the completion
of a new Torah, Dubrovna, Belarus (ca. early 20th century)**
Photo courtesy of ttp://litwackfamily.com/the_pale.htm

ℬ *Kuriza, the Chicken* ℭ

One day, Hasha came into the house carrying Kuriza (koor i sah'), Fradal's pet chicken. *Kuriza* is the word for chicken in Belarusian. Fradal never named her; they just called her Kuriza. Hasha said that there were soldiers in the town, and that they should be very careful. You could tell which army they were from by the color of their uniforms. Soldiers were frightening, and sometimes took things they wanted. Times were hard, and the soldiers were hungry too. As hungry as Fradal's family were, they never thought of Kuriza as a meal. It surprised Fradal when Hasha said that, but she thought it was better to be careful. Fradal didn't want Kuriza to be some soldier's dinner.

She had raised her from a tiny little chick. Fradal hand fed Kuriza grain and gave her all the food she could. Now that she was a big hen, she gave them a brown egg every day, which they shared. They often had very little other food. Fradal loved Kuriza. She used to talk to her and cuddled her. Fradal treated Kuriza like she was a puppy. It didn't matter to Fradal that she was just a chicken. Kuriza used to follow behind Fradal wherever she went. People used to point at her and say, look at that chicken following behind Fradal, just like a puppy dog.

One winter day, Fradal was in bed coughing and sneezing. She had a bad cold, and it was cold in the house. They had very little wood. It was hard for their mother and Hunia to get wood and chop enough for them, and they couldn't afford to buy any. When someone caught a cold it seemed to last forever. Chaiya Bailya's friend, Basha Perel had very kindly brought some honey for hot water for Fradal and she was sipping it slowly. They didn't have tea. Kuriza was cuddling up next to Fradal under her featherbed trying to keep warm.

Something in the other room was making a terrible noise. Fradal got scared. She didn't know what it could be. Their mother had warned them many times that it was wartime and that they should be very careful of everything. And after what Hasha had said the day before, Fradal wasn't taking any chances. She got out of her bed very quietly and went to look through the crack in the door. There he was - a uniformed soldier. Fradal never forgot him. He was tall and dark with a mean voice. He was going through their small, poor house looking for something, anything of value to take. Very quietly Fradal hid Kuriza under a straw grain sifter and pushed it under the bed. Terrified, not knowing what to do, she went back to bed and hid crying silently hiding under the quilt. She could hear her mama pleading with him not to harm them. Like thunder he came through the door in his big, black boots. He was searching for anything he could take away with him. He looked all through the little room, everywhere and under everything. He started to get down on his knees to look under the bed when Fradal started coughing. She thought he was going to get Kuriza. Her fear made her cough more. The German soldier seeing how badly she was coughing looked at her and asked, what was wrong with her. Fradal, coughing uncontrollably, put her hands up in a gesture to say 'who knows. Her mother told him to stay away from her because she was very sick. Frightened by Fradal's cough, the soldier stopped looking. He just got up and thundered out of the house, empty-handed.

Hasha, Fradal and their mama started laughing. He thought Fradal could have some terrible disease that he might catch. They took Kuriza out from under the bed. Fradal had made so much noise coughing that no one heard whether Kuriza had ever clucked or not, but she was safe. **CB**

✺ *Gedaliah's Father-In-Law* ❧

*U*nder the Czar, there were no real or formal city halls or town councils in most of the shtetlach. There were the governors of each of the provinces. Drohitchin is in the Grodno Province. So there was the Governor of the Grodno Province, but he was in the Capital city of Grodno, many miles north of Drohitchin. The famous Pyotr Stolypin was made the Governor of Grodno in 1902. He became famous much later, when Czar Nicholas II made him the Prime Minister of Russia. Once, when he was still the Grodno Governor he came to visit Drohitchin on his way to Pinsk. Pyotr Stolypin was the youngest governor they had ever appointed and the meanest. He had had so many men hanged during his time as governor, that they used to call the gallows "Stolypin's necktie."

There were the regional police. They weren't in Drohitchin all of the time, because they had the entire region to watch over. They, too, stayed mainly in Grodno. Then there was the much-hated Drohitchin constable riding around on his huge horse. Everyone was afraid of him. He was the one who took care of the Czar's laws and edicts in Drohitchin. On the orders from higher up in the Russian government, the constables sometimes instigated pogroms. When, the violence got out of hand, the constable would be the one to then stop them. Sometimes they used the Cossacks to start and stop the pogroms. The Czar had all kinds of laws. You needed permission to do anything and everything. If you did something that was against the law, the constable was supposed to take care of it, and there were a lot of restrictions just for the Jews.

Drohitchin didn't have a regular mayor; under the Czar's regime, there was the Jewish Elder. He was like a mayor but just for the Jews of the shtetlach. Fradal's cousin Gedaliah's father-in-law, Shmuel Yudel Piasetsky, was the last Jewish Elder of Drohitchin. He wasn't elected; he was appointed by the Russian authorities and paid out of the shtetl budget. The Russians reappointed him every three years. Shmuel Yudel Piasetsky was born in 1859 to a respected family. They gave him a good education - not just a Jewish education in the Talmud,[11] but a regular Russian education in addition to his Jewish learning. He was very good in his studies, especially Russian. In 1901 when Drohitchin needed a new elder, Shmuel Yudel asked the Russians for the appointment and they agreed to make him the new Elder of Drohitchin.

The Elder was the person who made sure that there was a doctor in town, that the firefighting equipment and the conditions of the Drohitchin bathhouse were ok. He made decisions about the roads. He also acted as mediator for the Jews of Drohitchin with the Russian authorities to alleviate the terrible decrees from the Czar. The Elder went and spoke on behalf of the poor when the tax collectors made their yearly trip to Drohitchin. He was usually not too successful, but would try to get them to waive their penalties and have a little pity. Shmuel Yudel Piasetsky, the Elder, a stout man, wore a gold chain around his neck that hung down to the middle of his chest. He wore it whenever he had important business to do. It gave him confidence, and he felt like it made him appear to have more authority.

---

[11] The **Talmud** – the ancient written record of rabbinic commentaries pertaining to Jewish law, ethics, customs, and history. It was compiled and written before the 8th Century, A.D. by Jewish rabbis. In the Jewish religious tradition, it is second only to the Torah (Bible) in importance and is the basis of most codes of rabbinic law and Jewish traditions.

The one time Governor Stolypin passed through Drohitchin, Shmuel Yudel heard about his coming in advance. He asked his wife Beila to bake bread for him to give to the governor. He thought it would be a good idea to make a good showing for him. Shmuel Yudel wanted the governor to know that the Jews of Drohitchin were not barbarians.

The day that the governor came, Beila woke up very early. It was almost the middle of the night. She baked a large round *challah* bread[12]. She brushed the top with egg yolk so the *challah* would glow. Putting extra raisins in, she braided the bread with a small hole at the top so that there was a place to put the salt dish. Beila placed her best embroidered white cloth on a tray. Then she put the bread on the tray with a small dish of salt on top. This she proudly made ready for Shmuel Yudel to take to the governor.

Shmuel Yudel put on his gold chain like he was putting on his office, and went with the rabbi, and the other leaders of the Jewish community, to welcome Governor Stolypin. They presented him with the bread and salt in the ancient, Eastern European custom of greeting somebody important, or on a special occasion, with this gesture of good luck and hospitality. When they met Governor Stolypin they offered him the bread and salt. The governor bowed his head in thanks and took the bread in both of his hands, and in the traditional way brought it up to his lips and kissed it. He then broke off a piece of bread and dipped it into the salt. He placed the bread and salt in his mouth and smiled. Governor Stolypin then thanked them for their hospitality.

This ancient, Eastern European welcoming custom of giving honored guests bread and salt is practiced by the poor and royalty alike. Traditionally bread and salt are the first things brought into a new Jewish home. The salt is a preservative and symbolizes longevity in relationships. Slavic brides and grooms are also presented with bread and salt to wish them good luck. In 1975, on

---

[12] *challah* - (hal' la) – special braided, egg and yeast rich white bread usually reserved for the Sabbath and holidays

the first joint flight of the U.S. and Soviet space programs, the Russian astronauts presented the Americans with crackers and salt tablets on the Apollo-Soyuz spaceship.

During Governor Stolypin's visit, Shmuel Yudel managed to convince the Governor to pave Drohitchin's horribly muddy roads. He told the governor truthfully that it would be better for trade. To Shmuel Yudel's own surprise, Stolypin agreed and the roads were paved. The Drohitchin roads still got flooded, but at least they weren't as muddy as before.

[Photo:] Józef Piłsudski the Marshal of Poland being welcomed
with bread and salt by the Jewish elders of Dęblin, Poland
after the liberation of the city from the Bolsheviks during
the Russo-Polish War   (ca. 1920)
Photo courtesy of Museum of Polish History, Warsaw, Poland

Once a year, the Elder had the hideous job of leading the recruiting committee in making up "the list." It was a list of Jewish young men who were chosen to be conscripted into the army whether they liked it or not, unless of course they could buy their way out.

In 1827, Czar Nicholas I had made the edict that for every 1,000 Jews in a shtetl, they had to send 10 Jewish boys to the Czar's army. The Gentiles only had to send seven boys for every 1,000 people.

Once in the Russian army, Jewish soldiers weren't treated very well. The Russians had a policy of placing the Jewish soldiers far from home and far from other Jews, in hopes that they would forget Judaism and become more Russian. Most of these boys would go off, never to be heard from again. Starting at the age of twelve, the Russian army drafted them for 25 years. They would die fighting somewhere far away. Most never saw their families again. Most of the Jewish soldiers didn't feel any allegiance to the Czar who treated Jews so badly, so they didn't want to go risk their lives for him. Jewish parents would do anything to keep their sons from being drafted. Frequently, when a Jewish boy's name came up, he would purposely maim himself, cutting off a toe or an ear. Some ran off - to America or Canada or Palestine – anything, not to have to go into the Czar's army. Even though there was a very heavy fine for this, half of the young boys who were drafted into the army deserted before they were actually inducted. The Jewish deserters were fined even worse than the Gentile boys that didn't want to join the army. The Jewish families had to pay 300 rubles - a fortune for them.

Shmuel Yudel would put on his gold chain and go to meet with the recruiting committee. None of the members of this committee wanted to be on this committee or do this. They had no choice; somebody had to do it. The committee had to decide which of these young men, whose parents didn't have the money to get them out of this awful fate, would have to go into the army.

The Elder was in charge of all sorts of things. Sometimes he could help people and sometimes he couldn't. As the Elder, Shmuel Yudel managed to get his son-in-law Gedaliah a job as a mailman.

In addition to the Elders keeping things orderly in the shtetlach, more importantly, there were the rabbis. The rabbis were the real community leaders for the Jewish community, and in charge of Jewish life. In addition to being in charge of the religious rituals, the rabbis had many other duties, including making sure that those who needed charity got it.

There were many traditions of charity and social welfare in the shtetlach. Jewish communities have always practiced social welfare; charity is mandatory in Jewish law. The Jewish people have always been required to give what they could to those who are less fortunate. The obligation of charity is commanded to us by the Torah and the Talmud and has always been considered a community responsibility. Even though the saying "From each according to his ability, to each according to his needs," was popularized by Karl Marx in 1875, mandatory charity was actually adopted by Jews before the common era.

In the shtetlach, there were welfare groups for everything. From the soup kitchen, to the burial society, to the dowry fund for poor girls, to money for schools, a group existed to help every need. They tried to take care of orphans, the aged, the sick, prisoners and all those who needed help. In bad times, it has always been the safety net for Jews.

Every Jewish shtetl home and every synagogue had a charity box. Money was placed in the charity box before Shabbos (the Sabbath) and the holidays and at sad, solemn and joyful occasions. It was emptied into the welfare fund and given to the needy. This system did not shame or glorify anyone; both the people making donations and those who received help remained anonymous.

It was usually the rabbi that made sure that the poor had money for food and for Passover flour. The rabbi had to make sure that orphans were taken care of and the charitable groups were doing what they could to help. The rabbi was also responsible for the birth, death, and marriage records for everybody. Each rabbi made sure that his community had a public bath, a ritual bath, and a doctor. The rabbi set up groups to take care of these things. He didn't have to be a great public speaker. Usually the rabbi only had to speak to everyone all together as a group twice a year: on the Saturday before Yom Kippur (the Day of Atonement) and the Saturday before Passover. What the rabbi had to be was learned in Jewish law, because he was also the community judge for the Jews and held court [the *Beit Din*]. He didn't just settle religious questions – he also decided divorces, and business arguments between Jews. The rabbi made all sorts of decisions, and, to the Jews in the shtetlach, what he said was law.　 beep

[Photo:] A *Beit Din* - a rabbinical court – a rabbi settling
a business dispute in Eastern Europe, (ca. 1922)
Photographer: Abraham Pisarek, Germany

ℬ *Bubba Rivka* ℛ

*F*radal's father must have been quite a kid. He was born Beryl Yosski Valevelsky. He hated school, and as a teenager ran off to Pinsk to see the world. He didn't go home to Drohitchin for many years. When he did go home, he had a wife and baby. His mother, Bubba Rivka, Fradal's bubby wasn't too pleased with him or his wife and kids, and didn't treat them particularly well. In Pinsk, he had gotten married without his parents arranging the marriage, or their permission, and without even telling them beforehand. Even worse than that, he had married a poor girl who was a maid. His father, Zelig Valevelsky, wasn't any too happy about it either, but a more good natured man, he wasn't as hard to please as his wife, Rivka.

Rivka was bigger than Zelig in every direction. Zelig was an unassuming, little man who was very gentle but also very respected by the community. He was a cabinet maker and made cabinets and other wooden furniture. But Rivka was an imposing stern woman.

[Photo:] Rivka Rafuse Valevelsky,
Fradal & Hasha's paternal grandmother
Drohitchin, Belarus (ca. 1921)

To make money, Rivka used to dye handmade yarn and cloth for the women of Drohitchin. The women made the cloth themselves, mainly linens from the flax that they grew. Some dyes Rivka made herself from different plants, but a lot of her dyes she bought from the itinerant peddlers who regularly came through Drohitchin. The dyes she bought came in these precious little sacks. Bubba Rivka dyed the cloth in great big tubs, and then hung the cloth out to dry on clothes lines. Everyone in Drohitchin brought their cloth to Rivka Rafuse Valevelsky to be dyed.

[Photo:] Shtetl woman carding flax to make into
linen cloth, Eastern Europe (ca. 1918)

Rivka also used to get things for people that she sold to them. She mostly sold notions, needles and pins, and stuff from other cities that you couldn't buy in Drohitchin. Rivka knew most of the people in Drohitchin, even the Gentiles. She was a hard-working woman and everyone came to her. Rivka and Zelig weren't rich; they had what they needed. But they lived in a house on the high ground next to the churchyard, which was where the people of Drohitchin who had money lived.

The local farmers, mainly goyim, used to bring their wagons full of fruits and vegetables to sell in town, especially on market day. Some would leave their wagons near the churchyard. During the war, it was hard times for them too. Sometimes, when Fradal was a little girl, and things were very hard for everyone, her Bubba Rivka would give her a basket and tell her to go get some stuff from the goyim's wagons in the churchyard for them to eat. Bubba Rivka told her "Don't take a lot, not so much that it would be missed." Bubba Rivka said that G_d made the fruit for everyone. Bubba Rivka knew who to pick for this task. Fradal was the youngest and the smallest child in the family that wasn't a baby - Fradal was the most likely person to do this. Fradal was very smart and also very gutsy. She was also very small for her age and always looked younger than she really was. There would be less trouble if Fradal got caught. A farmer would be more sympathetic to her than an older person. Fradal always felt shame doing this but she never got caught. ೞ

✂ *The Doctor* ✂

*B*ubba Rivka's maiden name was Rivka Reifuss (RAy' fUse). Rivka was the oldest daughter of Hershel Tzvi Reifuss and his wife Frayda. They were my mother Fradal's paternal great grandparents. Frada was my mother's paternal great-grandmother, and she was Frada's namesake. Hershel Tzvi Reifuss was known as Hershel the Doctor, and was one of the very few doctors that they had in Drohitchin and the surrounding area. A country doctor, he had been taught in the ways of Russian and Jewish folk medicine and healing by his father and was quite capable. He had a special room in the back of the house where he made all of the medicines and salves himself. Hershel the Doctor made a medicine that was a known cure for swollen tonsils, as well as cough syrups. He could also make all sorts of ointments to heal wounds. With his wife Frayda's help, he would put on cuppings[13] and leeches that he

---

13 Cuppings – (*bonkis* -bon'kissin Yiddish) - n. - medicinal cuppings, small glass cups that are heated and applied to the patient's back and then removed causing a suction pop. Cupping is used to treat an array of ailments, including muscular pain, joint pain, skin problems including eczema and acne, respiratory disorders, including the common cold, pneumonia and bronchitis, and has also been used as an alternative treatment for cancer. It's an old-world remedy, which has recently regained New Age popularity. It is still used today in many parts of the world and was used by athletes at the 2016 Olympics in Rio.

collected. Leeches can be found nearly everywhere that there is water - shallow ponds, lakes, and marshes. So there were plenty of leeches in Drohitchin.

Everyone called Hershel the Doctor when they were sick; even the Gentiles called him for help, even the *gallahck* (gal' lahck - rhymes w. bal lock), the priest. At one time or another he had taken care of almost everyone even lots of the farmers from the surrounding countryside. He had gone to their aid, frequently in the middle of the night, and in all kinds of weather. He even attended a good number of their births. Doctor Hershel was often paid with bags of potatoes and grain. He was right in thinking that his work was a great *mitzvah*[14] (mitz' vuh), a good deed.

Hershel the Doctor was a tall man with a long white beard, and he had thick eyebrows that made him look angry and fierce. He appeared to be very stern, but wasn't. He was really a *gooteh neshuma* (goot' teh • ne shu' mah) - a good soul with a kind heart. Whenever he could, he would help the needy, and he gave them more than he could afford. It was his habit when he heard that someone was in trouble and needed money, to offer them a small loan. Often, he deliberately forgot to collect the debt.

---

[14] *mitzvah* mitz' vuh - noun: lit. - commandment from G-d; any of the 613 commandments or precepts in the Bible and others of rabbinic origin that mainly relate to the religious and moral conduct of Jews; in common usage it means a good deed or charitable act

**[Photo:] Hershel Tzvi Reifuss – Hershel the Doctor
Fradal and Hasha Valevelsky's paternal great-grandfather,
Drohitchin, Belarus (ca. 1910)**

The doctor and his wife Frayda were always welcoming visitors to Drohitchin into their home, and taking travelers in. The poor and needy people in Drohitchin always knew they could turn to them for help, especially for the Sabbath. They knew that Frayda would give them a good meal. On Fridays, Frayda always cooked more food than they needed, and baked extra *challah* breads for Shabbos. She would bring the extra food to people who she knew were having a hard time. Frayda would quietly leave the challah and other food at their doorstep without knocking on their doors. This was so they wouldn't know who had left the food for them.

It is a Jewish tradition to give charity anonymously without expecting or receiving any gratitude. This is so the poor person who is receiving the charity isn't humiliated by having to look into the eyes of the person who gave it to him in order to thank him; instead he thanks G_d.

Everyone in Drohitchin liked Hershel the Doctor and trusted him to care for them when they were sick. So, it was a huge shock, when one day the constable came and took Hershel the Doctor off to jail. One of his patients had just died - a Gentile woman. Her husband was blaming Hershel Reifuss, saying that Hershel the Doctor had poisoned her. Hershel the Doctor yelled, "This couldn't be! How could this be? Why would anyone think I would do such a thing? What reason would I have to poison her?" He told them that when he had left her, she was feeling better.

There was to be a trial at the district court. Before the trial, Hershel's wife Frayda went to the rabbi to ask for a blessing. They were hopeful, but scared. All of Drohitchin was at the trial. The constable told the judge what had happened. The woman's husband said, that he had found the glass of poison near her bed that Hershel Reifuss had said was medicine. Of course, they took the husband's word for it; he was a Gentile. Even though he had taken good care of a lot of them when they needed him, nobody spoke up for Hershel the Doctor, a Jew. The Jews wouldn't speak against a Gentile; they were too scared. Nobody else was there to see that he took good care of the woman, his patient. Hershel the Doctor was being convicted purely on the patient's husband's say so and purely because he was a Gentile and Hershel Reifuss was a Jew.

At the trial, Hershel the Doctor said that he couldn't understand why the woman had died. She was feeling much better when he had left her. He pleaded with them, telling them that he was innocent, that he would never harm anyone, especially not one of his patients. Hershel the Doctor had no reason to harm her. He didn't know why she had died; he only tried to make her well. They were about to convict one of the village's only doctors, a Jew, of murder. Then, suddenly, a woman from the back of the courtroom started slowly coming forward. She walked up front to talk to the judge. The woman looked scared, and it was obvious that she was naturally shy, but the people in the crowded courtroom let her pass. A very quiet and humble woman, terrified by what was about to happen, she said that she was the patient's maid. She very quietly told the judge that Doctor Reifuss wasn't guilty; that he didn't do it. The patient's husband hadn't seen her, but she had seen him. He had poisoned his wife himself. She saw him put the poison in the glass after Doctor Hershel had left. The maid had no reason to lie. She was also a Gentile, everyone believed her. So, at that, they imprisoned the husband and released my mother's great-grandfather, Dr. Hershel Tzvi Reifuss.

The doctor came home, went into the little room in the back of his house, where he kept his medicines. He took each of the medicines that he had so carefully made, and threw each and every one out. He swore he would never practice medicine again. His wife, Frayda stopped him. She went and put back all the medicines. She knew he would keep using them, and that Hershel the Doctor would be there the next time somebody needed him.

Frayda and Hershel had one son. When he was drafted into the army, he fled Drohitchin. He ran off at his parents' urging, even though they knew they would probably never see him again. They all preferred that to having him drafted into the Czar's army, and dying for nothing G_d knows where.

They were right. They never did see him again. He ended up living out his days in Halifax, Nova Scotia, Canada. In Canada, he met and married his wife. They had six children: two sons, two daughters and twins (a boy named Dave and a girl named Miniver, who everyone called Minnie.)

His oldest and first-born son died when he was an old man. He was a bachelor. The two daughters married well and lived in Halifax. The second oldest son, Alkonie, got very rich in Halifax real estate.

Alkonie and his wife Rachel were wonderful people but never had children. They loved children and used to spoil me when I was a little girl. During World War II, Alkonie and Rachel had adopted a boy whom they were able to save from Hitler's madness. He was Rachel's cousin's son. They loved him and raised him as their own. Alkonie and Rachel gave him the world, but he resented them for not being able to save his parents from the death camps. They eventually became estranged. It broke Rachel's and Alkonie's hearts.

Minnie never married. As a young woman, she moved to Manhattan in the 1930s but couldn't get a job. She was a very qualified bookkeeper, but nobody wanted to hire her until she decided to start passing as a Gentile. Miniver Reifuss is not a Jewish sounding name. With her blond hair and blue eyes, it wasn't a problem to pass. She was born and educated in Halifax and spoke with a Canadian accent. Passing as a Canadian Gentile, she could get a very good position as a bookkeeper in a Wall Street law firm. Wall Street firms were notoriously anti-Semitic at that time. They never would have hired her if they had known she was Jewish. They never would have even given her an interview. But they did hire her when they thought she was a Gentile. Minnie worked at that same firm until she retired and moved back to Halifax. Although she worked in that office on Wall Street for over forty-five years; they never knew she was Jewish.

In addition to their son, Frayda and Hershel the Doctor had three other children, all daughters. Their oldest daughter, Rivka, was my mother's paternal grandmother. She married and had five children. Rivka and her husband Zelig Valevelsky never left Drohitchin.

Frayda Reifuss died in 1907. My mother was born in 1909 and was named Fradal after her great-grandmother, Frayda Reifuss. Hershel Tzvi Reifuss, the Doctor died in 1915, when he was 82 years old. He was buried in the Drohitchin cemetery next to his wife Frayda.   ⊂ઝ

ɞ *The Librarian* ɞ

ℱrayda and Hershel the Doctor's youngest daughter, Bobba, was married to Aaron Dovid Kaplan who was born in Khomsk – a small city in the south eastern corner of Belarus. After getting married, Aaron Dovid moved to Drohitchin where he opened a store. Aaron Dovid and Bobba had three sons and three daughters. Aaron Dovid was educated in Jewish studies and made sure that his sons were too. Their two youngest sons, Chaim and Yudel died young. First Chaim got sick and died, and then Yudel, their middle son who had a hunchback, died. Not having a lot of *mazel,* if losing two of their sons wasn't enough, the Kaplans lost their store and everything they had in the great Drohitchin fire of 1905.

Their oldest son Gedaliah, was born in 1895. My mother always spoke very fondly and proudly of her cousin Gedaliah. She said that he was a poet, but he was really so much more than that. Gedaliah was a gentle and good soul and was always helping people and doing good deeds. Like his father, he was very educated and thought of education as being one of the most important things in life. Because of his education, he was always able to get a job with the government. It also didn't hurt that his wife, Perel was the daughter of Shmuel Yudel Piasetsky, the third Elder of Drohitchin. At different times Gedaliah was the mailman, a clerk, and a policeman.

In 1910, Gedaliah helped in establishing the first public library in Drohitchin, and was the first librarian for the next five years. My mother said that it was just like Gedaliah to think of books and education as a priority, while in the middle of all that tumult. Drohitchin was poverty-stricken and war torn, people didn't always have food, and Gedaliah was building a library in addition to everything else he did.

That part of the world, as I have said, was always at war, and Belarus was a constant battleground. The surrounding countries seemed to take turns at power, and no matter who was in power, the Jews seemed to lose. In 1914, war broke out between the Russians and the Germans; it was the beginning of what we call World War I. The Germans marched into Drohitchin the first time, in the fall of 1915. They took over Drohitchin and didn't want the people who were the leadership of the villages under the Czar to continue to have any kind of authority. So, Shmuel Yudel couldn't continue to be the Elder, and he was actually in danger. He and his wife Beila fled to another shtetl not far from Drohitchin. He passed away not long after that. Shmuel Yudel Piasetsky was the last Jewish Elder in Drohitchin.

The Germans grabbed anybody they could to dig graves and to bury the horses that had died in the fighting. They made the people of Drohitchin do other work too. They didn't pay any money, and demanded that the people just work for free. Everyone was scared. They didn't dare say anything; they did what they were told.

Epidemics of disease always start during wartime and this was not different. Typhoid fever was running rampant in a terrible epidemic. Typhoid is caused by unsanitary conditions and contaminated food and water. The germ itself is carried by lice. During the bombings and fires it was hard enough to just stay alive let alone deal with keeping things sanitary. Typhoid killed children, adults and families. Lots of people died without any help. The disease wiped out many people not discriminating among the Belarusian Gentiles, the Germans and the Jews. Everyone was an eligible victim. Almost one fourth of Drohitchin was affected. The

German doctors didn't even bother to continue to register the deaths.

In an attempt to stop the epidemic, the Germans took over three Jewish houses in the alley near the church that led toward the church gardens, and quarantined them as a makeshift hospital. Naftali Steinberg, a teacher had the misfortune of having his house taken over by the Germans to be used as the morgue. They put a barbed wire fence around the area and brought in some German doctors and worked to stop the epidemic.

The Germans didn't seem to care much about Jewish lives, and the German doctors didn't seem willing to work very hard to save the Jewish patients. When the Jewish patients got worse they would say to forget them and let them die. If a Jew didn't show signs of a rapid recovery, the German doctor would give orders to give the patient a large dose of morphine to shorten his stay. The staff that were Jews frequently had to sneak care to save their friends and family from death. These brave volunteers surreptitiously ignored the German doctor's orders. They would put ice packs on the patients' heads and did what they could to bring down their fever. As soon as the German doctors left the hospital, they would do what they had to for the patients whose lives the doctors had given up on. They worked as long as necessary until those half dead, disease-ridden souls were better and opened their eyes or died. When the German doctors said to take those very sick patients who they presumed would die to the morgue, they were frequently surprised when they came back, and these people who were supposed to be dead, were feeling better and sitting up.

Gedaliah was a volunteer medic at this makeshift hospital. One of his responsibilities was bringing the sick people from their houses to the hospital, and taking the patients that had recovered home. Gedaliah worked night and day in that disease-ridden hospital until he himself caught typhoid. Gedaliah got well, but Gedaliah's parents both died in that typhoid epidemic.

When the epidemic was over and the Germans lost the war, the Polish government took over in Drohitchin and most of Belarus.

Gedaliah could speak Polish and could read and write; so he was made a policeman. Then the Ukrainians came into power, and, in 1921, the Bolsheviks took over from the Ukrainians. The Bolsheviks wanted to throw anyone who cooperated with the Polish authorities in jail; so Gedaliah and his wife Perel had no choice but to run away.

Gedaliah and Perel eventually made their way to New York City where they settled. In New York, Gedaliah got involved in community affairs and did what he could to help those that were needy just as he had done in Drohitchin. He worked hard to start the National Workers Union, and he was an activist for the Jewish National Fund. Always a zealous Zionist, Gedaliah worked ceaselessly for the creation of the state of Israel. Gedaliah also wrote articles and 42 poems that were published in the Amerikaner Magazine & Gazette – known by the Jews as *Der Amerikaner*. A Jewish, American family magazine and gazette, it was published in New York City from 1929 until 1945.

During the Shoah (Hebrew- the Holocaust), in Drohitchin and Bobruisk as in most of Eastern Europe, the Germans did not bother to ship the Jewish people off to camps to kill them. They just annihilated them all where they lived, destroying the entire Jewish shtetl way of life of Eastern Europe.

In the aftermath, many Jewish people who were overwhelmed with both the loss of their murdered families and the complete destruction of the shtetlach from which they had managed to escape, organized to memorialize and bear witness to the Jews and Jewish life and culture of the Jewish communities that had vanished in the Holocaust. In their unbearable grief, one of the ways they chose to memorialize the loss was to build a most appropriate and indestructible memorial. They, "the people of the book." chose to create gravestones in words and pictures by writing what were called *yizkor* books. Yizkor is the Hebrew word for "remember." The goal of the yizkor books was not just to bear witness to the annihilation of a way of life but also to prevent the loss from historic memory of an entire culture and to describe that history to future generations. Their rationale was that if there is one copy of each of these books left somewhere in the world, then their memorial and history survives.

In 1296, in a hideous twist of history, Nuremberg was where the first yizkor book was published. It was written to memorialize the Jews of Speyer, who were murdered by the knights of the Crusades in their killing spree across Europe. Those knights killed many thousands of Jews who were in their path while they were on their way to free the Holy Land for "good Christians."

The 20th century yizkor books were put together by yizkor book committees. The committees were groups of people who gathered to create yizkor books with descriptions and histories of the life in their shtetlach, their hometowns that had been destroyed. These books included historical data, biographies and all sorts of stories from the shtetlach, whatever they could remember, research and reconstruct. They also included family trees, photos, maps, and photos of every kind of memorabilia. After years of work most of these books were published in the 1950s and 60s. They are not only history books but also historical documents in themselves. There were yizkor books written about more than 1,000 shtetlach and areas in Eastern Europe. Most were written in Yiddish or Hebrew.

There is a yizkor book that was written about my father's city Bobruisk and the surrounding shtetlach (including Hlusk), where all of his relatives and any other Jews from that area that hadn't escaped were murdered. We lost many relatives. The Bobruisk yizkor book entitled "MEMORIAL BOOK OF THE COMMUNITY OF BOBRUISK AND ITS SURROUNDINGS" was published in Tel Aviv, Israel in 1967. It was written in Hebrew and Yiddish by Jews who had immigrated to Israel. It is 871 pages in two volumes with dark red hard covers.

Just before World War II the Jews of Drohitchin were fed up with all of the pogroms and anti-Semitism. The men organized and started a very brave vigilante group. They could stand up against the growing anti-Semitism, and because of this there were no pogroms during that time. But they were no match for the German military who marched into Drohitchin again in 1942. Except for the few who managed to escape and hide in the woods, the Germans with pre-planned, organized, almost systematic precision, killed the entire Jewish population of Drohitchin, over 5,000 people, in two days for no reason other than because they were Jewish. The first massacre was on July 25, 1942, and the second was a few months later, on October 17, 1942.

I am not surprised that a large part of the yizkor book about Drohitchin was organized and compiled by Gedaliah Kaplan, the librarian and poet. It was written in Yiddish by the Drohitchin yizkor book committee; Gedaliah was a leading member. The book was edited by Rabbi Dov Warshawsky. The Drohitchin yizkor book was published in Chicago in 1958 and is entitled *Drohiczhn: Five Hundred Years of Jewish Life.* ය

❧ *The Shtetl Week* ☙

$\mathcal{M}$ost days the people of the shtetl just worked to earn a living. The children went to school if they were lucky. The children also helped their parents with whatever they were asked to do. But Shabbos – the Sabbath (Saturday) was different for the Jews. The Ten Commandments says that we must ***"Remember the Sabbath day and keep it holy. For six days, you shall labor and do all your work. But the seventh day is a Sabbath to the Lord your G_d; you shall not do any work."*** Shabbos is supposed to be a day of rest and prayer. So, Shabbos was different from the rest of the week.

The Jews of the shtetl, in their observance of Shabbos (and observant Jews today), not only didn't work on Shabbos, they didn't ride or light fires; they didn't even cook. Pious Jews believe we are not supposed to buy anything or sell anything; in other words, you can't spend money. They believe that in observance of the Sabbath, you shouldn't even have money in your pocket on Shabbos. They are allowed to read, but not write anything. There are all sorts of things that they can't do; so in the shtetl they had a lot to do to prepare for Shabbos when they wouldn't be able to do those things that are religiously not permitted.

On Fridays, everyone in Drohitchin was very busy, just like in Jewish shtetlach all over Eastern Europe. From Sunday through

Thursday the shtetl Jews were busy scraping together the money they needed to make a living. But things were also different on Fridays because people had to get ready for Shabbos, when all work stopped. Friday mornings, the men were busy finishing the last bit of their work before they had to stop work and close their shops. Then the men went to wash up at the public bathhouse. The men and women of the shtetl took turns going to the public bath. Men went every week on Fridays, and the women went earlier in the week on another day. Early on Friday afternoons, the attendants from the public baths rushed through the streets calling the men to come to bathe, so that they could be clean for Shabbos.

Early Friday mornings, the women started cooking to prepare the Shabbos meal, the biggest and best meal of the week. If they were able, they would serve a little fish, some soup, some meat or chicken, wine, and challah bread. On Fridays, the women were very busy baking challah, and cooking the food for Shabbos. Fridays, the sweet smell of the challah and cakes baking filled the air. You could smell the cooking and the baking all over Drohitchin. You are not supposed to light a fire on Shabbos; not even to cook. A fire may be allowed to continue to burn and be used, as long as you lit the fire before Shabbos begins. So lots of women made casseroles that could sit on a low flame for a long time especially *cholent* (chOlnt). *Cholent* is a Shabbos stew that is baked for a long time. You can put anything you want in it, as long as you put in beans and barley. Usually it is made with beans, barley, some meat, a little potato, carrots, lots of garlic, mushrooms and onions. Some people bury whole eggs, shell and all in cholent as a treasure to find on the bottom. The casseroles and cholent were cooked very slowly overnight.

The housewives would put the cholent in a heavy cast iron pot. They then took their casseroles to the baker's oven. It would stay there all night and cook slowly. The baker's oven was so hot that it stayed hot all through Shabbos even though the flame wasn't stoked. The cholent would be finished cooking and ready to eat after the Shabbos morning services. When services were over, the housewives went to the baker and got the cholent and brought it home. It makes a wonderful mid-day Shabbos meal.

At the end of Friday afternoons, shortly before candle lighting, the man who took care of the shul, used to go around calling out that it was almost Shabbos. He called the men to the Friday evening shul prayer service. He was known as the Shabbos caller. In some villages, the man who announced the coming Sabbath would knock on the door or window shutter to tell people that Shabbos was about to begin, and in those places, he was called the Shabbos knocker.

On Fridays, *erev*[15] Shabbos, when you heard the Shabbos caller shout out, you knew that Shabbos was about to begin. Shabbos starts at sundown on the previous day, not at midnight. The day ends at sundown on the actual day, when three stars are seen in the sky. This is because in Genesis it says, **"And there was evening, and there was morning, one day."**

Fridays, the women would set the table for the Shabbos dinner. Then at least 18 minutes before sundown, they lit the candles and said the prayer to bless the candles. Fathers (and/or mothers) placed their hands over their children's heads, and said the prayer to bless them. The man of the house lifted his special *kiddish* cup full of wine and said *kiddish* - the blessing to sanctify the Sabbath. They then said a prayer for the challah, thanking G_d for the bread, and as a commemoration of receiving two portions of manna on Fridays, when the Jews were wandering in the dessert after the exodus from Egypt. After the blessing of the challah, it is broken or cut in pieces and everyone has a piece dipped in a small amount of salt.

The women saved the best food they had for Shabbos. So, if they were lucky, they ate a chicken dinner Friday night and cholent on Saturday afternoon. It was very quiet in Drohitchin on Shabbos.

---

[15] *erev* **er' ev** *n.* – Hebrew - literally eve, evening - the day before a Jewish holiday or the Jewish Sabbath, Friday evening before the Jewish Sabbath or the evening before a Jewish holiday

Nobody worked, all the shops were closed, and everybody went to shul.

Shabbos is supposed to be a day of rest and prayer. So what else was there to do, but to go to synagogue, like everyone else on Saturday morning? There were some Jewish people who didn't believe in it. They thought they were modern and enlightened, but even they stopped working and most went to shul. They didn't dare break the Shabbos. And where else were they going to go on Shabbos but to shul? In Drohitchin, that's the way it was.

You didn't ride on Shabbos, so everybody walked to shul even from far away. The women sat in the back of the shul, in the women's section, behind the curtain that separated the women's section from the men who sat in the front. The children sat in the women's section too. There were old women, young women, mothers nursing babies, little girls and little boys. The women took care of the children, of course. And they were, of course, not counted in the *minyan*. A *minyan* is the quorum of ten people you must have to be able to hold most religious services. Years ago, they only counted the men and the boys who had been bar mitzvahed in the minyan. Today most synagogues, other than the Orthodox Jews, also count women in the minyan.

At the Shabbos morning services, everybody from Drohitchin was there, so of course they had a minyan. Each of the men and all the boys who had already been bar mitzvahed took their own tallis[16](prayer shawl with fringes on the corners). They opened it with both hands. Holding it in front of themselves they said the Hebrew prayer- ***"Blessed are you, Lord, our G_d, sovereign of the universe, who has sanctified us with His commandments and commanded us to wrap ourselves in the fringes."*** After they said the blessing, they wrapped their shawls around their shoulders, holding it with both hands together in front of their face. Then they held their shawls over their heads for a

---

[16] *Tallis* - prayer shawl with fringes on the corners, worn at morning religious services. The fringes are called *tzitzi* and are made of *613* threads as a reminder of the 613 commandments from G_d that are in the Torah.

second, and then let their prayer shawls sit on their heads or on their shoulders and went to their seats. Everyone was facing the ark, where the Torah scrolls were kept behind the curtain on the eastern wall. The Rabbi was at the altar in the front. The men and the older boys sat in the men's section of the shul. The men who were the leaders of Drohitchin had the honor of sitting in the front near the eastern wall – in most places, the wall nearest to Jerusalem.

The rabbi led the services. They started with the blessings, and psalms. Everyone prayed and then, when the rabbi nodded, the congregation all stood up as the ark's curtain or doors were opened. Some of the men had the honor of taking the Torahs out. It is an honor to participate in any part of dealing with the Torah. Before they did anything, they would say a blessing. Still standing, everyone sang and, with the utmost respect, the rabbi and other honored men paraded the Torah around the shul with other honored men following behind. Everyone else turned to see the Torah go by, and if near enough reached out to touch one of the Torahs, and then to kiss their fingers that had touched the Torah. Some men came up to the Torah and touched it with their prayer book or their prayer shawls. With love, they kissed the spot on the book or prayer shawl that had touched the Torah.

They continued the procession to the altar at the front. There they unwrapped the Torah, getting it ready to be read. The reading was broken into seven parts, and a blessing was said before each part. When they finished reading, they retied and rewrapped the Torah, and then they paraded the Torah around the shul again, and again everyone reached out to touch it. The Torah was brought back and carefully replaced in the Ark. The congregation sang and chanted all in Hebrew and prayed. Everyone stood and said the prayer for anyone who was very sick. And almost at the end anyone in mourning stood up and said the mourner's *Kaddish*, the memorial prayer for the dead. Then the service was completed by the singing of the last hymn. The Shabbos morning service in the shtetl wasn't that different from the way it is done today in synagogues everywhere.

After the service, the congregation went to the back of the synagogue where the women had set up the wine and challah bread. Sometimes, on special occasions, there was a whole meal. The blessings for the wine and for the bread were said.

There was almost always something special happening on Shabbos besides it being Shabbos. There were reasons to cry and reasons to celebrate. Most of these occasions were and are included as part of the Shabbos service in the synagogue. A lot of times on Saturdays there are bar and bat mitzvahs. The bar mitzvah is the coming of age of a young person (bat mitzvah is the feminine form). It is usually marked by the first time a young boy of 13, or girl of 12, is given the honor of going up to the altar to say a blessing for the Torah or to read a portion of the service. At this age, they are now considered responsible adults in the synagogue (not at home), and are bar or bat mitzvahed regardless of whether they celebrate or mark the occasion or not.

Often on Saturdays there was a baby naming for a baby girl. Baby girls are given their names in shul. The father goes up to the altar on a Shabbos morning; he says a prayer for his family and says the baby girl's name for the first time in shul. Baby boys are given their names at their circumcision, usually when they are eight days old.

Sometimes there is an *ufruf.* An ufruf literally means call up. It is when they give the groom who is to be married the following week, the honor of being called up to the Torah to say a blessing for the Torah. After they finish reading the Torah, the congregation throws candy at the groom, cheering him with mazel tov (good luck, congratulations). Everybody sings *"Mazel Tov and Simon Tov."* It is a happy time. After the ufruf, the groom won't see the bride again till the wedding. His family usually makes the Shabbos snack after the ufruf, with wine, cake and challah. Sometimes they even serve cholent and a whole lunch.

Gedaliah's ufruf was in Drohitchin the week before he and his bride, Perel, got married. They had a big wedding for a shtetl.

After all, her father was Shmuel Yudel, the Elder. All of Drohitchin was there.

They had already made up the *ketubah*. The *ketubah* is the marriage contract. It is an ancient prenuptial agreement that was originally intended to protect women's rights. It states that the husband promises to provide food, clothing and marital relations to his wife, and that he will pay a specified sum of money (usually enough for her to live on for one year) if he divorces her.

The wedding was held in the late afternoon on a Tuesday, outside in the shul courtyard. The bride and groom each greeted their guests separately. Perel sat on one side where the women came to greet her.

Bobba Kaplan (Fradal's aunt), and Beila Piasetsky, the two mothers who were about to become mothers-in-law, each smashed a plate. This is the tradition that symbolizes a Jewish mother's break with her son or daughter who will then be forever in an unbroken relationship with their new spouse.

Gedaliah was on the opposite side of the courtyard, where the men were toasting him. Gedaliah and his father, Aaron David Kaplan, ceremoniously walked over to where Perel was sitting with the women and her family surrounding her. His mother Bobba was already there with the other women. Then they had the traditional *badeken*. The *badeken* is the ritual veiling of the bride by the groom. The custom stems from the bible story of Jacob who was tricked into marrying Leah instead of his true love Rachel. It is also a way of promising to take care of his wife and clothe her forever. Gedaliah took the veil, and with some embarrassed shyness, dropped it over Perel's face.

In a traditional Jewish wedding, both the bride and the groom are walked down the aisle by both their fathers and their mothers. Gedaliah's mother, Bobba, and his father, Aaron, on either side of him, each happily took one of Gedaliah's arms, and walked him to the wedding canopy where the rabbi was waiting to marry him and Perel.

As a symbol that they are marrying each other purely for themselves, and not for material wealth, the bride and groom don't wear any jewelry. Perel looked beautiful as her mother, Beila, and her father, Shmuel Yudel Piasetsky, the Elder, walked her to meet Gedaliah under the canopy. As G_d built the world in seven days, Perel circled her groom seven times in the symbolic building of their world together. Then Perel stood on Gedaliah's right side as the rabbi said the blessings and then gave them each some wine. Gedaliah gave Perel a gold ring, and placed it on her finger, as the rabbi told him to do. The rabbi read the ketubah (the marriage contract), and then handed it to Gedaliah, who handed it to Perel for safekeeping. The rabbi said the seven blessings, and then gave Gedaliah and Perel another cup of wine. A glass in a small bag was put on the floor, and Gedaliah smashed it with his foot. Everyone cheered mazel tov (good luck, congratulations). The celebration began with the klezmer musicians starting to play and everyone beginning to dance.

At almost every Jewish wedding, somebody always asks why the groom smashes a glass. The most widespread interpretation of the meaning of this ritual is that it symbolizes the destruction of the Temple in Jerusalem in 70 AD. Psalm 137 tells us to remember Jerusalem even when we are the most joyful. *If I forget you, O Jerusalem...............*

While this custom is still being practiced today, some believe it may have had its beginnings in near eastern superstition. At one time, it was common to smash glasses or dishes in gestures of smashing the powers of evil demons or ill-wishers. Some people believe that the ritual symbolizes how fragile relationships are and that we must be careful not to break them like glass. Others think it is a symbolic break with the past like the plates that the mothers break. And some think it is a gesture marking the beginning of a marriage that should last as long as that glass remains broken - forever.

There were wonderful gifts for the young couple. Someone gave them a kneading trough; somebody else gave them a bucket.

Fradal's grandmother Rivkah gave her nephew Gedaliah and his wife Perel, a noodle board that her husband Zelig had made for them. People gave the newlyweds all sorts of presents that they would need to start a home.

Then all of the guests ate and drank and said *L'chaim*! ('to life'- the traditional Jewish drinking toast). There were klezmer musicians playing *fraylocks* (happy songs). They played *Hava Nagila* ('come let us be glad'), and everybody sang and danced the circle dance, the *hora* (hO' ra). They danced the *hora* until they all nearly fell down. Some men did acrobatics and others did juggling tricks.

Some of the men dragged Gedaliah up on a chair, and they carried him around on the chair in the middle of the floor. Then some others put Perel up on a chair. The couple held a napkin between them as they were seated high on their chairs and paraded around. The guests all danced around them in a circle and cheered. That was a wonderful day.

Shabbos wasn't the only time that everyone went to shul. They went on all of the holidays, and especially the high holy days of Rosh Hashanah and Yom Kippur. On the holidays nobody worked or lit fires or rode, just like on Shabbos. The women prepared special foods to celebrate the holidays. It was a lot like Shabbos, only everyone stayed in shul and prayed even longer.

The high holy day of Rosh Hashanah is at the end of summer. It is the beginning of the Jewish New Year, considered by Jews to be the birthday of the world. It is on the first day of the Jewish month of *Tishrei*. It begins *the Days of Awe* - the ten days of repentance when Jews think about asking G_d for forgiveness.

The arrival of Rosh Hashanah and the high holy days is marked by the blowing of the *shofar*. The *shofar* horn, usually made from a ram's horn, is a trumpet that is one of the world's oldest wind instruments. The ancient sound of the shofar has been used by the Jewish people to sound attacks in battle, to put terror into the hearts of their enemies, and as a call to assembly. On Rosh Hashanah it is a call to repentance.

Traditionally during Rosh Hashanah, apples that have been dipped in honey are eaten, to symbolize our hopes for a "sweet" new year. The apple is dipped in honey, the blessing for eating tree fruits is recited, the apple is tasted, and then the apples and honey prayer is said.

A very special service at the end of the first day of Rosh Hashanah is *Tashlikh*. This is when the congregation goes to a body of moving water like the ocean or a river or stream. Prayers are said, then everyone takes the bread crumbs that they have placed in their pockets for this purpose and cast them on the water to symbolize throwing their sins into the sea.

The ten days between Rosh Hashanah and Yom Kippur are called the Days of Awe. It is a time of introspection and reflection. At sunset, on the ninth day, Yom Kippur, the Day of Atonement begins a fast. It then ends the next day at sunset with again the blowing of the shofar. The Jews of Drohitchin like Jews all over the world spent most of that time in shul.

After Yom Kippur, they spent the next four days before the 14th day of Tishrei building the *sukkahs*, the little huts that Jewish people eat in during the seven days of *Sukkot*. Sukkot is the Jewish harvest holiday. Sukkot is very similar to the American Thanksgiving Day. The Drohitchin sukkahs were decorated with flowers and branches that were collected in the forest and the Vion. The last day, the seventh day concludes Sukkot with the joyous holiday and celebrations of *Simchas Torah*.

Simchas Torah is the celebration and marking of the end and restarting the annual cycle of the reading of the Torah. On Simchas Torah, the last part of the Torah, Deuteronomy, is read and they again start to read the Torah from the beginning with the first words of Genesis, *"When G_d began to create heaven and earth..."*

Simchas Torah is a time for festivity and joy. The ark is opened and, with great care, all of the Torah scrolls are taken out. Then the Torahs are carried around and circle the shul seven times. Everyone standing and singing reaches out with a prayer book or their fingers to touch the Torahs and then kisses their own fingers that had touched the Torah. In Drohitchin there was always a lot of singing and dancing with the Torahs, just as we do here in America. The children are blessed under a large *tallis* and given treats. Sometimes, the Torahs were, (and are today), danced into the street, where the music of happiness and joy went on all night. ෬

❧ *The Thirty-Six* ❧

The first time Fradal and her family saw a car, she and her brother and sister were just children in Drohitchin. It didn't look like the cars of today. For one thing, that car made more noise than a whole box of firecrackers. In those days, when a car was coming, everybody knew about it before it got there. You could hear it coming. You didn't just get in and turn the key and, bingo, the car would go, as modern cars do. Oh no! You had to turn a crank in the front of the car until you made it go, like a wind-up toy. Sometimes, you had to get out and crank it many times before you got it to go. And you usually got very dirty from all the smoke and the dust from the roads. People used to wear special long coats and hats with goggles. The coats were similar to modern raincoats that we wear today. Only very rich people could afford cars then.

Fradal never forgot how scared her family was the first time they saw a car. They thought the devil was coming to get them. They didn't know what a car was. They had heard of buggies that could go by themselves, but never dreamt of seeing one right there in Drohitchin.

That first time was late at night and wartime. It was dark outside. In those days, you never knew what could happen to a person next. Fradal and her family could hear something coming down the road. It was making horrible unrecognizable noises, drowning out the croaking of the frogs and the sounds of the Vion.

They were sleeping; the noise woke them. They got up and, very carefully, looked outside. Fradal's mama said that they should not light a lamp, and that they should be careful. The noise scared her too. Something was coming towards their house. In the dark it looked as if it were a locomotive from a train. They never saw lights like that on anything else before. But it couldn't be a locomotive. The train tracks were on the other side of Drohitchin. How could it be? "*Kishuv!* It must be *kishuv*, (kis huv')– magic", Hasha whispered terrified. Chaiya Bailya was praying, "Please G_d we are good people. Don't let any harm come to my children. If something bad has to happen, better it should happen to me than to them." That horrible thing passed their little house and went on down the road without taking them. It only left a trail of smoke behind and did that smoke stink!

"We should thank G_d for not letting any horrible fate befall us," Fradal's mother had said, while they hugged and kissed each other. All four of them were relieved that whatever it was – was gone.

They didn't know what to do. In the morning, Fradal's mother told her children to get dressed as nicely as they could. They were going to see the Kholozhiner (hOl' e zEEn er). She said that she didn't know what he would do, but she didn't know who else to tell, maybe Shmuel Yudel, the Elder. She said that she wished their papa was there, and hadn't gone to America. This was his shtetl. He would know what to do, their mama said. "But we have to tell somebody about what we saw last night."

Fradal and her family walked up Kobriner Street to get to the Kholozhiner's house. Before they even got near the Kholozhiner's house, they saw a huge crowd right there in the middle of town. They didn't know there were so many people in Drohitchin. Everyone was there; even Gentiles were there in the Jewish section. Everybody was huddled all around something. No matter how hard they tried, they couldn't see what it was because it was so crowded. Then they heard that noise, that unmistakable noise. They had heard those noises only once before. "Oh, my G_d." Chaiya Bailya said clutching her family to her. When something started making noise again, everyone moved back as if they were all one body. Then they could see what it was. There was noise and smelly smoke coming out of both ends. It was a fancy buggy with a machine inside, but no horse.

Trying to get that crazy machine started was a big man with a short beard and a mustache. He was wearing a great coat with a fur collar. Even little Fradal knew the stranger must have been someone who was very rich and very important, even though they didn't know who he was. Hasha said, "Maybe he's a baron, or a count, or something." Chaiya Bailya was standing next to their neighbor, Mrs. Schwartz, from down the street. So she asked her who the man was. Mrs. Schwartz told their mama that she had heard that he was a businessman who had come all the way from Pinsk. He had come to speak to the Kholozhiner.

People believed that the Kholozhiner was a *Lamed-vovnik* (la med'-vuv nick). His real name was Eliyahu Mordechai Levinovitz. Everybody just called him *the Kholozhiner* or the Kholozhiner blacksmith, because he was a blacksmith and he was from Kholozhin. Kholozhin was a shtetl somewhere not far from Pinsk. *Lamed - vov* means 36 in Hebrew. The Jewish tradition teaches us that there are 36 truly special, just and righteous souls in the world. These extraordinary people sometimes know who they are, and sometimes who they are is hidden even from them, and only known by G_d. The tradition says that these 36 saintly people are born to take on the burden of the world's suffering. They carry all the sorrows and sins of the world in their hearts and on their shoulders. The rabbis say that for the sake of the Lamed-vovniks, G_d does not destroy the world even when people commit terrible sins.

Jewish people believe that G_d talks to the Lamed-vovniks, and that they know secret things. G_d must have talked to the Kholozhiner, the Lamed-vovnik they had right there in Drohitchin, because he seemed to know things that other people surely didn't know. When his daughter was pregnant, he told her that her baby would be a boy, and that they would name the baby after him. This was a strange thing to say, because Ashkenazie Jews usually don't give babies the names of people who are still alive, and the Kholozhiner wasn't even sick then. But he was sadly right, because he got sick and died before the baby was born. It happened just as he had said it would.

People used to come from all over to get the Kholozhiner's advice. Some people gave him a lot of money for his advice. The Kholozhiner used to give most of it away to charity, but he always kept a receipt. He saved all of the receipts in two bags that he hung on the wall. When he died, they put the two bags of receipts in the coffin with him, just as he had asked.

This Lamed-vovnik, the Kholozhiner blacksmith, wasn't a leader of a lot of Jews. He wasn't even a rabbi. He was a simple man. He could not even read Hebrew well. The Kholozhiner blacksmith read everything in Yiddish. He was very educated in Torah, but was really just a village blacksmith. Still, everyone came to him for all sorts of help. There were a lot of stories about him and not just the Jews; even the Gentiles thought he was a miracle-maker. The Gentiles used to talk about how their fields would grow overnight any time the Kholozhiner even walked by.

[Photo:] R. Eliyahu Mordechai Levinovitz -
the Kholozhiner
Drohitchin, Belarus (1846 –1932)

One day there was a fire, and a woman named Chayka
started yelling that it was going to burn her house down. When the
Kholozhiner saw what was happening, he lifted his cane up against
a wall of Chayka's house. You wouldn't believe it, but the fire stayed
in the air. It didn't touch the house, except that it singed one spot on
the wall he had touched. It was as if he had made the wind change

direction away from the house. That singed wall became a reminder of what had happened to everybody who had seen it.

Before the Russo-Polish War, the Polish leaders gave speeches about their coming independence from Russia. They talked about how everyone was going to be equal, Poles and Jews alike. They said it was going to be a democracy. Polish Jews even enlisted in the Polish Army to defend Poland against the Russians. They served under the Marshal of Poland, Józef Piłsudski, fighting on the same side against the Russian Bolsheviks. After the Polish city of Dęblin was liberated from the Bolsheviks, the Jewish elders of that city even welcomed Marshal Pilsudski with bread and salt.

During that war, the Poles gained control of Drohitchin and all of Belarus. Then Belarus was ruled by the laws of Poland. As soon as the Poles got power and declared the Republic of Poland, they started making restrictions against the Jews again. The new Polish laws were harsher than the old Russian laws, and the new restrictions against the Jewish population made things even harder than they had been before. After the war started the Poles of course lost the markets they had in Russia. It was hard to earn a living and they were at war. The Jews didn't do anything wrong, but the new Polish government had to have somebody to blame for the money troubles, so as always, they blamed their traditional scapegoats, the Jews.

The Polish officials made a law that said you couldn't cut down trees and sell firewood. They did this because they had lost a lot of their coal business in Russia, and they wanted people to buy their coal from the Polish coalmines in Silesia. In the summer, before this war, the Jews of the Polesia used to cut a cord of twelve loads of wood to warm their houses and cook during the winter months. For the first time ever, the people of Drohitchin were forced to heat their ovens with coal. They never had to do this before because there was a forest all around Drohitchin. With the steep increase in taxes that the Poles had raised and the very high cost of coal, the people of Drohitchin suffered the cold.

These "democratic" Polish officials watched the Jews with seven eyes. They made all sorts of anti-Semitic restrictions, including a ban on ritual slaughter. This meant that the kosher butchers couldn't kill the animals in the kosher way according to Jewish dietary laws. Then, of course, that meant that their meat wasn't kosher, so the Jewish butchers couldn't sell their meat to Jewish people who kept kosher. The Jews wouldn't eat it, so they wouldn't buy it. Jews stopped eating meat, because Jews are not supposed to eat meat from an animal that hasn't been killed according to Jewish law. In Drohitchin everyone, all the Jews, kept kosher. It wasn't a question. Even Jews who thought they were modern (and there weren't many of them), and didn't believe in the Jewish dietary laws kept kosher. A Jew could eat in any other Jew's house and know that it was kosher. That is the way that everyone in the shtetlach lived.

During the spring of 1919, the Polish Legionnaires beat back the Russians and fought their way into Drohitchin. The Poles were very anti-Semitic, and the even more horrible anti-Semitic White Guard[17] from Belarus, had volunteered to help the Poles against their enemies, the Bolsheviks.

The White Guard hated Jews, but hated the Russian Bolsheviks more, and they thought the Jews sided with the Bolsheviks. Always the scapegoats, after the Russian Revolution, the Jews were blamed by many for the Bolsheviks taking over in October 1917. There is an old Russian saying that explains how all of the Slavic and Polish people have felt about the Jews for centuries: "If the water in the sink is missing - it is because the Jews took it." They used this expression, and it is still in use today, even if the Jews are completely innocent, and frequently not even relevant to their problems. In other words, they all have always blamed the Jews for everything that happens to them that they don't like.

---

[17] The White Guard were a Belarusian volunteer army, fighting on the side of Poland. They all hated the Bolsheviks.

In the Polesia, the White Guard was led by General Bulak Balakhovitch. Under this anti-Semitic general, the murderous Balakhovitch gangs of the White Guard not only pushed back the Russians, but started pogroms of terror against the Jews. The Poles and the Balakhovitch gangs both came through the Polesia by force, taking anything they needed or wanted along the way. They broke into houses and killed people, beating the men and raping the women. The pogroms...who could stop them?

Businessmen, people from all over, from far away came to ask the Kholozhiner blacksmith for blessings and business advice, all sorts of advice. So, it was natural when Shimon Baum's son Avraham had trouble with the Poles, that he went to the Kholozhiner blacksmith to ask him what to do. The Baums were kosher butchers. They were having a lot of trouble earning a living with the new restrictions and the ban on ritual slaughter, and now they had more trouble. The Poles had taken a lot of their livestock to feed their soldiers. The Baums were having a hard time keeping bread on the table, and didn't know what to do.

The Kholozhiner scared Avraham with his answer to the problem, when he told Avraham to go ask the Poles to pay him for the animals that they had taken. Avraham Baum said no, he couldn't do that. He was afraid. Avraham didn't want to even try to imagine what the Poles would do to him, if he told them he wanted to be paid for the animals they took. The Kholozhiner told Avraham not to be afraid. He said, "Tell them, I'm your business partner."

Avraham didn't say anything, he just left. He didn't know what to do, but he was made strong by the Kholozhiner's words and advice. Avraham did what the Kholozhiner said. He went and asked the Poles for money for the animals they had taken, and he told them that the Kholozhiner was his partner, just as the Kholozhiner told him to do. To Avraham Baum's surprise, the Poles gave him the money.

He ran to tell the Kholozhiner. Avraham asked the Kholozhiner what he owed him for being a partner in the business. The Kholozhiner answered just a glass of wine for this Shabbos.

From then on, every Shabbos, Avraham Baum gave the Kholozhiner enough wine for everyone at the Kholozhiner's table.

The Kholozhiner was famous for his wisdom and the advice he gave people. They came from all over just to ask him for help with their questions, and for blessings. They came for all sorts of reasons; some people thought that he might be able to tell them where people were that were missing. During wartime a lot of people disappeared. So a lot of people came to ask where their loved ones were, and if the Kholozhiner knew where they could find them. They wanted him to tell them if he thought they would ever see their loved ones again.

Some people came on the train. They got off at the Drohitchin station. Most of the people who came to see the Kholozhiner came by horse and wagon. The rich businessman was the only one who ever came in a magic buggy. He had his little daughter with him. Many years later, Fradal could still remember them. That little girl was about Fradal's size and age, but she was beautiful. She had on a red coat with a white fur collar and a hat to match. Fradal couldn't take her eyes off of her. Fradal never felt so shabby as she did that day, standing there in her old horse blanket coat, that her mother had made with the army stamp on her *tuckhus* (tuck' us – behind). Boy did she want that red coat.

Fradal never got a coat like that, but when I was a little girl she got a red coat with a white fur collar for me. In my mother's eyes, I must have looked a lot like the little girl in the car. Would you believe it? I didn't like the coat at all. I wanted a green velvet one like my best friend had. My mother couldn't believe that I didn't like it. When my mother was a little girl, she would have given anything for a coat like that. Then my brother Marty came home, and so did my older sister Bea. They "oohed" and "aahed" at how I looked in the new coat. They said I looked just like a beautiful lady. So then I changed my mind. I liked the red coat after all.

So everyone wanted to know why the businessman had come to see the Kholozhiner, and what he wanted to know. Everyone always knew why people came. Either they themselves or someone would talk about it. Before long everyone in town would know, even little kids like Fradal. In a small village, everybody always knows from everyone else's business, but not that time. The businessman and his little girl didn't even stay the day. As soon as he got the car started, they were gone just as they came. The Lamed-vov never said a word about it to anyone. People asked him, but he wouldn't say. After a while people forgot about it.

But none of this compared to the first time the people of Drohitchin saw an airplane. It must have been in about 1918. It was during the day and all of Drohitchin could see it in the sky. That airplane looked like I don't know what. It was landing in an empty field nearby. Everyone in Drohitchin started running towards the field to see what this was. When it came down, everybody looked it over. They walked around and around it, to see what made it go. It was a German warplane. The Germans had been in Drohitchin almost since the beginning of World War I. Hunia said that he wished he could ride in that thing, and learn how to make it fly. ๛

[Photo:] **World War I German war plane, Eastern Europe (ca. 1918)**

ॐ *Hunia - Charlie in English* ॐ

There were almost always soldiers at war in Drohitchin. The Germans had come the first time in the autumn of 1915, when Fradal was just a six-year-old little girl. The Germans stayed more than three years until November 1918 when the First World War "the war to end all wars", ended. Then it didn't take even seven weeks until the Ukrainians marched into poor little Drohitchin; that was in December of 1918. The Ukrainians didn't stay long. They left after a few weeks when the Bolsheviks came in the winter of 1919. Whichever army was there it, was no good for the Jews. They all hated Jews. All of the armies caused the Jews trouble - the death, the destruction. They each took whatever they wanted. They raped a lot of women, and killed innocent people, or beat them up. Sometimes they scared people or caused trouble, just for the fun of it. Some fun!

When one army left, they would try to burn down the town behind them, so that the opposing army coming in wouldn't have shelter. When the bombing started, everyone became frightened and went and hid in the trenches, with everyone else from Drohitchin. The Drohitchin ground is always wet from the Vion, so of course the trenches were horribly cold and wet. The trenches had been covered on top with wood and earth, but that didn't stop them from being miserable, muddy hellholes. The cold mud was frequently knee deep. Sometimes the shtetl people stayed in those holes in the ground for a long time; it was safer there. The trenches were really nothing more than long, wet, deep grooves in the ground, but it gave them some protection from the bombs and shooting. The women and children went into the trenches first. There were many people there. It was very crowded, and there was very little room. People brought whatever they could with them. They brought their bundles and small animals. They knew they might need those things to live on. Nobody knew how long they would have to be there or what kind of devastation Drohitchin would suffer.

People pushed each other for a better spot. Tempers were high. Everyone was scared for themselves and their children. They could hear the hideous cannon fire explosions and the shells whistling over their heads. The machine gun fire didn't stop, sometimes not even at night. It was very dangerous. Everyone feared a bomb would hit the trench and kill them all. After a while, they got used to the sounds of war. Gradually everyone calmed down and waited for it to stop.

Finally, it did end, for then. The explosions and shelling stopped. The men who were above ground carefully watching could see that the soldiers were leaving Drohitchin on the other side of the shtetl. When the soldiers had completely withdrawn, the shtetl men went up above ground to look around. There were fires and smoke everywhere.

Afterwards, in the wake of this terrible nightmare there, it was followed by an outbreak of cholera. Lots of people, who had survived the bombings and the hunger from lack of food, died of disease. People were very much afraid of catching the dreaded disease and didn't go near people who had contracted it. Whole families died of cholera without anyone to help them.

It was so hard to just survive that everyone was in trouble. The shtetl welfare systems weren't working because everyone was having a hard time surviving. The *chevra kadisha* (the burial society hev' ra • cod dish' a) was kept very busy. They didn't know who to take care of first.

Reb Moshe Leizer Gratch was the leader of the Drohitchin chevra kadisha. They worked night and day, preparing all of the people who had died for burial. The chevra kadisha arranged for the graves to be dug at the Jewish cemetery. The men of the chevra kadisha hauled the water that was needed for the ritual bathing from the communal well.

Traditionally the chevra kadisha show proper deference for rich and poor alike. Everything is done for the person who has died with the utmost respect, insuring that the sanctity of the body is maintained. The chevra kadisha are so respectful that nothing is passed over the body, only around it. The women from the chevra kadisha take care of the women who have died, and the men take care of the men.

Everything in Drohitchin was done in the time-honored religiously Jewish way for the Jews. Talking in soothing terms to the body, they started the preparation for burial by softly saying the traditional prayers.

"The Lord has given and the Lord has taken, blessed be the Name of the Lord."

Then they undressed and washed the body; first to clean the body and then to purify the body before it went back to G_d. Out of modesty and respect for the person, they tried to keep the body covered as much as possible and always kept the face up.

After the ritual bathing, the body was dressed in a white robe, a shroud. The men were wrapped in their tallis (prayer shawl) as well. The tallis was first rendered useless by cutting off one of the fringes. The body with its eyes closed, was laid on the floor with candles all around it. The chevra kadisha remained all night watching the body while reading the psalms and speaking comfortingly to the soul.

The next day, they placed the body in the coffin. It was a plain wooden box that was made with wooden nails, and not fancy.

Jewish people are supposed to be buried without any display of ostentation that distinguishes the wealthy from the pauper.

The modest casket must be made of wood or other organic material, that will decompose in the ground, allowing the body to return to the earth as quickly as possible. **"And the dust returns to the earth as it was, and the spirit returns to God, Who gave it."**

The casket must not have metal parts because not only will it not disintegrate quickly, but because metal is the material of weapons and war weapons. Jewish people believe that it would not be appropriate to ascend to heaven bearing arms and aided by the elements of war.

Everyone walked behind the wagon that carried the coffin as it went past the synagogue courtyard to the Drohitchin Jewish cemetery. They stopped the traditional seven times to recite Psalm 91 before they reached the grave. They said the blessing, ***"Baruch atah Hashem Elokeinu melech haolam, dayan ha'emet,"*** **Blessed are you, Lord our G_d, Ruler of the universe, the true Judge.**

The close members of the family tore a part of their clothing when they first heard of the death or at the funeral. This was a traditional sign of their loss and a safe way to vent their anger. The rabbi recited psalms and the Mourner's *Kaddish* was said.

Sometimes damaged holy books that must be buried are placed in the grave with the coffin. This is not only because we dispose of holy books by burying them but so that the person who died will rise to heaven on the words of G_d.

Once the coffin was lowered into the grave, starting with the family, the mourners passed a shovel to each other after tossing shovels full of earth into the grave. Following the burial, the people formed two lines and as the mourners passed them by, they said the traditional condolence: ***"Hamakom y'nachem etchem b'toch sh'ar availai tziyon ee yerushalayim."*** **May G_d comfort you among all the mourners of Zion and Jerusalem.**

**[Photo:] Drohitchin funeral with horse-drawn cart carrying the coffin
(ca. early 20th century)**

[Photo:] Drohitchin cemetery (ca. early 20th century)

When they left the cemetery, everyone washed their hands before entering their homes to remove spiritual impurity and as a symbolic cleansing from death. A jar of water is left outside on the doorstep of the home of mourners for this purpose, so that all who went to the funeral could wash their hands. After the funeral, the family went home to sit *shiva* (the traditional first week of mourning). They lit the traditional large, seven-day candle to mark the shiva.

During the shiva all of the mirrors in the house are covered because the mourners are supposed to put aside any thought of vanity and think only about mourning. Some people believe that the tradition of covering the mirrors also stems from the fear of seeing ghosts in the mirrors.

When seated, the mourners sit on low stools or wooden boxes. They are not supposed to do anything but mourn. The bereaved are not supposed to worry about ordinary things. They are not even supposed to cook for themselves, especially the first meal after the funeral. So friends and other family members bring food for them. When the first meal is eaten after returning from the cemetery, friends are expected to stay and join in this meal. It is considered a mitzvah and act of charity to stay and comfort the grieving family. Traditionally, round foods such as eggs and round breads are served to symbolize the cyclical nature of life. Mourners don't even get up to answer the door to greet visitors. The door is left unlocked and visitors are expected to just enter.

Prayer services are frequently held where the family sits shiva. In the shtetl, the men made up the minyan. They came to the mourners' home so that the mourners would be able to say *Kaddish* (the mourners' prayer).The Mourner's *Kaddish* is a prayer that is a sanctification of G_d's name. It is also a prayer that asks G_d to give peace, grace, kindness, compassion, long life, and ample sustenance to His people, all of Israel. By rising from the depths of their grief to make a public declaration of the glory of G_d, the mourners transform their experience with death into an affirmation of life.

During that first week, mourners are traditionally exempt from all the usual activities of daily life, and not supposed to participate in its pleasures either. The close members of the family do not go to work or play; they don't go to the office or cook, unless absolutely necessary. In modern times, they are not supposed to watch TV, movies or work out. According to rabbis, the shiva is purely for exploring the emotional aspects of the relationship of the mourners to the person who died.

This is the way it was supposed to be done when things were normal. It was very hard to do anything in a usual way during the wars, when it was so difficult just to stay alive. People did the best they could to observe the traditions.

Fradal and her family had again lost everything in a fire in one of the bombings during the Russo-Polish War. Fradal was about nine years old when the Bolshevik army came into Drohitchin. They were lucky they weren't killed. During those bombings, even some of the richest people in Drohitchin lost everything. Bombed out buildings caught fire, and lots of people lost all of their property.

Their houses and what they owned had burned down. When they were able to leave the trenches, and go up to see what had happened, many found that they had nothing left but what they had brought with them to the trenches. Fradal's mother had grabbed the small bag of grain as they were leaving the house to go to the trenches.

In that fire, Fradal's family, like so many of the others, lost their home and everything they had. The house where they had lived was nothing but a pile of ashes. They moved in with two other families. There was the woman who owned the house and her daughter and there was the Neidick family. Mrs. Neidick was a widow with four sons, and there was Chaiya Bailya and her three children. There were eleven people, all living in four rooms. The floor was earthen like most of the houses of the poor. Wintertime the earthen floor gave off a chill. Only the well-off had wooden floors.

Everyone spent their time in that house sitting around the big wood burning stove in the middle of the main room just trying to warm up their bones. There was very little food. Little Fradal used to sit near the oven and pray for food. Once the Neidick boys found some frozen apples. When they weren't looking Fradal took the peals out of the garbage and she, Hunia and Hasha ate them. The Joint Jewish Distribution Committee in America sent them care packages from the U.S. Those packages of food and medicine saved many lives.

The landlady told Chaiya Bailya they would have to pay her rent. She had taken them in because it was an emergency and they had no place to live, but she couldn't support them forever. She didn't have any money either, and she would have to get a tenant who could pay her.

Chaiya Bailya had no money, so she went out and searched Drohitchin for a place for them to live. She found an empty house. The people that lived there had fled during the bombings. The house belonged to a Gentile family, and she was afraid to go in, but she did. She was afraid that they would come back and kill them, if they found them living in their house. Those people took everything they had with them except their wood. Every summer people would go into the forest to cut enough wood for the winter. They used to burn the wood to keep the houses warm and for cooking. The people who owned that house were poor too, so all Fradal, Hasha, Hunia and their mother had was a roof over their heads, and a place to keep warm.

It was just after the harvest time. The ground in the Polesia is wet and very rich. It is good for growing all kinds of vegetables. When times were good, people planted gardens. People planted potatoes, beets, peas, beans, cucumbers, cabbage, carrots, turnips, radishes, onions, even pumpkins. They had enough vegetables for themselves and to sell to other people. But when weren't times hard in Drohitchin?

After the harvest the women used to make pickles and sauerkraut. They pickled the cucumbers and cabbage in barrels, and saved it for the winter. People didn't have refrigerators. Those who had cellars would put their vegetables down there to keep them cold, so they would have vegetables for the winter. People who didn't have cellars used to dig a hole in the ground in the back of their house, and then put the vegetables in there until the winter. They would put the potatoes, the beets, the carrots, onions and what not in the hole. When winter came, they used to dig it all up. Some winters when people were not so lucky, the autumn floods would get into cellars and the holes and make everything wet, rotting all of the vegetables.

The Jews weren't allowed to own land but the Gentiles had farms. They planted fields of grain: barley, rye, oats, buckwheat. The starving people went out into the fields that had already been harvested and searched for anything left behind. Fradal, Hasha, Hunia and their mother found some grain and used it to make bread, and they found some apples in an orchard. By the time the Drohitchin ground was white with the winter's ice, they had nothing left. The floods had ruined the vegetables. With the fires from the cannon shelling and the terrible winter, and so many people hurt or sick with diseases, food, grain had become very dear.

The winter of 1919 was very hard for everyone, and everyone was desperate. One market day, Chaiya Bailya told her two daughters that she was very sorry, but she was going to have to sell their gold lockets. She said thank G_d they had them to sell. She had already sold her own locket. Until that day, Fradal and Hasha had worn those treasured little lockets on their necks and never took them off. Now they unhooked them and silently handed them to their mama. Chaiya Bailya took the little gold lockets to the market and sold them to a peddler who was passing through. She took the money he gave her and bought a large sack, a *pud* [36 lbs.], of grain with it. That would feed them through the winter.

Weeks later, the peddler came back to Drohitchin, and searched for Chaiya Bailya, until he found her at their house. The minute he was there, he started yelling at her that she had robbed him. He shouted that the lockets were not gold. They were nothing but plate. He pulled the two lockets out of his pocket and threw them on the floor. Chaiya Bailya said that she didn't know what he was talking about. She didn't even know what plate was. He wanted his money back. Chaiya Bailya told him she didn't have the money any more. She had bought food with the money. The peddler saw the sack of grain sitting in a corner. He went to take the sack. Hunia saw him walking towards the grain. Hunia quickly grabbed a kitchen knife. He ran over and stabbed the sack of grain, slitting the bag wide open. The grain scattered all over the floor. The peddler dropped the empty torn sack and stormed out. Chaiya Bailya bent down and picked up the lockets. She gave them back to Hasha and Fradal and told the girls they could put them back on.

In Drohitchin, Thursday was usually market day. The shtetl was filled with people on those days. They came from all of the farms surrounding the shtetl. The people gathered in the Marketplace. It was in an open area in the center of Drohitchin on the main road.

On Market Days everybody was selling something. The farmers (mostly goyim) would come to sell their animals, horses, calves, pigs, chickens, eggs. They sold potatoes, sacks of rye, oats, barley, buckwheat, seeds to make oil, wool from their sheep, and homemade linens from the flax they grew. People sold all kinds of things; they sold whatever people needed. There were women selling the clay pots that they made from Drohitchin clay. There is a lot of clay in Drohitchin. On market days, it was very crowded with people; people selling and people buying. If you had the money you could buy. They also sold sweaters, goatskin vests, hats, salt, fish oil for boots, candles, lamp oil. They sold tools, old ones, new ones, and tar for greasing wagon wheels. You name it; they had it for sale there. You would think it was 14th Street in Manhattan or Macy's.

Hunia and Fradal used to go into the forest together. Hunia always knew which way to go. They never got lost. Hunia taught Fradal to watch the sun to see where it was when they went into the forest so they would know how to go back. There were many kinds of animals in the forest. There were wolves, foxes, deer. Sometimes these animals would come out of the woods and bother and even hurt the villagers. So they knew that there were dangerous animals, even bears, in the forest. But Hunia and Fradal never saw a bear. They just heard about them being in the woods.

In the forest, they picked blueberries or whatever fruit was in season. Hunia taught Fradal to pick the plump, full blueberries with a light gray-blue color. He used to say not to bother with the berries with even a little hint of red because they weren't ripe yet.

After they went berry picking, they went and sold them by the cupful, especially on market day to get a few *kopecks*. In the village square, Hunia would play *fraylock* (happy) songs on his *dudki* to get people to come over and Fradal would sell them the blueberries. He used to play the songs that the *klezmer* musicians played and that everyone knew.

[Photo:] A typical shtetl market day, Eastern Europe (ca. 1915)
Photo courtesy of YIVO Archives, NY

**[Photo:] Shtetl women selling *challahs* and other breads on market day,
Eastern Europe (ca. early 20th century)**
Photo courtesy of Museum of Polish History, Warsaw, Poland

Hunia was a wonderful boy. The sort of boy who - when he found out that there were two Jewish prisoners in the local jail one Friday - brought them some food. He did this even though his family didn't have much for themselves. Hunia was studying at the *Beit Midrash* (house of study), that Friday afternoon shortly before his bar mitzvah. In the shtetl, during the mid-week, the life of the men who were learned was spent mostly in the house of study. The rabbi and scholars studied the Torah and the Talmud there. They spent a lot of time there. And that is where most news was discussed and spread.

Hunia was there studying, when he heard the men talking about the two Jewish prisoners that the police had arrested and put in jail. Those men were strangers who were passing through. People were often put in jail just because they were strangers and didn't have the right papers. It could then take quite a few days until a regional judge would see them and decide to release them. People said that the two men wouldn't be fed until the next day and perhaps not for two or three days. Hunia was afraid that they wouldn't have food for Shabbos, if then. They didn't have family in Drohitchin to bring them food. Hunia knew what hunger was. He went home and took what he could and brought it to the two men at the jailhouse. When Hunia told his mother what he was doing, she didn't tell him no. It was probably the only food those men had that day or the next.

It was almost spring 1919, when the Polish Legionnaires marched into Drohitchin on the heels of the Bolsheviks fleeing. It seemed that one army left the helpless little shtetl on one side of Drohitchin, and before the poor people ever got a chance to know what peace was, another army came from the other side of Drohitchin to take its place. Hunia's bar mitzvah was shortly after the Polish Legionnaires had come. Whenever there wasn't any fighting in the streets, people went to shul on Shabbos. Hunia's bar mitzvah was on one of those Saturday mornings.

During the week before Hunia's bar mitzvah their grandfather, Zaidy Zelig (Fradal's father's father), came to the house. He never used to come to visit. They always saw him at his house or in synagogue. That day, he came to see Hunia. He had a package he was carrying under his arm.

Chaiya Bailya asked him to sit down and she offered him some tea. He accepted. He wasn't in a hurry. His grandchildren wanted to know what was in the package and why he was there, but they wouldn't dare be so rude as to ask. They were all standing around when Zaidy Zelig started to talk. He turned to Hunia and said, "You know, Hunia, this Shabbos we will go to shul and you will be bar mitzvahed. Then you will be a man in the shul. You will be obligated to remember the mitzvahs and to be a good Jew. You know there are 613 mitzvahs - the 613 commandments in the Torah – not just the Ten Commandments.

"Before your father went to America, he gave me his old *tallis*, the prayer shawl from when he was a boy. He said that if he couldn't send for you before, I should save it for you and give it to you when you are bar mitzvahed. I have it here for you. This is your father's *tallis*, his prayer shawl from when he was bar mitzvahed.

"A Jewish man usually gets two prayer shawls in his life. The first one he gets when he is bar mitzvahed. The second prayer shawl, a much bigger one, he gets when he takes a wife and gets married. That is when you are really expected to be a man in life, not just in synagogue. That prayer shawl lasts the rest of your life. It is the only thing you get to take with you to the after-life.

"Your father wanted you should have this. He has the prayer shawl that his mama, your Bubba Rifka, and me gave him when he got married."

Hunia already knew how to put the *tallis* on. Zaidy Zelig and the other men had taught him and the other boys at the house of study. He had been watching the men put their prayer shawls on all of his life, knowing that one day he would put one on too. Hunia knew that they didn't have money so he didn't know where he was going to get one. He didn't know that he would have the pleasure of having his own father's prayer shawl.

Hunia took it and started to finger it and feel the tassels. "Good!" Zaidy Zelig said. "You are supposed to finger the tassels. That is why they are there." Zaidy Zelig said, 'The fringes are made with 613 threads, so you will remember the 613 mitzvahs - the 613 commandments in the Torah to be a good Jew."

That Saturday the family went to shul and Hunia put on his prayer shawl. They were grateful and happy and proud of Hunia. They all said *Shehecheyanu - "He gave us life,"* the customary prayer of thanksgiving over something new and special. It is how Jewish people thank G_d for their living to be able to have a specific experience. ***"Blessed are You, Lord our G_d, King of the Universe who has given us life and kept us and brought us to this time."***

In Drohitchin, people didn't have the kind of big fancy bar mitzvahs people have here in America today. The bar mitzvah boy would be called up to the Torah and just do a reading. Afterwards there was a small celebration.

Hunia just read the passage for that day from the Book of the Prophets. He had studied it so he would get it just right and he did. Then the rabbi and all of the men shook his hand and congratulated him on doing a good job. Hunia's father was in America so he wasn't there to say the father's prayer thanking G_d for making his son a man (and not a girl).

Now Hunia was obligated to remember the 613 commandments from the Torah, just like all other Jewish men. Everyone shouted Mazel Tov! Hunia was now one of the men and to be counted in the minyan. Fradal, Hasha, and their mama sat there watching in the women's section behind the curtain that separated the women from the men. Their bubby, Bubba Rivka, their papa's mother, was sitting next to them and their papa's sisters and nieces and all of their children sat with them behind the traditional curtain, as they did every Saturday. Bubba Rivka sat beaming with pride and she wasn't easy to please. Zaidy Zelig was in the front with the men. The men were all saying mazel tov to him too, as the proud grandfather. The whole family was very proud of the job Hunia did. Their papa's whole family was there, but their papa was in America, of course. He would have been proud too if he were there with them. Afterwards, they said the blessings for the wine and the challah that the women had managed to put together. When they toasted Hunia with the wine, everyone shouted L'chaim!

It was 1919, about two months after Hunia's bar mitzvah, when the letter came. When any letter from America came, it was always a special occasion, but this time it was different. You could see this letter was different. It was much fatter than any other letter their father had ever sent. Chaiya Bailya thought she knew what was in it. They had waited for so long. They were hoping they weren't wrong. Chaiya Bailya opened it very carefully. Some money fell out. Fradal picked it all up and gave it to her mama. They weren't wrong. There were the papers from their papa for the four of them to go to America. In the letter their papa gave instructions for what they were supposed to do in order to go. There were papers to give to the officials that said who they were and that he was Chaiya Bailya's husband and their father. Each paper had three copies.

And there was a picture of their papa. He wrote in the letter that he wanted them to be able to recognize him without his beard. It was more than eight years since their papa had left to go to America. Their mama said she didn't recognize him. He was wearing *Americaner* clothes and his beard was gone. Their mama told them that their papa looked like a different man from the one that left to go to America.

[Photo:] Barney Levine, New York City (ca. 1919)

It cost about $200 for one person to come to America from Eastern Europe. In those days, that was a king's ransom. In America, a good week's wages were about $12. Fradal's father was a very poor man; he must have worked night and day to save the money for the four of them to come.

In the letter, their papa reminded them that when he got to America, the officials changed his name from Berel Yosski Valevelsky to Barney Levine. He decided that it would be better if he chose their American names for them, then to have the officials do it. Their papa figured if you had an American name that the officials could read and pronounce, they wouldn't change it. So their father got somebody in America to help him pick new American names for them, and that is what their names were on the papers. Fradal's name, Fradal Valevelsky was changed to the American name Frieda Levine. Hunia was now going to be called Charlie Levine, and Hasha's name, Hasha Devorah Valevelsky, was changed to Anna Levine. Their mother, Chaiya Bailya Valevelsky, became Mrs. Bella Levine.

They danced around the little house until they almost fell down. They were going to have a new life in America, without war and soldiers. They were even going to have new names. They would have enough food and clothes to keep them warm and dry. Enough food, oh! They were going to eat challah every day. But best of all they would be with their papa. They were so excited. The four of them started dancing around their little kitchen. They were going to have a new life.

One day soon after that, Hunia came running home. He was hot and sweaty but in his hand were the photographs. The four of them had gone to the *fotographer,* like their papa said they should in the letter, and had their pictures taken. They had never had their pictures taken before. Their mama had sent Hunia to see if the pictures were ready.

**[Passport photo:] Chaiya Bailya Valevelsky,
Drohitchin, Belarus – 1920**

[Passport photos:] Sisters - Fradal and Hasha Valevelsky,
Drohitchin, Belarus – 1920

"Why are you so hot from running? Are you ok? Hunia, you
don't look so good. Your face is all red. Hunia, you come sit down
and open your shirt." his mama said. Hunia said that his throat hurt
in the morning when he got up, and now it was worse. She looked
at his chest it was all red. Their mama feared what was happening.
She told Hunia to get into bed, and she told Fradal to take the bucket
and go get water from the well. She said, "Don't tell anyone, not
anyone, that Hunia has fever!" Fradal knew better than to disobey
her mother when she used that voice, but she wouldn't have told
anyone anyway. She knew better. There was an epidemic of scarlet
fever. They feared that they would take Hunia away to be
quarantined, and that he could die there. Chaiya Bailya knew she
could give him better care if she took care of him herself. She did

whatever she could that would get the fever down. She took care of Hunia nonstop. She did not let Hasha or Fradal help her, and she wouldn't let them near Hunia. She feared that they would get scarlet fever, too. The girls just kept bringing water from the well for the cold compresses. They didn't tell anyone anything.

Hunia wouldn't eat. He was too weak to even shake his head no, and tell them that his throat hurt too much. Chaiya Bailya finally did tell Fradal to go get Bubba Rivka and Zaidy Zelig. She said to tell them Hunia needed a doctor.

Before the week was over, Hunia was gone from them. He never saw another Shabbos. The day after he died, his mother and sisters watched while he was wrapped in his prayer shawl, now with the one cut fringe. He was buried in Drohitchin's Jewish cemetery. They had seen a lot of death but never thought it would touch them by taking their Hunia.

After Hunia's funeral, Fradal, Hasha and their mother went back home to sit shiva -the week of mourning. They washed their hands outside before they went into the house, like you are supposed to after going to a cemetery. During the first meal, they ate the hard-boiled eggs and round bread that their papa's sisters had brought them. Those are the traditional foods that symbolize the cyclical nature of life that are eaten after a funeral. Usually people come to the house to pay their respects and to comfort the mourners when they are sitting shiva. But nothing could comfort them. They were heartbroken in their grief.

People usually also come so the mourners can say *Kaddish*, the mourner's prayer. You need a minyan to say Kaddish. When Jews stand and say the Kaddish, they are praising G_d's greatness in spite of their loss. It is supposed to help raise the soul of the person who died up to heaven. You are supposed to stand up and say the Kaddish during the services every day for one month for a relative. You say Kaddish for eleven months, out of more respect, for a mother or father.

People who are sitting shivah are not supposed to do a lot of different things to take care of themselves during that week.

Traditionally, friends of the family come to help and to pray with the mourners. Because of the war and all of the illness, there were so many people sitting shivah in Drohitchin that not many people were able to come to their house for the minyan. And also, people were afraid to go into the house where someone had died of scarlet fever. When Chaiya Bailya and her daughters were sitting shivah for Hunia, not enough men came so they could have a minyan at home, so they went to shul to say Kaddish for Hunia. There were a lot of people in synagogue because so many people needed to say Kaddish for their loved ones.   ೮ঙ

❦ *Pinsk* ❧

*C*haiya Bailya wasn't a very big woman. She had dark hair and a kind face. After Hunia died, the deep sadness she felt never left her eyes. When Hunia was gone more than one month, Chaiya Bailya, with a will of iron, pulled herself together. She said that it was time for them to get going. They were going to their papa in America. But before they went, she wanted to go say goodbye to her sisters and family in Pinsk. She said that in this world who knew when she would ever see them again. Chaiya Bailya was born in Pinsk in 1886. That is where she had met and married Fradal's papa. She was 18 years old and their papa was 21 when they got married. Their papa was having trouble making ends meet, so after his wife became pregnant with Hasha, he thought it would be better for them to leave Pinsk and move to Drohitchin where his family lived.

Chaiya Bailya had two sisters who lived in Pinsk and a younger brother, Yankel (Yonk' el). They were very poor. Chaiya Bailya's father had died when she was a little girl and then their mother had died. They all worked as maids.

Yankel had once come to see them in Drohitchin. It was when he was drafted into the Czars' army. He didn't have the money to pay off the conscription agents, so he had to go fight for the Czar. Fradal remembered him. He was very handsome. He was dark and had a dark mustache and when he smiled he had a devilish twinkle in his eye. Yankel wanted to see his sister Chaiya Bailya and meet her children before he went off to war, because he didn't know when he would ever be able to come back. They never heard from him again after that.

Chaiya Bailya took Fradal with her to Pinsk. She told Hasha to stay in Drohitchin. Hasha was still working for the scribe and his family. The wife had a difficult birth, and now there were six children to take care of.

Chaiya Bailya and Fradal went to the Drohitchin train station and waited for the eastern bound train. Pinsk was about 72km, maybe 45 miles, east on the train. Fradal had never been on the train before. It was very exciting. Then she thought about Hunia and knew that he would have loved riding on the train too. She missed him terribly and still couldn't believe that he was gone forever.

[Photo:] Street in city of Pinsk, Belarus (ca. 1910)
Photo courtesy of www. rymaszewski.iinet.net.au

When they got to Pinsk, Fradal's mama said it still looked almost the same as when she left in 1904 to move to Drohitchin. Drohitchin was a very small shtetl, but Pinsk is a city. It's on the Pripyat River. There were big buildings and some factories. It even smelled different from Drohitchin. You smelled the smoke from the coal burning chimneys at the factories. And they had a lot of people. Pinsk had more than 24,000 people living there. Fradal never saw anything like it before.

Fradal and her mother walked from the Pinsk train station to where her family lived. Her sisters were still there. Fradal met their husbands and their children. They were happy to see them and very sorry to hear about Hunia. When Chaiya Bailya asked about Yankel, her sisters told her that they hadn't heard from him since he left either. Chaiya Bailya said that when they got back to Drohitchin she would go ask the Kholozhiner about him. Her sisters seemed to know all about the Kholozhiner. He was famous even in Pinsk.

The next day, Fradal and her mother left to go home. They kissed them all goodbye, and Chaiya Bailya said she would try to send them all the papers to come to America. Waving goodbye, they left. When they got to the end of the street, Fradal's mother turned and went in a different direction from the train station. Fradal asked her mama, where they were going. Her mother told her that she was going to see a big doctor about her stomach pain. Chaiya Bailya seemed to know where she was going. She said that she had heard about him. When they got to his office, Chaiya Bailya went in. She told Fradal that she should sit quietly and wait for her outside.

Chaiya Bailya's stomach always hurt her, but seemed to bother her even more since Hunia died, but she didn't complain. She tried to hide it, but Fradal could tell. A while later she came out. Fradal asked her mother what the doctor had said. Her mama just said, "What does he know? Nothing more than they do in Drohitchin." He just gave her some medicine. Fradal's mama told her not to worry about her. She was going to be fine. Then they turned and went in the direction of the train station and went home to Drohitchin.   ೞ

**[Photo:] left: Fradal's maternal grandmother,
right: Fradal's mother's sisters
Pinsk, Belarus (ca. 1903)**

[Back of photo:] Fradal's maternal family
Pinsk, Belarus (ca. 1903)

ഔ *Shnippistolk* ങ

They knew they were going to have a hard time getting to America. They had lost their *mazel*, their luck, in the snow. Packing their few things and the papers from their papa, and the passport pictures they had taken, they said good-by to all of their friends and relatives, and they got ready to go.

They said good-by to their father's family - Bubba Rivka and Zaideh Zelig, their father's brothers, their uncles Aaron and Zolmon, and to their uncle Zolmon's daughter, their cousin Sonia, who now lives in Israel. Their papa's sister, Chaiya Bailya's sister-in-law Maitta, was the oldest. She lived in the next town with her husband and their seven children. They came to Drohitchin to say good-by to Chaiya Bailya and the girls. And they said good-by to their father's younger sister, aunt Yenta, and her family. Yenta had a twisted mouth but was a very good soul. She had married a widower with two daughters. One of her step-daughters is their cousin Broucha, who now has a chicken farm in Springfield, Massachusetts. Bubba Rivka gave Chaiya Bailya pictures of the family that she wanted her daughter-in-law to give to her son. Everyone said, *"Zol nor zein mit glick."* That means that things should go well for them, and they should only have good luck.

Hasha's dearest friend, Ruchel begged them to send her their old clothes when they got to America. They told her of course they would. Who didn't know that in America no one ever wore old *shmattas* (shmot' tess – rags)? They were happy to be going even though Hunia wasn't going with them. All of their friends were happy for them, but every one of them would have been even happier if they were going in their place.

[Photo:] Fradal and Hasha's father's brother, uncle Aaron
and his family, Drohichyn, Belarus (ca. 1920)

Last of all they went to pay their respect and say good-by to the Kholozhiner. His house was near the other side of Drohitchin, on one of the main streets. It was one of the bigger houses in the shtetl, but he wasn't rich and, for an important person, his house was very plain. People were always coming to him for advice and with their troubles, and he would help them. Chaiya Bailya and her daughters went to ask about her brother Yankel, to say good-by, but also and more important to ask for a blessing.

They told the Kholozhiner that the papers and money had come from their papa for them to go to America. They had waited so long, but finally they were going to the "golden land."

Like everybody else, he had a relative in America. He wanted they should bring his cousin, his regards and a letter with a picture from the family. Chaiya Bailya said that, of course, they would be happy to. They never saw his cousin because it turned out he lived in Chicago, and they never went there. When they got to New York and found out how far Chicago was, they mailed the letter to him. Who knew Chicago wasn't around the corner from Delancey Street?

"I hear from him once in a year, but I haven't seen him since he ran away from the Czar's army." the Lamed-vovnick sighed, "I miss him. He should only live and be well." Chaiya Bailya told him, that one of the reasons they had come to him was to ask about her brother Yankel. He wasn't so lucky as to be able to run away. Yankel became a soldier for the Czar, and they hadn't heard from him since he left. She asked the Kholozhiner if he thought that Yankel was ok. The Kholozhiner said "From land you come back. From sand you don't come back." It was the Kholozhiner's way of telling her that Yankel had died. About a year, later they heard that the Kholozhiner was right; that Yankel had died.

Chaiya Bailya said, "We are going to miss everything we have ever known, and all of our friends and the family. We will probably never see any of you again. *Oy,* what a life! To have to go away from everything and everybody, to have to go so far, just to have a little peace. To tell you the truth, I'm afraid to go. I came here, from Pinsk, years ago, after I got married; I've never been anywhere else.

Whoever expected to really be going to the other side of the world? Besides, who knows what could happen along the way? Maybe we wouldn't even get to America. Well, you'll pray for me and for my girls, that we should have a little mazel."

"Of course I will pray for you." the Kholozhiner said. "And I am sure you will all be all right. What's here to miss? You'll be with your husband. You'll be fine. What could be bad? You are going to the "golden land" and you will have a golden life there. I know you will. Here take this coin, I found it. It is a lucky coin. It will bring you mazel and lead you in the right way."

They thanked the Lamed-vov for his blessings, and good hopes for them, and for the good luck piece. They felt better about leaving their home after being blessed by the Lamed-vov. As they were walking back to their house, Hasha asked if she could see the coin. Their mama had wrapped the lucky coin in her hanky and was about to put it in her pocket. She stopped walking and showed it to the two girls. Their mama said that Hasha should be very careful with it, that it was going to bring them good luck. Chaiya Bailya gave Hasha the coin. It didn't take a minute; she didn't even get a chance to look on it. It slipped from her hands and fell right into the snow. They right away quick bent down and looked for it, but it was gone, like it never was. Disappeared, who knows where and that was the end of it. Finished! And with it, went their luck.

The time came. Finally, they were almost all packed and ready. They were going to take the train to go to America. One morning before they left, Hasha and Fradal got up; their mama was still in bed. She always woke up before them. Their mother, Chaiya Bailya, was very hot and sweating, and doubled over in pain. She asked Fradal to get her some water and her medicine. She was very thirsty. Even Fradal could see she was very sick. Hasha went for a glass of water, and told Fradal that she should hurry up quick and go get Bubba Rivka. Fradal really didn't like Bubba Rivka. She was her papa's mother, but a scary woman. Fradal never wanted to have to tell her anything bad, but she went.

Their mama was very sick for I don't know how long. Her skin and eyes seemed to turn yellow, and she kept throwing up. She was in a lot of pain. There was no hospital, no more medicine. Their grandmother, Bubba Rivka gave their mother something to drink; nothing helped. The doctor came but he didn't seem to know what to do. Nobody knew what to do. She kept getting worse and worse, and then she died. Bubba Rivka sent someone to get the chevra kadisha, the burial society.

The next day, Fradal and Hasha watched while their mother was buried in Drohitchin's Jewish cemetery next to Hunia. Chaiya Bailya was only 34 years old. Everyone said she should be a guardian angel for her girls. Fradal was ten years old then, but even when she herself was an old lady, it was still painful to talk about her mother.

Hasha and Fradal walked home holding each other tightly. They were all they had except for their papa, and he was on the other side of the world and didn't know about their mama. Hasha wrote him a letter and told him about their mama dying. She told Fradal that their mother had made her promise to take care of Fradal, and that they should go to America. I don't know what made Hasha so strong. She was fifteen, not much more than a little girl herself. I guess when you have to be strong you are, because you didn't have a choice.

They sat shivah at Bubba Rivka and Zaidy Zelig's house. Fradal went to shul twice every day to say Kaddish for her mama, just as they had done for Hunia. But Hasha refused to go. No one could change her mind. Not even Zaidy Zelig could persuade her to go say Kaddish. You go to say Kaddish to say that even though a member of your family has died, you still revere G_d. Hasha asked why G_d had let their mama and Hunia die? Why did he let so many other people die and suffer? For what? Zaidy Zelig didn't force her to go say Kaddish. To him she was just a girl anyway. It wasn't as if she were a son who was unwilling to say Kaddish. Hasha's anger scared Fradal. So Fradal went to shul alone to say Kaddish. Sometimes Zaidy Zelig went with her. Once in a while, she saw the

Kholozhiner there. He tried to comfort Fradal, but nothing did. She didn't say anything to him.

Hasha told their grandparents and uncles not to worry; they wouldn't have to take care of them. They had the papers and money from their papa, and they were going to America to be there with him. Their family seemed relieved. Hasha and Fradal knew that their mother had wanted them to go. She told them before she died that they had to go. And they knew it would have been hard for their family to have two more mouths to feed.

They were never really that close to their father's family. Bubba Rivka always called their father a *trumbanick* (trum' ba nick-a bum). She said he was always running off and leaving what he was supposed to do. He didn't like to go to school. He wasn't like her other two sons. He had run off as a boy and then came home years later with a wife and baby. He didn't even have a marriage matchmaker.

Hasha and Fradal kept close together. Fradal asked Hasha who was going to take care of them. Hasha said that until they got to their papa, she would take care of them, just as she had promised their mama she would. I don't know how, but she did. She became Fradal's mother and her father. They became each other's whole family.

It was still dark out when the two young girls took the train. They had been to the station before, but Hasha had never gotten on the train. She had only looked on it before. Now they were riding all the way to some place called Warsaw, just the two of them. The two sisters called it *shnippistolk*. Shnippistolk is a Yiddish word for a distant place that does not really exist and is hard to imagine what it is actually like. It was a very long trip and they were frightened. Everything frightened Fradal then. Hasha was afraid too but didn't show it. Nothing ever seemed to scare her or at least she would never show it.

Warsaw - they had never seen anything like it. Who knew from such things? Drohitchin was a small shtetl, a country village, far from anything. What did they know? They were plain people.

Who would expect there should be such things as they saw in Warsaw?

Just the hoo-ha, the tumult, they never heard anything like it. Even Russian chicken yards didn't sound like the streets of Warsaw. And all of the streets were paved. In Drohitchin only the main street was paved. Drohitchin still had mud puddles with wooden boards placed over them to walk on. Even Pinsk wasn't such a big city. And Pinsk didn't have as many beautiful big buildings as Warsaw. There were so many people in the streets hurrying around; Fradal and Hasha couldn't imagine where they could all be going. And a lot of them were dressed so fancy and in the middle of the week yet!

Hasha asked directions from a man with a long beard and coat. She thought he looked Jewish. She was right. He answered them in Yiddish. He told them that the area where they wanted to go was the Jewish section, on the other side of Warsaw. He said they should take a streetcar there. The man called it the *tram vise*. He pointed across the street at it. It looked a lot like a train but only one car. The motorman took their money and told them where to get off. Somehow they understood him. They managed to get to their Uncle Zolmon's friend's brother's house. He was a glazier and lived with his wife Malka in Warsaw. His name was Pinya Brodsky.

Their father had told their mama, in his letter, to write to Pinya Brodsky, and ask if they could stay with him and his wife while they were in Warsaw. They would, of course, pay him. Their father had stayed with them when he was in Warsaw. And if not, if he knew some nice kosher people they could stay with. He wrote back saying, that he and his wife would be happy to have them stay with them. They would make a place for them.

The Brodskys lived in a tiny, little apartment, all the way up on the third floor, in a dirty, old building. They lived alone in that apartment, just the two of them. It was such a pity, that they never had had children. They were nice people if you shouldn't need anything, and didn't mind Mrs. Brodsky yelling on you.

After they finally got there, the Brodskys didn't want to let the girls stay with them. When they heard that their mama had died, they didn't want to be responsible for two girls. But Hasha told them they would pay them extra, and they would help out. She pleaded. They had nowhere else to go until they could get their visas, and that would only be a short time. So, the Brodskys let them stay.

Pinya and Malka Brodsky had two rooms, their bedroom, and a bigger room in the front where the four of them ate. Since Pinya was a glazier, there were always some sheets of glass standing up in the corner that he stored at home. They had to be careful not to break any of it. The toilet was in the house, not outside. It was out in the hallway; they shared it with the other families that lived there. Hasha and Fradal shared a bed in the front room. They didn't have anywhere they could call their own. It was crowded. It was the best they had money for, and they were lucky to have that. Anyway, where else could they go, two girls, alone? It didn't matter. They were going to America in a few days. They would be fine until then.

Fradal and Hasha thought it was a miracle. Right there, in the Brodsky's kitchen, they had water coming out of the wall. They never saw a sink before. In Drohitchin, they used to walk to get water from a well outside that they shared with other families. Then they had to first *schlep* (drag) it back home. They kept the water in a wooden barrel. The Brodskys had water right there in the house. They just turned the spigot when they wanted water, and it came out of the faucet. They also had gaslights instead of oil lamps. The girls had heard about gas lights but had never seen them before. Almost every day they saw something new and different in Warsaw.

After their first day, they went to the market street. Hasha said that in their papa's letter he had told them that they should buy some new clothes. They shouldn't go to America in old *shmattas* (old clothes, rags), not to mention the American Consulate. The officials there shouldn't, G_d forbid, think they were beggars, and then not give them the visas. The Brodskys told the girls that they should go to Kopelman for clothes. They said he would give them a good price if they would bargain with him, and then threaten to leave without buying anything, if he didn't lower his prices. So, that's where they went. They knew where the market street was; they had seen it the day before while going to the Brodskys' house. It wasn't far.

They walked down the street looking at everything, and trying to make their way through the crowded streets. They weren't accustomed to so many people. The street was full of people, and most of them were either buying something or selling something. In Drohitchin, there were no stores. You wanted a pair of shoes - you went to the shoemaker's house and told him what you wanted. He would measure and measure, and then he would make a pair of shoes for you. Everything else was like that too. Or you waited till market day to get what you wanted. But in Warsaw, things were different. There they had regular shops, all sorts. And there were people with stands and pushcarts selling things on the street all the time, not just on market day. Oh, what they didn't sell: food, clothes and things for the house, all kinds of *chotchkes* (chotch' kess - knickknacks). There was a big woman selling fruit and vegetables, and a homely, pock-marked man selling candied apples on sticks. There were people that had stands with bags of roasted nuts, and some with little cakes. A man selling fish from his stand was sprinkling fresh water on the barely alive, but still breathing, fish.

There were people selling clothes from carts right there in the street, but the two girls were looking for Kopelman's store. On their way, they passed a store that had a long marble counter inside. The girls could see that they sold ice cream there, and all sorts of sweets. It was their first glimpse of an ice cream parlor. They only went in there once, but it wasn't on that day. They were afraid it would cost too much. It was so fancy. Besides, they were looking for Kopelman's store. Once in a while, they would splurge and buy little cakes from a man that had a stand in the street. They would stand outside the ice cream parlor and look in through the big window. They used to eat their little cakes and imagine what it would be like to be inside. Then one day they went in and bought one ice cream. They shared it. Fradal didn't remember whether it really tasted so good, or maybe they never had had anything like it in Drohitchin. But that was the best thing they had ever eaten in their lives. Everything tasted so good in Warsaw. There was a kosher delicatessen store there that had smoked meats. They had goose salami you couldn't stop eating it, it was so good.

They ate lunch outside, because the Brodskys only gave them food two times a day; a roll or something in the morning and a hot supper at the end of the day. The girls paid for it, of course, and they helped out. The Brodskys wouldn't give away ice in winter, but they were nice people anyway. So when the girls were hungry at lunch time, they used to go to the dairy and buy a piece of cheese and then they would go to the bread man and get a couple of rolls or buckwheat buns, a piece of pumpernickel from his cart or a bagel. Sometimes they got eggs from the dairy. They used to eat them raw, right out of the shell. They used to take the food they bought, and go and sit on the edge of the street.

Fradal and Hasha spied Kopelman's Store. They looked around to make sure that it was the right place, and when they were sure, they went in. They told the man in there they wanted some new clothes. He said, of course, what else would they be doing in his store? But how did two young girls like them expect to pay for new clothes? He wanted to know. Hasha told him that they had money; that their papa had sent them money to come to him in America. When he heard, they had money, then he sang a different tune. "Oh! Of course," he said, "If you are going to America you have to have new clothes. You can't go to America in those old *shmattas* you are wearing. They wouldn't even let you in." Mr. Kopelman heard the word money, so all of a sudden, he was very nice.

He helped the girls pick out what they needed. Fradal picked out a dark blue dress with a white lace collar. The day before she had seen a girl on the tram vise wearing a dress like that. The girl had pink ribbons in her hair. Who knew that she would, the very next day, be wearing a dress like that? She chose some long white stockings, a warm coat, some pink ribbons for her braids, and her very first pair of real shoes. Hasha picked out a more grown-up looking outfit. Suddenly, she looked like a lady. She looked more like their mama. Fradal nearly started to cry, but she wouldn't let herself.

Mr. Kopelman said, "Well, well you don't look like so green anymore. No one would guess what you looked like before."

Hasha tried to bargain with Mr. Kopelman but it was no use. She even threatened to take off the beautiful things and leave, but he didn't believe they would really leave. So, he only came down a few rubles. Fradal and Hasha took everything anyway. Hasha told him to wrap them up. They were saving them to go to the American Consulate.

Hasha told Mr. Kopelman that they needed to have their picture taken to send to their papa. It was years since he had seen them. Mr. Kopelman told them to where their new clothes to go to a photographer. He told the girls to tell the photographer that he had sent them. Mr. Kopelman instructed them not to change their clothes, that they should go have their pictures taken wearing the new clothes. He told them that when they had finished, they should come back to the store and then he would wrap up the new clothes for them.

At the photographer's studio, Hasha told Fradal that they should take their lockets out and wear them on top of their dresses, so that you could see them. Until then, the girls had never stopped wearing their lockets under their clothing, where they couldn't be seen. Hasha said that she thought that their papa would like to see that they were wearing the gold lockets that he had sent them. In the picture, Fradal is the one on the left with the ribbons in her braids, and Hasha is the taller girl. You can see in the photo that they were wearing the little gold lockets that their papa had sent them.

**[Photo:] Fradal and Hasha Valevelsky after buying the new clothes
(they are wearing their little gold plated lockets),
Warsaw, Poland 1921**

The next day, the Brodskys told them how to go to the American Consulate. Hasha and Fradal were all dressed up in their new outfits. They felt like they looked just as fancy as the people they saw in the streets; except their feet hurt. They weren't used to wearing real leather shoes. In Drohitchin, they used to wear their homemade rubber shoes. But they were willing to overlook the pain in their feet.

Hasha and Fradal took a tram vise part way, and then got off and walked. They recognized the American Consulate, because it had soldiers standing guard in the front, just as the Brodskys had told them there would be. They knew they weren't Polish soldiers because they could recognize Polish soldiers. They used to have Polish soldiers in Drohitchin. And also, they had a big flag with red and white stripes and stars like Pinya Brodsky had described to them. The two young scared sisters were afraid to go in. The building was so fancy with marble on the floors. To them it looked like what they imagined a palace would look like. A guard came over and asked them what they wanted Hasha just said, 'visas'. He immediately knew what they wanted, and pointed which way they should go.

One official after another talked to them, all asking where they were going in America and what they would do there. Hasha told each one that their papa was in New York, and he had sent for them. She showed each one the papers from their father and his picture. When they finished with one official, he sent them to another one. Hasha and Fradal had a long wait for each one. They waited on long benches before they were called. The two sisters sat there with other people, everyone holding their papers just like them. It was cold and damp there. There were radiators hissing near the walls that scared Fradal, but they didn't do much to heat the place up. There were children and babies from the other families. Hasha and Fradal sat quietly on the bench afraid to move. They didn't want someone to, G_d forbid, notice them and tell them that they didn't belong there, and that they should leave.

Finally, their names were called. They heard them yell, not

Hasha and Fradal Valevelsky, but the not yet familiar, "Levine, Anna and Frieda Levine...this way." The official that called out their names sent the two girls to another part of the building: the medical rooms. They needed health certificates to show that they were healthy and didn't have a disease. When they got there, they had to wait again. Then a nurse called them. Their mother had gone that time in Pinsk, but the girls had never been to a real doctor before. Hasha said that they shouldn't be afraid. No one was going to hurt them, but Fradal didn't think that Hasha believed it herself. What did she know?

The doctor called them to come over to him. He and the nurse looked the girls over, up and down, from head to foot. They didn't talk to them, except to tell them what to do and which way to turn. They didn't talk between themselves either. Then the doctor was finished.

The doctor told Hasha and Fradal that he was sorry, but that Fradal had a disease in her eyes that other people could catch. He couldn't give them their health certificates, and not only that, but if they didn't take care on Fradal's eyes, she could even go blind from it. The doctor called the disease trachoma. He described the disease as having wild growths in her eyes. They never in their lives had ever heard of trachoma. Fradal started saying that it couldn't be; her eyes were fine. She didn't have any trouble with her eyes, they didn't hurt, she could see fine, and that he must be wrong. Hasha was almost crying, but she would never give in. She started to plead with the doctor for the health certificates. Hasha told him that they were on their way to their father. That their mother had just died and they didn't have anyone else in the world to take care of them. Fradal stood there crying with guilt and fear. Hasha begged him to give them the health certificates so they could go. He absolutely refused and that was all. Hasha pleaded "But what should we do? We don't know anyone here. We are from Belarus." He told her, "You should go to Dr. Brygida Zawadzki. She will probably be able to do something for your sister's eyes." He took a piece of paper and wrote down the address for them. He said, "Here is the doctor's name and the address. Don't go today, it is too late. Wait till tomorrow. When her eyes are cured, Dr. Zawadzki will give you a letter. Then you can come back here to me, and I will give you the health certificates."

That night, back at the Brodsky's apartment, Fradal and Hasha didn't eat and they didn't sleep, they were so scared by what the doctor had said. Practically before it was light out, they got up and got dressed. They waited till the Brodskys got up, and then asked them how to get to Dr. Zawadzki's address. The girls didn't tell the Brodskys, that the doctor had said that somebody could catch what Fradal had. They just said, that the inspectors wanted them to go for a regular examination. Fradal didn't seem sick, so they believed the two sisters. The Brodskys didn't even realize that they had any reason to be scared. The Brodskys made them eat breakfast before they went, and they wished the girls good hopes.

Hasha was sleeping in the same bed with Fradal. Fradal was afraid that Hasha could catch trachoma from her, and also go blind. Hasha was wonderful. Fradal didn't know if she was scared or not too. Hasha told her not to worry ... that they would both be fine. She didn't see any growths in Fradal's eyes.

Hasha and Fradal took the tram vise to Gansha Gas - the street the doctor from the consulate told them to go to. Funny, Fradal could always remember that street, but not Dr. Zawadzki's office so well. Probably because she spent so much time there with her eyes closed. After she had examined Fradal, Dr. Zawadzki said that yes, she had trachoma. The doctor told them that she would try to cure it, but it would take a long time. She couldn't cure it in a minute, but that they shouldn't worry. She told them that Fradal would be ok, and she wouldn't go blind if she got the treatments. The treatments were terrible. They burned and itched and Fradal couldn't touch her eyes and she couldn't scratch. Worst of all she had to wear a patch on one eye from one visit to the next, and then switch the patch to the other eye on the next visit. Fradal always felt like people were looking at her. First Dr. Zawadzki used to squeeze out what she called the wild growths. Fradal never knew they were there before. The doctor used something like tweezers. She used to rub Fradal's eyelids with these white sticks, and then she would put drops in her eyes. Fradal quietly cried because it hurt, but Hasha used to sit with her and comfort her.

They used to take the tram vise there two, sometimes three times a week. Each time they had to pay Dr. Zawadzki. Each time she said that soon Fradal would be cured, but that soon never seemed to come. The girls kept asking her how much longer, and the doctor kept saying soon, and that they had to be patient. They needed the letter to bring to the doctor at the consulate in order to get their health certificates, so they kept going to Dr. Zawadzki.

Hasha was worried that they would run out of money. So she asked Mrs. Brodsky if she knew of anyone who needed help, where she could get a job. Mrs. Brodsky said that it was a good idea for her to work. They couldn't afford to support them if they needed money. Mrs. Brodsky asked a few people, and the next day she heard about a woman who did need help. Hasha got the job as a maid and went to work. She left in the mornings and then came back at night. She took off from work to go with Fradal when she had to go to Dr. Zawadzki. But otherwise Hasha worked every day but Saturday. She was gone most of each day.

Fradal missed Hasha during those days. She wandered around the Warsaw streets alone. Sometimes she enjoyed the new and exciting things she saw. It took her mind off missing her mother and Hunia. A lot of times when she couldn't stop crying, she would find a corner somewhere to sit by herself. It was hard when she thought of never seeing her mother or Hunia again or anyone from Drohitchin. She felt very scared and very much alone.

Then there was the night the bed got wet. The girls had been at the Brodskys apartment for about three weeks. While Fradal was sleeping, she suddenly felt something wet. It woke her up. She tapped Hasha to see what was wet. Hasha woke up and realized that it was blood and that it came from her. Fradal said, "Oh my G_d! Are you ok? What is that?" Hasha said she was fine, that she just had her period. That she would clean up the mess.

Fradal knew about such things because animals would bleed like that, but it still made her feel unclean. She did not want to go back to bed with Hasha there like that. Her sister whispered, so as not to wake the Brodskys, "You will see, little Fradal, when you are older one day, you will get your period too. Just like all women. The first time it will be a happy day." Hasha told her that it happened once a month.

Fradal realized that Hasha was like a mother to her. Fradal didn't know what she would have done without Hasha. Her sister could have left her and gone to America without her, but she didn't. Hasha was even willing to sleep in the same bed as Fradal when there was a possibility of catching trachoma from her. But it didn't make it easier for Fradal to sleep in the same bed with Hasha when she had her period. And the thought of getting her period herself one day didn't make her any happier. When Hasha finished cleaning up, they both got back into bed, but Fradal couldn't sleep. She realized that she was being a silly girl for feeling dirty, but it didn't help her sleep.

While Fradal and Hasha were in Warsaw, they did many things that they had never done before. They had some time to spend between the visits to the doctor when Hasha wasn't working. Sometimes, they went to look at the fancy stores on the other side of the city. They couldn't believe how beautiful everything was, the buildings and the clothes. Once, they even went to the movies. The Brodskys had told them about it, but they wanted to see for themselves what it was like. They paid this lady outside. She was sitting in a glass cage and then they went into this dark room. Everybody was sitting in chairs looking at the wall where the performers moved around. Fradal took off her eye patch while in there so she could see better. It was a silent movie with the words written in Polish, and they couldn't read Polish too well. It was a love story but Hasha and Fradal giggled.

They used to help Mrs. Brodsky with the housework and sometimes the shopping. Once, she asked them to go buy a chicken, for Shabbos. Hasha and Fradal went to the chicken market. There was a store that sold chickens, down on the other side of the market street. Hasha and Fradal went into the shop. It was full of cackling chickens in wooden cages. The smell of burnt feathers and chicken droppings was overpowering. They were glad to go out to the back, where they had a live chicken yard, to find the owner of the store. Hasha told the chicken man that Mrs. Brodsky wanted a spring chicken; it should be nice and juicy. He said, they should take their choice and he would catch it for them. Hasha showed him a nice fat one, and the chicken man went and caught it for us. Fradal turned her head away, when he very quickly tucked the chicken under his arm. He held the chicken's head so that the blood drained down, when he slit the chicken's throat, in the kosher way.

He asked, if they wanted with the feathers or without? Hasha said, "With, how else?" He wrapped the fresh killed hen and they took it back to Mrs. Brodsky. The girls didn't even set their feet in the door yet, when Mrs. Brodsky started to yell on them. She said that they should get that chicken out of her house, and take it back to the chicken man right away quick. She said that they should have the chicken cleaned by the chicken plucker. He should take off the feathers and he could keep the lice himself. She didn't want them. At home, their mama used to take the feathers off herself, that's when they were lucky enough to eat chicken. Who else was there to clean it? They never heard of a chicken plucker before. Their mama washed herself up afterwards but sometimes she caught fleas anyway and it itched and she scratched. They weren't lucky enough to have chicken very often, so the problem wasn't so much of a problem.

Finally, Hasha felt that enough was enough. They had been to visit Dr. Zawadzki. Again, Hasha asked how much longer it would be, and again Dr. Zawadzki said soon Fradal would be cured. Hasha told her that they didn't have enough money to stay in Warsaw forever, but again the doctor told them they should come back in a few days.

Hasha thought there must be something they could do. They talked about going to another doctor. But who wanted to start up with another doctor, and who knew from another doctor that could give them the letter? The girls both thought that Fradal must be cured already. Except for the miserable treatments and the horrible patch, her eyes never bothered her in the first place, and they weren't any different after so many treatments.

They expected to be in Warsaw one week, maybe two, but there they were over two months later. It didn't look as if they were ever getting out of Warsaw. If they didn't go to America, to their papa soon, they would not have any money left and then they would be begging in the street.

They couldn't keep the eye problem a secret from the Brodskys. They had known that Fradal was wearing a patch on her eye since her first visit to the doctor. There was no way Fradal could hide it. Dr. Zawadzki had told her that she had to wear the patch all the time, except for when she slept. So, the girls had no choice but to tell the Brodskys about it. They didn't know if the Brodskys knew about trachoma, but even if the Brodskys might have known about it, and that it is contagious, the girls didn't tell them what the actual problem was. They had agreed to never mention the word trachoma. They never mentioned trachoma, and they absolutely never said that it was supposed to be contagious and could cause someone to go blind. The Brodskys would have thrown them out.

Since they didn't know what the eye problem was, the Brodskys weren't afraid to catch what Fradal had. So, Hasha and Fradal decided it would be ok to ask Pinya Brodsky what they should do.

Pinya Brodsky was a glazier, and he spent most of his time fixing windows, but in the evening, he liked to sit home and take a little snuff. Pinya was sitting at the table, like he always did after dinner, taking out his little box. He took the snuffbox with his left hand, and then tapped the side of it to make the snuff settle down. He didn't want to lose a bit of his precious treasure when he opened the box. He then opened the clasp and lifted the lid. The glazier dug his stubby, constantly cut, fingers inside the box, and took out a pinch of tobacco. He closed the lid, and then put the snuff on the back of his left hand. Pinya then snorted it right up into his nose. He made a lot of noise sneezing while rubbing his nose. Then Pinya blew his nose. A very quiet man, that was usually the only noise he ever made.

Pinya Brodsky never used to talk a lot, his wife used to do all the talking. Maybe one should say yelling. When Pinya Brodsky did talk, it was something for people to listen to. Everybody would be quiet when he would talk, even his wife. That's why Hasha figured that they would talk to him about their problem. He would know something smart to do. They didn't tell him everything, only that they were having trouble getting their papers. What he said was that he didn't know from such things. He never in his life had to deal with officials and he thought that was his good *mazel* (luck). But if they wanted to talk to someone who knew from such things they should maybe go to HIAS. They would know what to do. HIAS, the Hebrew Immigrant Aid Society - helping people who want to go to America was their business. That's what they do. Mr. Brodsky told the girls that HIAS was a group of Russian Jews from New York, America, who helped Jewish immigrants.

So, that's what they did. They went to HIAS. It wasn't too far, just on the other side of the Jewish section, at Muranowska 34. HIAS was in a building with a courtyard. When they got there, the courtyard was crowded with people waiting on a very long line. Hasha and Fradal started looking for someone to talk to - to ask what they should do. The people on line said that they should just wait on line and one by one the HIAS people would talk to them. The line was so long, and so slow that it was called "the snail walk." After many hours, they got to the front of the line.

When it was finally their turn, a lady called to them in Yiddish that they should come over to her desk. She asked how she could help them. She didn't look Jewish, but she was, and she was very kind to them. The girls poured out their hearts to her. They told her that their mama and brother had died, and that they were trying to go to their papa in America, but the officials wouldn't let them. They told her about the doctors and what they said. Hasha told her that they didn't know who to turn to or what to do. In a very low voice, so only the girls could hear what she said, she told them what to do. She said, that maybe the solution would be to go back to the first official, and tell him that Fradal was all cured. Just to make sure that he understood, they should put some money in an envelope, and give him the envelope when he asked for Dr. Zawadzki's letter.

The HIAS lady also told them, that if they had the money, they should buy ships tickets in 2nd class, not 3rd class steerage. She said, the officials didn't look as carefully at the 2nd class passengers as they did at the people in steerage, because the 2nd class tickets cost more. She asked the girls if they had the money to give to the official, and if they could afford to buy the more expensive ships tickets in 2nd class. They told her that they had the money that was supposed to pay for four tickets. But because their mama and Hunia had died, they only needed to buy two tickets. She told them that because Fradal was small for her age, that she could get away with getting a child's ticket, even though she had already passed her tenth birthday. The child's ticket was half price, but you weren't supposed to be more than ten years old. Fradal didn't look as if she was even that old, so they took her advice. She told them not to tell anyone, not even other passengers, that Fradal was older than ten, till they got off the ship. So, then they had the money to give the bribe to the official at the American Consulate, and to buy one and a half 2nd class ships tickets. The HIAS lady gave them an envelope to put the money in, and told them how much they needed to bribe the official. She wished them well. They thanked her, and told her how grateful they were for her help, and they left.

The next day, Fradal took off the eye patch. They got dressed in their fancy clothes, and their first real shoes, and went back to see the first official they had seen at the consulate's medical office. They waited a long time for him, and finally they got to see him. They told him that they had gone to Dr. Brygida Zawadzki, like the other doctor told them to do. Hasha said that Dr. Zawadzki had treated Fradal, and now she was cured. When he asked them for the doctor's letter, Hasha didn't say anything. She just took the envelope with the money, out of her pocket. She quietly put it on the desk. The official didn't say anything. After he looked in the envelope, he just started filling out the visas for them. He handed Hasha the visas, and wished the girls good luck, and that's all.

The lady from HIAS had told them to go to the Red Star Line office, after they got their visas. They did exactly as she had told them to do. They went to the Red Line Shipping Company's ticket office, and Hasha bought their tickets in second class. The ship was leaving from Antwerp, Belgium. Now they had to get to Antwerp, wherever that was. They never heard from Antwerp before, but they knew it was a port on the other side of Europe. Their ship's tickets included the tickets for the train. It was a 1,156 km (718 miles) trip from Warsaw to Antwerp.

Hasha and Fradal were grateful that they were finally able to leave Warsaw. They thought they would never get out from there. Well they were on their way. They said good-by to the Brodskys and left. Carrying nothing more than their meager clothes, and the pictures from the family in their sacks, they took the train across half of Europe.

The nice lady from HIAS warned them to be careful. She said that like any port or big city, Antwerp was full of thieves, and swindlers at every turn. They were careful, and lucky; nobody ever bothered them.

After they got to the Red Line office in Antwerp, the officials there took their bags from them. They didn't have much, and they didn't know what the officials did with their things. The officials told them that they were going to disinfect and delouse their things. The girls didn't know what that meant or what they were going to do. They were told that they would give them their things back after they had finished.

Antwerp is a beautiful city in Belgium. The people of Belgium speak French, and the girls couldn't understand them, but they weren't there long. They had to wait there until their ship was ready to leave. They only stayed in Antwerp for a few days. After Warsaw, and their train trip across half of Europe, the girls weren't surprised by Antwerp, except for the water. The girls were startled by the sight of the very large river and then by seeing the ocean for the first time. Fradal used to stand and watch the waves. Antwerp is a port on the Scheldt River not far from the ocean. It has a very deep harbor enabling the large steam ships to come there from all over the world. The ocean is something you can't describe if you haven't seen it. Fradal said, "Who could imagine such big water?" She was afraid a big wave was going to come and wash them into the sea. She knew it wasn't so, but she thought it anyway.

The big ships coming into the port were loaded with things from all over the world. There was even a ship there from South America. That ship had a lot of black sailors. Hasha and Fradal had never seen a black person in their lives before. They couldn't take their eyes off them. They just looked and looked. Fradal and Hasha had heard about them before. Black people are mentioned in the Bible, and they also heard that there were people in the world that were dark like a piece of wood, but those sailors still looked strange to the girls. The South American sailors were also unloading things the girls had never seen until then: crates of grapefruit, and big bunches of bananas. A sailor they asked told them that the bananas were fruit, and delicious.

**[Postcard:] Passengers waiting on dock to board ship,
Antwerp, Belgium (ca. early 20th century)**
Photo courtesy of the Public Library of Antwerp, Belgium

It took about 16 days to cross the ocean. On the day they boarded their ship to leave Europe, it rained and poured. The rain didn't stop anything; the docks were still crowded with people, all waving good-by as the big ship started to move, and blow its very loud whistle.

All of the passengers on the ship were at the railings, also waving good-by. Fradal and Hasha didn't know anybody, but they waved too, at nobody in particular. They just waved. Why not? They were sad that their mama and Hunia were not there with them. But they did know that they would probably never see Europe again, and that they felt was a good thing.

Later, they went down to see their room again, and to make themselves at home. They had crossed half of Europe, and now they were going across the ocean on a big fancy steam ship. They still weren't used to it. In second class, they had been given a good clean room, just for the two of them. It was far from the best room on the ship, but it was the best they had ever been in. And so clean! The sailors were always washing and scrubbing everything. Hasha and Fradal were afraid to touch something; it shouldn't get dirty. The sisters laughed to each other that it was so clean; you could eat from the floor. You didn't have to go to the big dining room.

The dining room had big tables. The girls sat and ate with other people. It was so fine and, with so much tableware on the table, that they didn't know which spoon to use. The food was delicious, and they gave so much food. The girls didn't care; they just ate. They even had bananas. Fradal took a bite out of one before someone showed her how to peel it.

Though it rained the first day, the rest of the time it took to cross was lovely. The water was very calm. Even so, some people got seasick. Hasha had to be one of them. Poor Hasha after the first day, she barely ate anything. The sailors told them to bring her up on deck. They said that she would feel better in the fresh air. And that they should give her tea to drink. Hasha couldn't even look at food, not even the bananas that Fradal brought her from the dining room. Hasha spent almost the whole trip in a chair on deck.

Fradal helped some of the other people that were sick like Hasha and sitting up on deck. She brought them blankets and pillows. She brought some of them tea and crackers and went around making friends. Fradal played with a boy named Dovid, Dovid Greenburg. Fradal and Hasha had made friends with his family in Antwerp. They were going to America too. They were going to stay with Mrs. Greenburg's brother. Dovid's father had died. Dovid's sister, Shifra, was also seasick like Hasha. Hasha, Shifra and Mrs. Greenburg all sat up on deck together while Dovid and Fradal played cards. Dovid taught Fradal how to play pinochle. The happiest day Fradal had on the ship was when she found a small American coin. She was so excited and happy she couldn't wait to show Hasha. Hasha said, "It is a sign that our luck has changed, and we are going to know only good times in America. We aren't even there yet, and already you are finding money on the ground. See I told you, everything is going to be ok." That seemed to cheer Hasha up. But she still felt seasick.

The sailors told them that they would know when they were near New York. They would see a big statue of a lady sticking out of the water. Most of the passengers had heard about that statue before. The Jews all seemed to have heard that there was a saying written on the bottom of the statue – a poem that was actually written by a Jewish woman, Emma Lazarus. They said that the poem welcomed immigrants like them to America. When they were near, most of the passengers came up on deck to see it. It was the Statue of Liberty (1921 - only 35 years old). When they saw it, everyone cheered. Someone yelled, "Long live Columbus!!!"

Like most of the Jews on the ship, Hasha and Fradal said the prayer: *"Shehekianu"* – *"Blessed are you, creator of the universe for bringing us to this time."*   ❧

ഔ *So Close and Still So Far* ൔ

The ship landed in New York harbor on Wednesday, September 21, 1921. They couldn't leave the docks to go wherever they wanted to. They had to take another ship, a smaller one, a ferry. Only the American citizens and some very rich people could just leave. Those passengers had been processed on the ship. The poor immigrants mostly steerage, had to go to Ellis Island to be inspected all over again. Ellis Island was then the American immigration center, where all of the poor, scared immigrants who landed in New York had to go to be able to live in the United States. Finally, the ferry landed. They were there on Ellis Island. You could see New York, America off in the distance, so close but out of touch for nobody knew how long. Fradal had heard someone on the ship say that Ellis Island wasn't always so big. That they built the island with the earth they dug out of the ground, when they built the subway in Manhattan, in the 1890s.But that's another story.

Hasha and Fradal were two of the thousands and thousands of immigrants who walked off the ferry at those docks, with the frequently mean Ellis Island officials hurrying them along. Some days, there were as many as 10,000 people there. More than twelve million people had passed through Ellis Island before it was closed in 1954.

The immigrants were told to wait their turn in the big hall. When it was their turn, they were then told to go upstairs. Officials pointed to the big staircase at the end of the hall, but they already knew they were supposed to walk up that staircase. The immigrants had been watching them send people up those stairs for more than an hour. What they didn't know was that the doctors at the top of the stairs, watched everyone, as they walked up that long staircase. It was the beginning of the examination, to see if they were healthy. The officials called it "the six-second physical." The doctors inspected every immigrant who walked up those stairs. They watched for weakness, limping, blindness, wheezing or heavy breathing, and mental problems. When the immigrants got to the top of the stairs, the doctors examined everyone for more than fifty different symptoms. They sent some people who they thought weren't "all there mentally" for more tests. One of those tests was a wooden puzzle that they had to put together. Hasha and Fradal didn't have to do that. Those people who were sick were sent to the Ellis Island hospital. But those people who the doctors thought were incurable, that they couldn't heal, were sent back to wherever they came from. The doctors wanted to make sure that the immigrants didn't have something that was contagious. The immigrants were looked over from head to foot.

Hasha and Fradal were scared in case they shouldn't find something again. They heard the disease that they sent the most people back for was trachoma. Even though Hasha and Fradal believed that Fradal never had trachoma in the first place, they were now afraid that the doctors would find something in their papers that said that she was kept back in Warsaw because of trachoma, and that they would deport her because of it. The two sisters didn't whisper a word of their fears to anyone. They were scared. Fradal was now really terrified. She asked herself, what would they do? Where would she go alone if Hasha didn't go back with her? She wondered if Hasha would really go back to Europe with her if she were forced to leave, or would she stay in America without her. Hasha had promised her and their mama that they would stay together no matter what. Fradal was only 11 years old. She had heard that when they deported children that were under twelve they made at least one parent go with them. But Hasha wasn't her parent. Fradal wondered if they would make Hasha go with her, or make her go back alone? Fradal was scared, and so was Hasha, but they didn't talk about it.

On Ellis Island, they had interpreters helping people that spoke every language. And in every language, the inspectors searched their scalps for fleas, for rashes, for itches. Looking for cripples to deport, they watched everyone walk again. The inspectors told people to open their mouths and stick out their tongues. They told them to stick out their hands and to turn them over. People were barred from remaining in the United States if the doctors saw signs of mental illness, cholera, tuberculosis, epilepsy or trachoma. If the doctor saw that something was wrong, they marked your shoulder with a chalk mark. The letter E was for something wrong with the eyes, F for feet, CT for trachoma. About two out of ten people got marks on their clothes. They didn't know what the marks meant. Most of them couldn't read English. Those who were marked were sent for more examinations. The inspectors didn't mark Fradal or Hasha. They thought they looked healthy. But the girls hadn't seen the eye doctor yet; that was next.

Ellis Island Chalk Marks

X	Suspected Mental Defect
Circled X	Definite Signs of Mental Defect
B	Back
C	Conjunctivitis
CT	Trachoma
E	Eyes
F	Face
FT	Feet
G	Goiter
H	Heart
K	Hernia
N	Neck
L	Lameness
P	Physical and Lungs
PG	Pregnancy
SC	Scalp (Fungus)
S	Senility
SI	Special Inquiry

[Photo:] Ellis Island diagnostic code chart
Photo courtesy of the Ellis Island archives

After the doctor's examination, everyone who had not been sent to the hospital, or sent somewhere else, was sent to the eye inspectors. They were the ones who looked for trachoma. The immigrants had to wait on line for everything on Ellis Island including the eye examination. While they waited their turn to be examined, the immigrants could see how the inspectors looked in everyone's eyes. They waited on a long line to have their eyes examined. Everyone was afraid of the eye inspectors; not just Fradal. They called the doctors who did this the button-hook men. The Ellis Island eye inspectors didn't look at people's eyes the way that Dr. Zawadzki, the Polish doctor looked at Fradal's eyes. The button-hook men used a long narrow iron stick that was curled at one end into a hook. It was really meant to be used to button shoes and clothing. Holding the button-hook against each of the immigrants' eyelids, the eye inspectors twirled their eyelids inside out, around the hook, so they could see if there was any swelling or growths under the lid. Then he did the same thing to the other eye. This was very painful. He did this one by one, to everyone on the line using the same unwashed hook. Some people got poked and shouted out. It was frightening just to watch. When he got to Fradal, she was terrified that she would be hurt and even more terrified that he would find something wrong with her eyes and deport her. She wanted to scream but didn't say anything. She didn't make one sound. The button-hook man looked in each of her eyes, and then told her to move on. No chalk marks on her clothes and no deportation. He didn't see anything wrong. Hasha and Fradal both silently said thanks G_d to themselves. Not wanting to call attention to themselves, they didn't say anything out loud to anyone, until they were alone. When they were finally able to find a corner to talk quietly, they hugged each other in joy.

[Photo:] Button hook similar to those used to examine the immigrants'
eyes for trachoma at Ellis Island (ca. early 20th century)
Photo courtesy of the Ellis Island archives

[Photo:] Ellis Island Inspectors doing the dreaded eye exam
with a shoe button hook (ca. early 20th century)
Photo courtesy of the Ellis Island archives

After the medical examinations, they were sent into the Registry Hall. The hall was huge and cold. It was the biggest building they had ever been in. The size of the place made them feel even smaller than they were. They followed the guard's directions to go sit on the benches. They waited on those benches a long time until the inspectors looked at their papers. The officials questioned everyone again and again. Person by person, they questioned, and questioned and questioned, and, very frightened, the immigrants waited, and waited their turns. Those officials were only supposed to spend one minute with each immigrant, but they asked a lot of questions in that one minute. They asked all sorts of questions: where did they come from, where were they going, who did they have here in America, their ages. The immigrants were asked questions like: how many legs on a pig, how many legs does a chicken have? Men were asked if they had skills or a job waiting for them here. The officials wanted to make sure that the refugees were normal and smart enough not to become a drain on the American society. They also asked the men how many wives they had because it is against the law in America to have more than one wife or husband. They wanted to know if people were trouble makers, or had been in jail in the old country. Fradal and Hasha asked each other, "What kind of dumbbell would tell them the truth about that?"

The girls passed the doctor's exams, but were scared, like everyone there, that the inspectors shouldn't find some other reason to keep them there, or maybe even, G_d forbid, send them back to Europe. They also got scared when they heard that women couldn't come in alone, without men. For a while, Hasha and Fradal thought they were going to make them go back to Europe for that reason. Everyone knew that they made people go back for any crazy reason. They heard that women couldn't leave with men to who they were not related. Some single women found men right there on Ellis Island and got married. Then they heard that women could stay if they had a relative here in this country. Fradal and Hasha had their papa. When the girls heard that, they were relieved. They knew they were two of the lucky ones.

Finally, Fradal and Hasha were able to show the officials their papers. The uniformed inspectors, with their starched faces, looked at all of the information that was in the sisters' papers, and on the ship's manifest. They were able to say their names, because their father had given them new American names and they had practiced saying those names. The officials didn't have trouble with them and didn't change their names when they wrote them down in their log.

There is a belief that some people's names were changed by the officials at Ellis Island. The Ellis Island archivists and historians claim that this is a myth. They say that because of their procedures the Ellis Island inspectors could not have done this. I don't know, but somehow, somewhere my grandfather's name was changed from Beryl Yosski Valevelsky to Barney Levine. Did he change it himself or did some official change it along his journey to America? I don't know. If the officials got their names wrong, who would tell them that they didn't get it right? The immigrants thought disagreeing with the inspectors in any way, might interfere with their getting off Ellis Island, and might even mean being sent back to Europe, G_d forbid. So, after finally landing in America, many people ended up spending the rest of their lives with new names. There is a rumor, and I don't know if it is or isn't a myth. I have attempted to research this and still don't know the truth. The story is that there were some Jewish people who couldn't remember how to spell their names and said in Yiddish, *"shen forgossen"* (they already forgot). To some of those officials, those Yiddish words sounded a lot like the Irish name Sean Ferguson. Supposedly, officials would write down Sean Ferguson, and "supposedly" quite a few Jewish people started their new lives in America with that Irish name.

After Hasha and Fradal were questioned, they had to sign their names on their papers. They wrote their names in Yiddish. Many people who couldn't write, signed their names with an X. Lots of Jews didn't like to sign with an X, because they thought it looked too much like a cross. Jewish people who didn't know how to write would sign their names with a small circle instead of the X. That is where that terrible racist slur of calling Jews –*"kikes"* came from, because the Yiddish word for circle is *keikl* (kI-kle).

Despite the lengthy list of guidelines that the new immigrants had to comply with, the number of people that were actually deported from Ellis Island was quite low. Of the 12 million people who were examined at Ellis Island between 1892 and its closing in 1954, only about two percent were denied the right to remain in the United States. But most of the immigrants didn't know that. They were all afraid that it would be them for some reason, that they may or may not have known, that would cause the officials to send them back.

Most of the immigrants were allowed to leave before the end of the day. Two thirds of them bought railroad tickets right there, and took the ferry to Hoboken, New Jersey. From there they took a train, and went on to other parts of the country. One third of people took the ferry back to Manhattan. Hasha and Fradal had to stay on Ellis Island longer because they had to wait for their father to come get them.

Hasha and Fradal were taken to the dormitories with the other people who weren't able to leave. The guards took them with other women and girls and children to a women's dormitory. There they had rows and rows of metal-framed, canvas cots, all triple-tiered and stacked up one on top of the other. They spent their nights sleeping there until they could leave. Fradal had to climb up a ladder to the cot above Hasha's cot. The men were taken to the men's dormitory on the other side of the building.

There was a room for showers like Hasha and Fradal had never seen before. Who knew from a shower in Drohitchin or even such a thing in Warsaw? They were very strict. They forced everyone to shower. Some people didn't want to. They didn't like taking off their clothes in front of other people – not even other women. Then the immigrants were given food in a big dining room.

There were long tables and benches. But mainly they spent their time at Ellis Island waiting.

When their papa had sent the money and papers for them to come, he had also put in a picture of himself, so they would know him. Hasha said that he had changed after all these years; Fradal couldn't remember what he looked like. She was only three years old when he left, too young for her to remember. In the picture, he didn't have his beard anymore. He said that it was always getting in his way. When he ate, his beard ate too, and in America, not everybody wears a beard. Fradal and Hasha looked for their papa in the faces of all the strangers they saw there. They didn't recognize anyone. They didn't see their father. Before they had left Warsaw, they had written to him, to tell him when they were coming. Hasha had told him which ship and everything. Then the Ellis Island officials said that they would send him a telegram, telling him to come get them.

The two sisters didn't know what they would do if he didn't come. They felt like crying almost the whole time they were on Ellis Island. They were afraid that, even if the officials let them stay, they would have nowhere to live. Their papa wasn't there to meet them. They thought maybe he didn't get the letter, maybe he didn't know they were there. Hasha and Fradal didn't have anyone but their papa in this country. What should they do? They didn't know. Neither girl voiced her fears, but they both feared that maybe their papa was dead. They were afraid to even say such a thing, but they both thought it. Their mama and Hunia had died. So Hasha and Fradal waited and waited and then waited some more.

A few days later, an official called out their new names. He shouted 'Levine, Levine, Anna and Frieda Levine...' again and again. Then Hasha realized he was calling them. As they tried to push their way from the bench they were on, over to the official's desk, the sisters could see that standing next to the official, was a man holding his hat in his hand. The official told them, "This is Barney Levine." In their fear, they forgot their new names. They didn't know who Barney Levine was for a minute. Their father's name was

Beryl Yosski Valevelsky. The strange man looked a lot like the man in their papa's picture. The stranger said, 'Hasha, my little Fradalli, is that you?' He started to kiss and hug them, and they were hugging the strange man back. Fradal started showing him the coin she had found on the ship. The American man was their papa. They thought he was very American, but he was their papa. He had come to take them to their new home.   ෪

⁊ *The Lower East Side* ⳉ

*F*radal was born during Chanukah, 1909. She was the third child and the baby in the family. Her father was having a very hard time. As hard as he struggled, he just couldn't seem to make a living. Fradal was about three when he left them in Drohitchin and went to Warsaw. From Warsaw, he went to America to find a way to make a better life for them. He promised he would send for the four of them as soon as he could.

When he got to America, lots of things changed. Like many of the twelve million people who disembarked in Manhattan, by way of Ellis Island, he metamorphosed. His name was changed along his journey, from Beryl Yosski Valevelsky to the much more American, but still Jewish sounding, name Barney Levine. He shaved his beard, and learned to fit in. He became an American.

Barney Levine was 30 years old in 1912 when he left Drohitchin. He didn't want to leave his wife and three children, but what could he do? In America, he hoped he would find a chance for them to have a better life. Barney was a short, stocky, strong man and a very good man. And he was determined to do whatever it took to bring his wife Chaiya Bailya and the children over from Europe, and to make a home for them.

Once in America, like many immigrants, Barney didn't move far from where he landed. He stayed with his cousin Golda and her husband Jacob, and their six children on Manhattan's Lower East Side. Jacob worked in a small clothing factory on Essex Street. He helped Barney find a job there. After Barney saved up some money, he found a place to live not far from them on Cherry Street, near Jackson Street. He made his way among the thousands of East European Jews who lived on the Lower East Side of New York.

There were immigrants from all over the world living on the Lower East Side. There were Italians living in Little Italy on Mulberry Street. Chinese people were living on Mott Street. There were Germans, Polish and other Slavic people, Hungarians. By the time Barney landed in New York, more than two million Jews had come to this country from Eastern Europe. Most of the immigrants on the Lower East Side were Jewish. Many of the street signs were in English and the languages of other immigrants, but an enormous number of signs were in Yiddish and some in Russian. The Lower East Side was a slum, but it was mainly a Jewish slum. It was odd and wonderful for Jews on the Lower East Side to live in a place where Jews were in the majority.

For a while, Barney worked at the job in the garment industry sweatshop that Jacob had gotten for him. When there wasn't enough work for him, he was laid off. A lot of poor Jewish immigrants of that day worked in those infamous sweatshops, even the children. Barney tried to find steady work in other sweatshops, but he hated it, and he wasn't good on the machines. He didn't have the patience to do that kind of work, and he didn't like having a boss. Barney had a good friend named Mendel. They met in Warsaw. Mendel was one of Pinya Brodsky, the glazier's, neighbors. Barney met Mendel when Barney lived in Warsaw with the Brodskys. He and Mendel became good friends when they both realized they would be better off in America. They remained friends from then on. They even took the same ship to New York. Barney and everyone used to tease Mendel by calling him "Mendel with the *fendel*." A *fendel* is the Yiddish word for a pot. It was natural to tease him with that nickname because Mendel was a peddler, and what Mendel peddled were pots and pans and household goods. He was peddling pots and pans in Warsaw, when Barney met him. When Barney was having trouble finding work in New York, Mendel talked him into also becoming a peddler.

The Lower East Side had all kinds of peddlers, selling all kinds of things. There were those peddlers who always stayed on the same spot with their carts or stands, and those who wandered around the streets searching for customers. There were peddlers walking around hawking clothing with their sing song shout of "I sell Clothes," and men shouting that they sold junk, and household things that everybody needed.

Barney's mother (Bubba Rivka), always managed to make money selling stuff, so he thought this might be a good idea. It was not easy working outside. In the winter, New York was, and is, bitter cold, and in the summer it is very hot. But Barney liked it better than working in the sweatshops. After a while, Barney found that he could make a humble living as a peddler. And he liked not having a boss and not having to answer to anyone. He worked his way up to buying and selling junk, and used things that were made out of iron and other metals. But these things were heavy, and he needed a horse and wagon. He woke up early and went to the stables, where he rented the same horse and wagon every morning.

The horse was called Fresser. A *fresser* in Yiddish is a person who eats a lot – someone who eats like a horse. Barney put cowbells on the wagon posts, so people could hear him coming, and went out and peddled his wares. The horse was an old mare, but he liked her company. He used to talk to her while he rode the streets of the Lower East Side looking for his next customer.

Barney rented a bed from a man named Tuvia. Tuvia was a fiddler. Barney had met him one day, while Tuvia was playing his fiddle on a street corner. Tuvia had just taken an apartment because he had saved enough money to bring his wife Blooma over from Europe. But to make it easier to pay the rent, he wanted a border. Barney didn't like his landlady, and Tuvia was just a few buildings away, so Barney moved in with him. Tuvia worked mainly at night. Sometimes when he didn't have money, he would stand on a busy corner in the market and play his fiddle for the few coins people dropped into his fiddle case. He played the klezmer music from home and American songs. He made the most money when he played a *fraylock* (a happy song). The passersby would stop and crowd around, the hardships of life forgotten for a few minutes in the joyous melodies of the remembered songs from the shtetlach.

Tuvia's narrow little apartment was in a typical Lower East Side tenement. The building, like most of the tenement buildings, had a permanent smell of dampness and mold. It was two dark rooms. One was the kitchen - living room, and the other was a tiny windowless bedroom in the back. Barney slept in the living room.

They had indoor plumbing, but the water had to be heated on the stove. There was nothing that you could call privacy, especially after Blooma came. The only way for Barney to get a hot bath was at the Russian baths, or public bathhouses. He loved the *schvitz* they had there. The word *schvitz* is Yiddish for "sweat" and also for "steam bath." Barney, like most people who know of the schvitz, thought that it made you feel better, especially if you were sick, but even if you weren't. He thought that the schvitz was good for you, because it makes you sweat out all of the poisons in your body.

But Barney wouldn't spend the extra nickel on the schvitz. He was saving every penny in order to bring his family over from Europe. The bath was five cents and for another five cents you got a little soap and a towel. But there was no choice. The Russian baths were the only way for him, and a lot of other poor immigrants from the Lower East Side, to get a bath.

In 1912, the average wage in the U.S. was 22 cents per hour. The average U.S. worker made between $200 and $600 per year. Barney saved not only to be able to send money to his wife for her and the children to live on, but also to be able to bring them to America. He never spent a penny for himself that he didn't think about, and rethink, over and over again. Another peddler he knew, a fat woman named Ruthie, offered him a little heart-shaped gold locket for his girlfriend. He told Ruthie, he didn't have a girlfriend.

He had a wife and three beautiful kids, thanks G_d. Ruthie said, so buy it for your wife. It wasn't real gold, it was only plate, but it was a pretty little thing. You could open it up and put little pictures inside. He couldn't resist; he missed Chaiya Bailya and his children. He bought one for his Chaiya Bailya. Ruthie, hearing he had two daughters, told Barney that she could make him a real good deal for three lockets, all the same. He took all three.

Barney only spent a penny he absolutely didn't have to, twice. Once when he bought the three lockets, and the second time, a short time after that. It was when he saw a man from Belarus playing a dudki. The man made dudkis, and sold them on the street. Barney was always lonely and homesick in this new and strange world. The dudki music from homemade Barney even lonelier. He missed his wife Chaiya Bailya, and his three children. Barney bought a dudki, and sent it to his boy Hunia, with the three lockets. He thought that they should remember that they had a father who loved them.

Being a junk peddler didn't make Barney rich, but at least he could make some money. It was better than working in a sweatshop for somebody else, like most of the people he knew were doing. It was better than starving in Drohitchin. Barney spent nine long years, working very hard, and saving every penny he could scrape together, until he had the money he needed to send for his family.

Mendel didn't have a family but he knew that Barney missed his. Barney had been almost starving himself, and working from morning till night, to save the money to bring them over. But when he finally had the money, he didn't know how to go about it. When Mendel heard that some guy had gotten advice from HIAS about how to bring his family over, he right away told Barney that he should write to HIAS. Barney didn't know how to write; so, he asked Tuvia, who knew how to write, to write the letter for him. Tuvia wrote the letter to HIAS for Barney and HIAS answered him.

The letter from HIAS gave Barney the instructions on what to do. It said that he needed to go to a Notary Public, and make out an affidavit saying who he was. It also had to say that he was Chaiya Bailya's husband, and the children's father. He needed three copies. One copy was needed when they went for the passport, and another copy was for the American Consulate when they applied for a visa. The third copy they were supposed to keep – just in case they needed it. The letter said that the transportation cost would be about $200 each for anyone who was over ten years old, and $100 for a child. Barney figured that if Fradal was ten then her passage would cost the $100, and he needed another $600 for the other three passages. Altogether he needed more than $700. This amount of money in a time when the average weekly salary was about $15 was an unthinkable fortune. And Barney knew he had to do it before Fradal got much older and couldn't pass for under ten anymore. But Barney worked very hard and managed to save it all up. It had taken him nine years of denying himself, and scrimping since he came to America. When he had saved enough money, he got the papers and sent for the four of them to come.

Barney sent the money with the instructions that he got from HIAS, and a picture of himself in the photographer's rented suit, and without the beard. Not long after he sent the money and papers to Chaiya Bailya, he got a letter back from her, saying that they were very excited, and that they would come as soon as possible. He couldn't wait; he was overjoyed. Now he worked even harder than before. He started saving to be able to get an apartment for them to live in. He couldn't have his family living like him, sleeping on a day bed in someone else's kitchen.

Sept. 23, 1920

Mr. H. Forman
c/o I. S. Kibrick
106 Main Street
Brockton, Mass.

Dear Mr. Forman:

In reply to your letter of recent date, we would suggest that you fill out an affidavit in triplicate similar to one of the enclosed, sworn to before a Notary Public or Commissioner of Deeds, using form 'A' if you are a citizen and 'B' if you are a declarant.

Two copies of this affidavit should be sent to the guardian of the child to be used by him when applying for a passport to the authorities of the country to which the child owes allegiance, and also when applying for a visa to the American Consul. The third copy of the affidavit should be kept by you for future reference.

The approximate cost of transportation per adult is $200.00, while for a child below the age of ten, it is half of that amount.

Money may be sent through the Joint Distribution Committee, 1133 Broadway, New York City, or any bank or trust company doing business in international exchange.

Very sincerely yours,

General Manager.

GF

[Copy of letter:] This standard letter has the instructions for bringing a family to America from Belarus and is similar to the letter Barney received from HIAS. (1920) Photo courtesy of the HIAS Archives

Then he got a second letter from his wife a few weeks later. This one wasn't so joyous. This letter from Chaiya Bailya said that Hunia had died of scarlet fever. Barney didn't know what to do with himself. He started screaming. He tore his jacket and started pulling on his hair. Barney had been planning all the things he was going to do with his boy. His son had been growing up without him, without him there to help him. Barney had been picturing himself taking Hunia with him out on the wagon, teaching him about horses. He could just see him playing the dudki, while sitting up there on the wagon beside him. Barney used to watch other little boys in the street and think of his son. Now he would never see him again. Before he stopped mourning Hunia, he received another letter from Europe. This one was from Hasha. It said that Chaiya Bailya had died. In this letter, Hasha told him that before she died, their mother had made her promise to take Fradal and go to America. Now just the two of them were coming. ☙

✎ *Disha* ✎

*L*onely and homesick for so long after his wife Chaiya Bailya, and Hunia had died, Barney remarried to a woman named Disha Dorsky (Dora in English). We called her Bubba Disha.

Disha grew up in Vilna, the capital of Lithuania. Barney was her second husband. Her first husband left her in Vilna and went to America. Her first husband wasn't madly in love with her, and, once he was in America, he refused to bring her over to this country. Disha's two brothers sent for her and paid her passage. After she arrived in New York, her husband didn't want to know her, and he gave her a *gett*, a divorce. They went to a *Beit Din* - a Jewish court. A religiously observant Jewish man can give his wife a divorce for any reason, if she agrees. But if the wife wants a divorce, she must ask her husband to give her one, and hope he is willing. If he is not willing to give her a divorce, there is very little she can do about it. She would have to go to a *Beit Din* and prove that he was horrible to her. There was no problem here with Disha because her husband was the one who wanted the divorce.

Disha had an aunt that was a marriage matchmaker, and she had a lot of money. Her aunt knew Barney Levine from their neighborhood. Disha's aunt was the neighborhood *yenta* (busybody). It was part of her business to know who was who, and what was going on in everyone else's kitchen, because she was a *shadchan* – a matchmaker. Being a yenta was her stock in trade, so to speak. She knew that Barney Levine was poor, and that his wife had died, and that his two young daughters were coming over from Europe. Disha's aunt approached him with the arrangement of marrying Disha. She convinced him that two young girls needed a woman, a mother. How could he bring them up by himself? The matchmaker gave him the extra needed incentive of a substantial dowry. He was scared he wouldn't know how to take care of Fradal and Hasha. He hadn't even seen them in many years and they were coming to America, G_d willing, soon. Being a poor man, and not exactly being a bargain himself, he agreed to this arrangement. Soon after Fradal and Hasha arrived in New York, Barney and Disha got married.

Bubba Disha was a real character, a Renaissance woman, a jack-of-all-trades. She used to do almost anything to make money. She even learned to be a matchmaker from her aunt. Years later when my parents met, Disha wanted to match my father up with someone else when my mother (Fradal) wasn't sure she wanted to marry him. My father was very handsome as a young man, and Disha said she could get a very good match for him. It made my mother more interested in my father and angry with Disha. My mother said that Disha could connive a nickel out of a piece of wood. Disha also told people's fortune with cards, and by reading melting wax like tea leaves. There were always a lot of people coming to Bubba Disha for her to do fortune telling for them. She earned most of the money that she and Barney had in this way, and she believed that she was telling them the truth. Surprisingly, she was proven correct quite often.

The Lower East Side was an ugly, stinking place with little grass and few trees. It was sidewalk to sky, bricks and stone and squalor. The streets were all dark, windowless tenements, block after block of crowded ugly buildings, and no fresh air. It was the most crowded place that Fradal and Hasha had ever been. In the summer, it was very hot with no way to cool off. With so little grass and few trees, the sidewalks and cobblestone streets just heated you more. The smells of the city from garbage and animal dung went through your head and crept into your clothes; so there was no escape. Some nights, it was so hot that people would sleep on their fire escapes. People even went and slept in the park to catch a bit of breeze, and to be able to cool off a little, sleeping on the grass. It is amazing to me that in those days nobody bothered them.

In the winter, it was cold, and damp, and miserable with few ways to warm up. It was always an open-ended debate as to which was worse – summer or winter.

Disha searched for and found them an apartment in Brooklyn. It was cheaper and bigger than the one they had in Manhattan. So, the four of them moved from the Lower East Side to the Brownsville part of Brooklyn.

Next, Disha arranged for Fradal and Hasha to work in a garment factory, as did a great number of poor children. Hasha was sixteen by then, and had been working a long time in Europe, but Fradal was only eleven. Disha convinced Barney that Fradal wasn't too young to help out, and bring some money into the house. You had to be fourteen to get working papers. Fradal was underage by more than three years. It was against the law to hire her, but she went to work anyway. She would hide under a bushel, or in a closet, when they thought the inspector or a school truant officer was coming.

Actually, it was Disha's aunt who got Fradal and Hasha their first jobs. Disha's aunt knew some people, the Chernoffs, who made bow ties. They had a small factory in their apartment on 9th Avenue in the Borough Park section of Brooklyn. It was Fradal's job to poke out the corners, and then turn the ties right side out. At first, the Chernoffs didn't want to hire her because she was small for her age, and looked much younger than she was. They didn't believe that she was even eleven. The Chernoffs told them that they didn't need babies. They needed people who could really do the work, and that Fradal didn't look like she was even ten years old. Fradal spoke up and defended herself, saying she was twelve, and that they should give her a chance and try her. Her gutsy attitude made them give her that chance. Of course, children worked for a lot less money than adults did. They hired Fradal to see if she would work out, and she did. Fradal and Hasha took the streetcar to work every day, but not on Saturday - Shabbos. Fradal said that the Chernoffs weren't too terrible to her, as long as, she kept doing her work. Fradal's friend Mirele, who lived on their street, and was also about eleven years old, worked for some other bosses. They were always pulling her hair and pinching her ear. Mirele said, that they were always complaining that she didn't work fast enough. She had to listen to a constant stream of tongue lashings. Mirele was the oldest of six children. Her father had died, and Mirele had to work to help feed everyone at home. So, she put up with their meanness, and never said anything. She was afraid they would fire her if she complained.

Before getting this job making bowties, Fradal became friends with two girls from the neighborhood - Bertha and Fanny Goldman. After getting the job, she had very little time to spend with them. Fradal was really friends with Bertha, the older one, but Mrs. Goldman, their mother, used to make Bertha take her younger sister Fanny along.

Bertha and Fanny introduced Fradal to the public library. Fradal couldn't believe that it had so many books, and that they let you borrow them, and take them home with you for free, even if you were an immigrant. Fradal could read and write in Yiddish, but she could barely understand English. She wished she could understand and read English, so she could read those books. Fradal promised herself that one day she would understand English and know how to read those books.

[Photo:] Fradal (far right) and her schoolgirl friends, Fanny & Bertha Goldman walking home after visit to the Brooklyn Public Library Brooklyn, New York (ca. summertime 1922)

Bertha and Fanny's father, Mr. Goldman, used to buy and sell used jewelry and watches. He walked through the tenement streets with his singsong call of the peddler yelling "I cash gold! I cash gold!" He was like a walking jewelry store.

Fradal didn't work on Saturdays, so she was able to see Bertha and Fanny then. One Saturday, at the end of the summer, before the High Holy Days, Bertha and Fanny came running to see her. They told her that they were moving to Palestine. They were going to be in Jerusalem before Rosh Hashanah. Their father had a brother there, and they were going to be with his family until they could make their way. Both Mr. and Mrs. Goldman were staunch Zionists. They thought they would have a more meaningful life in Israel, living with other Jews. Bertha and Fanny were gone before the next Saturday. Fradal never heard from them again.

Fradal worked for the Chernoffs for a few years. After working all day in the factory, she and Hasha went to night school in the evenings. They were learning how to speak English, the alphabet, and even how to read a little. School was free for everyone in America. They didn't have to pay anything and anyone could go, even immigrants, even Jews.

The teacher tried to teach them as much as she could in the short time they had in the evenings. She taught them about American history, and the Constitution. She talked about the rights people had in this country, that they didn't have anywhere else. It was 1921. They had started school soon after they had moved to Brooklyn. The teacher was very excited that the Nineteenth Amendment to the Constitution had just passed the year before. It gave women the right to vote. She told the class about the women who had fought for their rights. They even fought against men who didn't think women should vote. She said that women had fought for the right to vote for many years. Many women had gone to prison, and women had been beaten, but they didn't give up. Their teacher said, "Wasn't it wonderful, that they were all so lucky to be living in America?" She told her class that she was going to vote in the next election, and that one day, when they were old enough, and citizens, they would be able to vote too. Fradal and Hasha agreed. They wanted to be citizens in this wonderful country.

They were learning how to speak like Americans, and how to be Americans. To each other, they always remained Fradal and Hasha, but to the rest of the world they started using their American names, and became Frieda and Anna Levine.

I write about my aunt Hasha, referring to her by her Jewish name Hasha, because that is what my mother always called her. I refer to my mother by her American name, Frieda, because that is how she was known in the world I was familiar with.

On the first night at school, they met Sarah Leah. She was an old friend from Drohitchin. They were walking through the hall, looking for their classroom, when they saw her. She was able to tell them which room to go to. Sarah Leah was not really a friend. She was a little older than Hasha. After Sarah Leah was gone, Hasha said that she really didn't like her – not that she didn't like her, but she didn't like her actions. Hasha never really told Frieda exactly what about Sarah Leah's actions she didn't like. Hasha didn't actually come out and tell Frieda that she was a *kurveh* (kur' veh – a prostitute/whore). She just implied it, in her way of whispering on a side about something that is shameful, and never to be spoken of. Still, it was always good to see someone from Drohitchin. They gave each other a big hug. Sarah Leah took their address, and said she would find them. They could get together some evening after work.

Years earlier, Sarah Leah's father, Yitzhak, had left Drohitchin to come to America. When he found that the streets weren't paved with gold, and it was very hard to make a living here too, he turned around, and went back to Drohitchin. People didn't do this. They went to America and stayed there. They were supposed to send for their families. The people who went to America weren't supposed to come back to the shtetl. But Yitzhak did come back, and his wife, Sarah Leah's mother, Brouka, was furious. She never stopped telling him how disappointed she was, and that he was a failure. She told him they could have starved in Drohitchin without him. They didn't need his help to do that.

Sarah Leah and her mother didn't seem to starve when he was gone. In Drohitchin, they lived in a house on the other side of the fields, near the mill. It wasn't far from where there were soldiers living in a makeshift barracks. Sarah Leah used to be nice to the soldiers, and they were nice to her. She was a very pretty girl with beautiful, red hair. The Jewish boys were always chasing her until she started hanging out with the goyishe soldiers. Not many people were nice to Sarah Leah after that, but the soldiers gave her food and even money. So, she and her mother didn't starve.

Hasha and her mother, Chaiya Bailya, a very good woman, were always nice to Brouka and Sarah Leah, even though they didn't approve of Sarah Leah being friends with the soldiers. Chaiya Bailya told Hasha and Fradal that she would rather starve than go with the soldiers. At the time, Fradal really didn't know what her mother was talking about. But she understood that it wasn't ok to be friends with the soldiers. Sarah Leah used to invite Hasha to go with her to the parties in the soldiers' barracks, but Hasha always said no.

After her father came back from America, one of the soldiers nearly killed Yitzhak. He had thrown the money the soldier had given Sarah Leah in his face, and tried to stop Sarah Leah from going with him again. Brouka and Yitzhak took Sarah Leah and managed to run away. They eventually made their way to Brooklyn.

Sarah Leah came to visit Frieda and Hasha a few days after meeting them at night school. She brought ice cream, and taught them to play a new card game. She said it was good to see a friendly face from Drohitchin. Sarah Leah started coming to visit every once in a while. She was always laughing and fun, and always brought a *nosh* (a tasty treat). It became a treat to visit with her. She became a real friend.

One night, a few months later, she came and asked if we could help her get a job, in the factory where we worked. She had been fired from her job in the garment factory where she worked. This was because her boss's wife caught the boss trying to kiss her. She had been fired even though Sarah Leah was trying to push him away. She said it was a curse to be pretty. Hasha told her that they would ask her boss, but she knew that it was useless. The factory they worked in didn't need more workers. Hasha told Sarah Leah to look in the Yiddish newspaper, the <u>Morgan Journal,</u> for a job. Hasha told her that she heard from a girl at work that a lot of the big factories put notices there when they needed help. They usually read the *Forvitz* newspaper (the <u>Jewish Daily Forward</u>), but for jobs she thought the <u>Morgan Journal</u> was maybe better.

Around 1916, the golden age of Yiddish journalism, when most of the people living on the Lower East Side were Jewish, there were five daily Jewish newspapers written in Yiddish. They had more than five hundred thousand readers. There was the *Forvitz, a* very liberal paper that was read by the secular Jews and those interested in the problems of labor. It was also read by people who wanted to read the very popular advice column *"A Bintel Brief"* ("A Bundle of Letters"). Years before the *"Ann Landers"* and *"Dear*

Abby" advice columns were thought of, the *Forvitz* delivered practical, sage advice to those writing them letters asking for their guidance. The *Forvitz* wrote answering their readers' questions about everything from family and relationship problems to the trials and dilemmas of living in (to them) a foreign country. *The Tagablatt* (*The* Daily Sheet) which was a non-political paper, was read by the extreme orthodox. People who were observant but less extreme and Republicans read *Der Morgan Jornal* (The Morning Journal). The labor movement's paper was the *Freie Arbeiter Shtime* (Free Workers' Time). *Der Tag* (The Day) published every day including Saturday, was the paper that Democrats and everybody else read.

About a month later, Sarah Leah came again. This time she was all dolled up and asked Hasha to go to a party with her. Hasha asked, "What kind of party?" Sarah Leah told her that she was going to a party with some sailors she had met down near the docks. She said they were very nice and gave her presents. Hasha told her that she couldn't go. She had to go to work in the morning. Hasha didn't tell Sarah Leah that she wouldn't go no matter what, even if she could go. She also didn't tell Sarah Leah what she really thought, which was that she didn't approve.

They didn't hear from Sarah Leah again for a few months, and then they heard from her mother, Brouka. Brouka got a friend to come, and tell them to come to the funeral. Sarah Leah had died. She had become pregnant, and didn't know who the father was; it was some sailor. Sarah Leah was scared and ashamed. She was afraid that she wouldn't be able to take care of herself and a baby. She knew that people would shun her. How would they live? Abortions wouldn't be legal in America for another fifty years. Rich women who had unwanted pregnancies always had the where with all and the money to pay a real doctor for illegal services, but poor girls like Sarah Leah didn't have that option. They frequently went to unscrupulous and sometimes incompetent back alley abortionists who butchered them. Sarah Leah went to the drug store and asked the man there what to do. She paid him a lot of money and he gave her a bottle of something to get rid of the pregnancy. A few days later the beautiful Sarah Leah started bleeding and it didn't stop.　　ᲝᲒ

❧ *The Flappers* ☙

The clothing factories in New York weren't called sweatshops for nothing. The work was very hard and extremely tedious. Most of the people working in the sweatshops spent all day bending over a sewing machine, trying to make a piece of clothing faster and faster, in order to be able to buy some food and have a roof over their heads. At best, it was boring; at worst you don't want to know about it. The factory owners weren't all very rich. Some of them were, of course – the ones with the big factories, but many were just scraping out a living too. There were many people in tenements like the Chernoffs' that had a little business in their own apartment. Most of the people who worked in factories were there because they had no other way to earn a living, and they were grateful to have that job.

The Chernoffs taught Hasha how to sew on a sewing machine, and after about a year of working on that sewing machine, Hasha was able to get a better job. She kept getting better and better, learning more and more complicated machines. And she kept getting better and better jobs. From Hasha's example, Frieda did the same thing. Frieda eventually even learned how to sew on a flatlock machine making ladies underwear. It had four needles and nine threads.

Frieda and Hasha were still kosher, of course, and made they were sure to be home on Friday nights for Shabbos dinner. They went to shul on the High Holy Days, Rosh Hashanah and Yom

Kippur. They tried not to miss the fun of Simchas Torah. But it was a long time since they had gone to shul on Shabbos morning. Shabbos was the only day they didn't go to the factory to work. They had gotten out of the habit of going to shul on Shabbos during their journey to America.

Like a lot of American Jews, without a government's forced conversion or threat of violent anti-Semitism, Barney, Disha and his girls stopped practicing a lot of the Jewish ways that were part of their everyday lives in the shtetl. In the shtetl people told other people that were leaving to go to America that they should remember who and what they were, and that the most important thing was that they were Jews. This was a real concern. Once the people from the shtetlach emigrated to America and were in safe environments, mixing with people who were not Jewish, many did assimilate completely forgetting Judaism.

Now in America, Frieda and Hasha, their father and Disha never forgot that they were Jewish. They never stopped being kosher, they lit the Friday night candles, and the girls said kaddish for Hunia and their mother. Barney went to shul on Shabbos, but frequently, Hasha and Frieda found more interesting things to do on Shabbos, which was their only day off from work.

They made friends with other immigrant girls and were building a modern American life. In a very short time, they went from life in a restrictive, 17th century medieval, Russian shtetl in the Pale, to the freedom of the modern new world of New York City in the 1920s. They worked hard at abandoning their not very useful, and somewhat outlandish, shtetl beliefs, to adapt to this new urban life. They were doing what they could to become real Americans, and leave their greenhorn[18] ways and some Jewish modesty behind.

---

[18] greenhorn - (antiquated Amer. slang) *n.* foreigner, newcomer unacquainted with local manners and customs; someone who is young, inexperienced or immature, naïve and green, especially one who is easily deceived, (origin: from animal with young horns).

With the small prosperity they had from their jobs, they bought some machine ready-made clothing. It was the Roaring Twenties. Women were cutting their hair and wearing pants like men. Some women were even smoking. Hasha and Frieda were still very modest but wanted to be modern. Disha said it was shameful for girls to dress like men. Hasha told her that was the way people their age dressed in America. Barney told his wife it was okay. "It is a new world in America." He saw that they dressed like that in uptown Manhattan. He told Disha, *"Americana,* rich ladies dress like that."

[Photo:] Hasha (21 years old) very fashionably dressed
in knickers and men's style shirt and tie,
Prospect Park, Brooklyn, New York (ca. 1927)

[Photo:] Frieda (18 years old) - left and Hasha looking very
fashionably modern in their short dresses
on their rooftop, Brooklyn, New York (ca. 1927)

Hasha and some of her girlfriends bobbed their hair in the new fashion and bought the very new cloche hats. You could only wear a cloche hat if you had short hair because it fit very close to the head. There just wasn't any room for long hair under there. That was the point. You wore it with the brim pulled low over your eyes so you had to hold your head back in order to see where you were walking. But the world could see how modern you were with your hair cut short.

[Photo:] Hasha wearing a cloche hat and short dress
on the roof where they lived, Brooklyn, New York (ca. 1927)

**[Photo:] Frieda wearing a cloche hat and short dress
on the roof where they lived, Brooklyn, New York (ca. 1927)**

Frieda was young yet, but she wanted to look modern too. She cut her hair, but not as short as Hasha and her friends. Frieda didn't cut her hair quite as short as the fashion dictated because she had beautiful light brown curls that she kept in long banana curls to her shoulders. It would have been a pity to cut them off. Disha and her father both had what to say about it, but it was too late. What was done was done. Frieda was happy with the way she looked and she bought a cloche hat too.

Just about then the fashionable women in New York City started wearing make-up. Not just loose women, streetwalkers, and actors were wearing make-up, but nice girls started to wear make-up too.

Hasha and her friends bought some lipstick and face powder. They practiced putting it on in the way the lady in the drug store had shown them. The powder came loose in a small round box with a large powder puff. They powdered their faces with the puff. The first girl who tried put too much on and started coughing. The next girl put on less and more gently. Then they all tried it. Hasha tried to put on the lipstick as the salesgirl had shown them. She held her lips back and slightly open in a crazy smile that tightened and smoothed out her lips. The other girls did this too. It was hard to do because they were all laughing so hard. After they actually put on the make-up and looked at themselves and each other, they stopped laughing. Their Jewish modesty got the best of them. They decided they didn't want to be that modern. It was a long time before any of them tried lipstick again, but they eventually did, and started wearing it regularly.

After the misery of freezing in the cold of the city's winter, you got a short break in the spring with beautiful, and sometimes rainy, weather. But come summer, it was the worst; you just couldn't escape the heat or the stink of the city. Their small tenement apartment had very little fresh air and the sweatshop factory wasn't any better.

One way they escaped the heat a little was to go to Coney Island. The first time Hasha and Frieda saw it, they couldn't believe such a wondrous place existed, and was real. It was too fantastical to be real. They had never seen anything like it. Frieda and Hasha had heard it was wonderful, but were still surprised by all of the lights and colors, the music coming out of everywhere. Coney Island was built in the late 1800s, and at that time it was the most popular summer resort in the whole country. The girls didn't spend the money to go on the rides or anything. They just walked around; they couldn't stop looking at everything. They were fascinated with the Ferris wheel that took people into the sky, and the carousel with the beautiful hand carved, painted horses.

The sisters walked along the wooden board walk, and saw the people on the beach wearing beach clothes. Hasha and Frieda saved their money, and then went to a store where they bought bathing clothes to wear at the beach. Their next day off they went to the beach. The beach was free for everyone. At first, they were too shy to take off the layer of clothes they had covering their bathing suits. After a while, they forced themselves to disrobe and get used to wearing so little clothes. They had fun on the beach and shyly tiptoeing into the cold surf.

Winter and summer their everyday life was hard. They worked from seven in the morning till six at night, and then went to night school. A few years after working in factories like this, Hasha and Frieda decided to go on a vacation for a few days, during the summer. They wanted to get away from the noise and heat, and the stink of the city, and the boredom, and dread of the unending race to do more in the sweatshops. One of Hasha's friends had saved her money, and had gone to the mountains, to a Jewish camp for young people. She said it was wonderful with fresh air, and the mountains weren't as hot as Brooklyn. That summer Hasha told Frieda that they would do the same thing the following summer. She convinced other friends to save up and join them. Hasha and Frieda saved all the money they could to go to camp with their friends.

Two young girls going away on vacation didn't sound right to Disha. She didn't have to argue with Barney about it. He didn't like the idea at all either. Hasha told them that she was going and that she was taking Frieda with her. She said they had worked hard, and were entitled to a little fun away from the city. The camp was Jewish and kosher, and they would be okay. There was nothing wrong with it. They would have fresh air and farm fresh food. Hasha and Frieda had come all the way from Europe alone, when they were a lot younger. They had saved their money for the last ten months to be able to go. Hasha was not taking no for an answer.

The girls took the O & W railroad to the Catskill Mountains, the "Jewish Alps," and went to camp. The camp had a lake where they were able to go swimming. Hasha and Frieda didn't really know how to swim. They just splashed around in the shallow part of the water, and went rowing out on the lake. The girls went hiking, and were just happy to be away from the city. In the evening, they sat around and sang Yiddish songs. They sang the popular American songs too like "I'M SITTING ON TOP OF THE WORLD," "AIN'T SHE SWEET," "YES SIR, THAT'S MY BABY," " SHOW ME THE WAY TO GO HOME." They had a carefree few days away from the dreary sweatshop. Mainly, they enjoyed being outside in the countryside, with clean fresh air, away from the heat, the noise, and the stink of the city.

At home in New York, they were doing other things that were modern too. A friend of Hasha's took her and Frieda to a Jewish social club, to meet nice Jewish, young men. This was really very modern – no matchmakers, no *shidduchs* (Yiddish – an arranged marriage or business match). Young people just introducing themselves to each other, people who were strangers. The young people had a good time there.

It was still the roaring twenties, and prohibition was still in effect. There were clubs called speakeasies, but Hasha and Frieda never saw the inside of any of those places. They didn't really even know much about them. The social clubs that they went to didn't sell liquor openly, but they sold a little schnapps in the back. Hasha and Frieda didn't drink. It was mostly the young men who would have some, not a lot, just a little. Nobody ever really got drunk there.

Drunkenness was very strongly frowned upon as being something that nice Jewish people never did.

The social club was just a big room, with a man playing a phonograph so that people could dance. They had straight backed wooden chairs lined up along the walls. That's where the wallflowers sat. They were the girls that were either too shy to talk to anyone, or they weren't pretty, and no one asked them to dance. The men stood in small groups, chatting with each other, trying to get up the courage to go ask a girl to dance, or to even just talk to one.

What was really modern was that not only did the girls dance together, but the young men and young women danced together, without anyone properly introducing them. It was not like in Europe, where the men danced with the men, and the women danced with the women, on the other side of a curtain. These young people danced modern dances like the waltz, and some did the polka. Some very daring girls even did the black bottom, and the charleston, which were new dances sweeping the country. A young man could politely come up to a girl and ask her to dance, even if he didn't know her. If she said yes, he would take her hand. She would go to the center of the room with him, where there were other couples dancing. The couple would dance together, even holding on to each other.

Some of the dancers were quite good. It looked like fun. Hasha and Frieda didn't know how to dance. They stood in the corner watching the couples dance. After a while, they went home, and practiced what they saw the dancers doing. They practiced dancing until they felt comfortable; then a couple of weeks later, they went back to the social club.

Frieda loved dancing, but hated the social club. She was shy with the young men. Frieda was very smart and not usually shy. But she was shy with the boys. She never knew what to say to them. And to make matters worse, her feelings were hurt at the social club more than once. Frieda was very pretty with beautiful brown curls, and big green eyes, but she was very short in stature. A few times young men saw her sitting and admired her. They came over, and asked her to dance, and then rejected her when she stood up, because she was so short.

Lots of young couples met at the social clubs, and got married, without the aid of a matchmaker. Disha didn't like the idea of Hasha and Frieda going to such a place, where people did such things. But it didn't stop her from saying that if they met somebody who needed a little help, they should remember to tell them to come to her; that she would find them someone nice, and make them a good match in the right way.

Hasha met Nathan at one of these dances. Nathan Sheinhouse was the middle son of a poor immigrant family. Nathan was a presser on cloaks and, like Hasha, he worked in a cloak factory sweatshop. He wasn't Prince Charming but she was 25. It was time she should get married already. They were married at the end of 1930.

After Hasha met Nathan, she, of course, stopped going to the social club. Frieda stopped going too.   ❧

ဘ *Fox* ର

*H*asha and Nathan got married, and took a small apartment in Brooklyn. Frieda missed her sister very much after she and Nathan got married. Lonely, Frieda sometimes went to visit their friend Libby, an older woman, who was a friend from Drohitchin.

At one point Frieda, her sister Hasha, their brother Hunia, and their mother lived in Libby's parents' home in Drohitchin. Libby's parents, her mother, Basha Perel, and her father, Binyamin, were very kind people. After one of the fires from the bombings, Frieda's family lost everything, and didn't have a place to live. They had walked out of that fire with just their clothes on their backs. Libby's family were close neighbors. Basha Perel and Binyamin took them in and told Chaiya Bailya not to worry. She and her children could live with them as long as they needed to.

Binyamin could barely walk. He had fallen on one of the many wooden boards that covered the mud puddles of Drohitchin. One Friday night, Binyamin had been late. He was running to get to shul for Friday night service, when he fell on a slippery, broken board. He broke his leg, and it never really healed.

Binyamin and Basha Perel took pity on Chaiya Bailya and her children. It was wartime and things were so hard. Even though they didn't have much more, Basha Perel and Binyamin were very kind, and always shared what they had. They all lived together in the three-room house near Pinsker Street until Chaiya Bailya found an abandoned house for herself and her children to live in.

Libby and her husband, Shlemy, came to America from Drohitchin together. He managed to run away from the Czar's army, after being drafted. He and Libby left Drohitchin and found their way to Antwerp, where they lived, until they were able to get on a ship and come to America.

Once here, they lived on the Lower East Side, on Columbia Street near Delancy. Shlemy was a very decent and gentle man. He worked as a coal man in the winter, and an iceman in the summer. Shlemy used to deliver the coal with a horse and wagon. At each of his stops during the winter, he would shovel the coal into the steel trap doors in the sides of buildings that opened up into long chutes that traveled to the inner cellars of the houses on his route. Most people in New York City heated their homes with coal that was shoveled into large boilers. The boilers held the fires that were housed in their basements. The fire heated the water in the boilers, creating steam that rose up into pipes and circled up through the buildings making them warm.

In summer, Shlemy would carry large blocks of ice on his back, up the stairs of those same houses for his customers' ice boxes. It was the 1920's and 30's - refrigerators weren't in widespread use until the 1940's. People kept their food cold in their metal or wooden metal lined ice boxes. Every week, the ice man came, and brought a fresh block of ice. Delivering coal and ice was hard work, but Shlemy always fed his family.

Libby was sick a lot when she was younger; and they only had one child, a boy named Benjamin. He was named after Libby's father, who had died in Drohitchin.

In those days, unmarried girls didn't live on their own, unless their parents lived far away. Frieda lived with her stepmother, Disha, and her father in Brooklyn, in their small Brownsville apartment. After Hasha had gotten married and moved out, Disha found a smaller, cheaper apartment for them on Stone Avenue.

When Frieda wanted to visit Libby on the Lower East Side, she would take the elevated subway train, called the El, from Brooklyn to Delancey Street. Libby kept saying that it was time for Frieda to marry already; she wasn't getting any younger. She was already over twenty years old. Libby told Frieda that she would talk to their rabbi about her. He had also come from Drohitchin. Libby used to take her son, Benjamin, to study at the rabbi's house. She planned to ask him if he knew of a nice man for a *shidduch* for Frieda, the next time she went.

Well, she did ask the rabbi if he knew of someone for Frieda. Libby told the rabbi that Frieda's mother had died, and she was poor, but very pretty and sweet. The rabbi told Libby that he did know of a nice man. He knew him from the ship they had both come over on. He would try to arrange a meeting with him. Libby said that she thought it best if she met him first. So, the rabbi made the arrangements, and Libby met this man at the rabbi's house. His name was Moshe Fox, and he lived in the Bronx. He worked as a bunch maker in a cigar factory. After meeting him, Libby told Moshe that she would talk to Frieda about him.

Libby told Frieda what she knew about Moshe Fox. She said that he wasn't very good looking; he wore glasses, but seemed to be a nice man, and the rabbi had said very nice things about him. She thought that Frieda should meet him. Frieda agreed to it. So Libby told the rabbi, and they made the arrangements for the young couple to meet.

Frieda was going to bring her friend Esther, and Moshe was going to bring a friend too. They would all meet at Frieda's house in Brownsville that Saturday night, and then go to the movies. They made these arrangements by way of the telephone. It was the spring of 1931; not that many people had telephones, especially not poor people. People called each other from telephones in corner candy stores, or the grocery store in their neighborhood. Frieda told Libby to have Moshe call her at the candy store down the street from her house. Libby had the number. She gave it to the rabbi to give to Moshe. Moshe called the store. Someone at the grocery store went and told Frieda that she had a phone call from someone named Moshe. Frieda ran out of the house to the grocery store to get the call. She had all sorts of questions she wanted to ask him about himself, but she didn't. Those questions would have to wait. Frieda and Moshe didn't talk long. They were both shy, but they wouldn't have talked long anyway; it cost too much money. They only spoke about the arrangements of where and when to meet, and then quickly said good-by.   ଔ

ᔆ *Sam* ᔆ

𝓕rieda was supposed to bring her friend, Esther - a girl for Moshe's friend, Sam. But at the last minute, Esther couldn't come, and Frieda couldn't find another girl who could come. She had no way to reach Moshe to tell him. Moshe didn't have a telephone, and even if he did, she didn't have the number.

Moshe and Sam came all the way down to Brooklyn on the El, from the Bronx. Moshe was a shy, quiet man and didn't know how to talk to girls. He was afraid to be alone with Frieda. He convinced Sam to stay. Rather than go home alone, Sam stayed and the three of them went out together. They went to the movies on Pitkin Avenue and saw a talkie called *Monkey Business*. All three of them laughed at the crazy Marx Brothers. The Marx Brothers were Jewish too. Afterwards, they walked down Pitkin Avenue and went into an ice cream parlor.

The gas lit ice cream parlor had mirrored walls and little round, marble topped tables with twisted wire, scroll back chairs. The long marble topped, mahogany counter followed one side of the parlor. Frieda had some pistachio ice cream.

Moshe carried the faint, but annoying, smell of the cigar maker about him, and he had yellow stained fingers from the tobacco. He had dark hair, and his dark eyes, behind his wire rimmed glasses, showed a sad and angry man. His smiling friend Sam was very handsome with an upbeat and joking way about him. Sam was not very tall. He was a stocky, strongly built man with thick dark, blond hair and laughing, warm blue eyes.

It was obvious that Frieda liked Moshe's friend Sam better than she liked him. She paid much more attention to him and laughed at his jokes. It made Moshe angry.

The two men walked Frieda back home together. Frieda lived with her father and Disha up on the fourth floor. When they got to her building, Moshe said good-by to Frieda on the sidewalk. He was about to leave, when his friend Sam asked him why he wasn't walking his date upstairs. Moshe responded, "I don't walk up no four floors for no skirt!" Sam said that wasn't right, and if Moshe wouldn't take her upstairs, he would. Sam then walked Frieda upstairs. When they got to the top of the stairs, Sam asked Frieda if she would like to go out with him the following Saturday, and Frieda said yes.

Frieda and Sam, my parents were married the following October 31st in the Minford Place Synagogue. It was Halloween 1931. In those days Halloween was a minor holiday and completely irrelevant to Jews. It was the day before my father's 26th birthday; it was a great present for him.

Hasha had borrowed her wedding gown from a friend. But Hasha was much taller than Frieda. Frieda was smaller than all of their friends, and couldn't borrow a gown from anyone. So Hasha went with Frieda to S. Kleins on Union Square, at 14th Street in Manhattan. They sold ready-made clothes, and other soft goods, and had very good prices. Kleins was an "underselling" business - one of the first discount stores in the country. Frieda and Hasha searched through the overflowing racks and Frieda bought a white chiffon dress with pale flowers.

Abie, Sam's younger brother, was his best man. They wore rented tuxedos. Abie reminded Sam to buy a bouquet of flowers for Frieda. In the morning on their wedding day, Frieda and Sam went to a photographer's studio and had their wedding picture taken.

Sam's stepmother Miasha started making wine for the wedding as soon as she heard they were getting married. It was Prohibition but you can't get married without a little wine. Some *schnapps* – whiskey, they bought from Leo, the neighborhood bootlegger. He gave them a good price when he heard it was for a wedding. He said it was a wedding gift. They should have a lot of luck. Everybody made a dish to bring. Miasha didn't stop cooking. Sam hired an accordion player who played music all evening.

Both his father and birth mother were gone, so Sam's stepmother Miasha walked him down the aisle. It saddened my mother that her mother wasn't there to give her away. Disha and her father walked Frieda down the aisle.

My cousin Sylvia, Aunt Lena's oldest daughter, was the flower girl. Her four-year-old, little sister Mae got up on a table and sang Yiddish songs and "LIFE IS JUST A BOWL OF CHERRIES."

Sometime, after they had all danced the *hora*, somebody grabbed a chair and a bunch of the men pushed the seated groom on a chair, up into the air, and danced around with him in the middle of this circle of cheering, clapping family and friends. Another bunch of men grabbed Frieda and put her up in the air on a chair too. Sam took a handkerchief and tossed a corner of it to Frieda. The bride and groom held the handkerchief between them, while they were carried around in time to the music. The men danced around with the couple up on chairs until the men carrying them were too tired to keep it up.

Hasha remembered that Frieda was the youngest of their family. She told them they had to sing the "*mizinka.*" A *mizinka* (me zink' a – Yiddish – *n.*) is the youngest child in a family. To celebrate the parents not having to worry about marrying off another child, the gathering traditionally sings this joyous Yiddish song. The first words of the song are *"The youngest was given away, play fiddlers play."*

After they were married, Frieda moved to the Bronx. It was during the Great Depression and the young couple didn't have a lot of money. So they lived with Sam's stepmother Miasha and his family on Charlotte Street. Moshe Fox lived in that neighborhood too. He was very jealous and angry at Frieda and Sam. He spread untrue rumors about Frieda all over their Bronx neighborhood.

Before her arrival, Frieda's welcome to the Bronx was to hear these rumors being spread by the Charlotte Street *yenta-telebentas*[19]. Across the street from where they lived, there was a woman named Itkie. Itkie had wanted Sam to marry her daughter, Gert. After seeing Frieda, Itkie jealously said, "He had to go to Brooklyn to get a girl with curls? A *pitchiroochi* (pitch e' roo chEE – Yiddish - a nothing) from Brownsville! A nothing!" ❦

---

[19] *Yenta Telebenta* (yen' ta • tell' e ben ta)*n.* –a gossip who could be a reporter for "Page 6." "Mrs. National Enquirer." a bigger blabbermouth than a *yenta*. From the play of the same name, written by the famous Jewish humorist Jacob Adler for the Yiddish theater. Jacob Adler was also a columnist for the <u>Jewish Daily Forward</u> newspaper where he was the first to popularize the use of the ordinary Jewish woman's name Yenta as a synonym for a gossip monger.

**[Photo:] Frieda and Sam Mnuskin's wedding,
New York City, October 31, 1931**

ೞ *The Mikvah* ೞ

Sam's father, Mikhel Mnushkin, was born in Hlusk, Belarus, in 1875. Hlusk was a small shtetl about 56 kilometers, give or take 35 miles east of the city of Bobruisk. His family was well off for shtetl Jews. They had a small inn on the road from Hlusk to obruisk.

Mikhel was very smart, and learned in the Torah. Being a scholar was considered one of the greatest honors one could have. Jewish parents were (and are) proudest of their sons who are scholars, and Mikhel knew nothing else. From the time that Mikhel was three years old, when he was taught the Hebrew alphabet, that was who he was. He was taught the Hebrew alphabet in the traditional shtetl way, of the child licking the letters written in honey, so that the child would know that learning was sweet. His parents could see that he was very smart, and they encouraged him in his studies.

Mikhel was dark, with a dark beard, thin, and of average height. As a young man, with his parents' urging, Mikhel left Hlusk, and moved to Bobruisk, to study and become a rabbi. There, he entered one of the yeshivas and became a *yeshiva bukher* - a Talmudic scholar. A yeshiva[20] is a Jewish college and seminary.

---

[20] yeshiva - 1. An Orthodox Jewish seminary; 2. a college for Talmudic study and higher Jewish learning; 3. In America a Jewish children's day school for religious and secular studies

At the end of the 19th century, there were more than 300 students studying in twenty small yeshivas in Bobruisk. After moving to Bobruisk, Mikhel joined them and spent his days studying the Torah and the Talmud. The modest life of a yeshiva scholar was not an easy life. It was extremely demanding, rigorously studying the ancient texts from early morning to late at night. The students never stopped thinking about the words of the Torah. When humble yeshiva scholars were seen walking in the street with their scraggly beards and ear locks, it was usually with their eyes looking down in concentration on a remembered Talmudic passage. They were generally pale and stooped over from long hours of studying indoors, and the lack of sunlight and fresh air. Their hands were soft, and their bodies weren't strong because they lived their lives mostly inside the yeshivas, bent over their books. Part of their studies involved long discussions on the different Talmudic passages. They did (and still do) mental gymnastics arguing over the hair-splitting meaning of a phrase, or even just one word. The Hebrew word for this kind of studious nit picking and penetrating semantic investigation is *"pilpul"* (rhymes with fill full). It always makes me think of pulling tiny little pills apart. That nit picking is something like what they are doing. The lifestyle of these scrawny scholars didn't (and still doesn't) make their bodies strong, but it did make for rapid theoretical thinking and very strong minds. Mikhel eventually obtained his *semikhah* – the rabbinical ordination.

The yeshiva students were supported by the community. In order for the students to have kosher meals and a place to sleep, local families took turns feeding and boarding them. It was considered an act of piety, a mitzvah, and an honor to feed and board these young men. After all, they were studying the Torah and the Talmud. It was prearranged that the families gave one or two students dinner and a bed once a week, usually the same night each week. These days were called *essen teg* - "eating days." They went from home to home, eating and sleeping in a different family's home each night. Lots of poor students, who were unlucky in finding a place to board for the night, slept on the benches at the yeshiva, and had little to eat. When they could, the yeshiva boys went to the same seven different families for dinner each week. If they were very lucky, they were able to have a warm bed there too.

Like most of the other yeshiva students, Mikhel would have dinner with the host families. One of the families he had dinner with happened to be a family that had originally come from Hlusk. They were his father's distant cousins. At that house, Mikhel met their daughter, Sima Razel. Her name, Sima Razel, means treasured rose, and like her name, she was as beautiful as a rose. She was not very tall, but had big blue eyes, and long, blond curls circling her porcelain, white face. He was smitten at first sight. She saw how he shyly looked at her and didn't mind. Yeshiva scholars were considered good matches – a matrimonial prize. Mikhel came from a well off family, and wasn't bad looking. Sima Razel's parents were very proud to make such a match.

Mikhel and Sima Razel were married in 1896. After the wedding, Mikhel moved in with Sima Razel and her parents. It was not uncommon for yeshiva scholars to live with their parents or in-laws after getting married. Within what seemed like a dreamlike time, Mikhel had a beautiful wife, Sima Razel, and then within a short time, three beautiful little daughters - Elka, Layah and Fagel (fAy' gell). Fagel, his youngest daughter with her blue eyes and long blond curls was the prettiest of the three, and looked just like his beautiful wife Sima Razel.

Sima Razel's parents moved back to Hlusk in 1902, shortly after the great fire that had burned down her father's business, and half of Bobruisk. They gave Mikhel and Sima Razel what was left of their house.

Finally, on a Wednesday in the middle of the night, November 1, 1905, their first son, my father, Zolmon Ellie Mnushkin (Sam) was born. Zolmon Ellie was their fourth child, but the first boy. Even though it was a very hard birth, everyone was very excited. There was joy; finally, a boy, a son.

November first is the middle of winter in Bobruisk, Belarus; it is extremely cold. Six weeks after giving birth, a religious Jewish woman must go to the *mikvah*, the ritual bathing, before she can have marital bliss with her husband. The mikvah is not for purposes of cleansing the body but for cleansing the soul. In fact, people are required to bathe their bodies scrupulously before entering a mikvah. Jewish brides are supposed to go to a mikvah for the first time on their wedding day, and then again, every month after their menstruation has passed, and six weeks after the birth of a child. Men go to the mikvah for ritual purity before the high holy days, before their wedding day, and before their sons are circumcised. People who convert to Judaism go to a mikvah just before their conversion. And people dip food utensils into a mikvah to make them kosher after they have become unkosher.

Most mikvahs did not have the best, indoor heated plumbing in 1905, Belarus. When my father's mother, a very religious woman, went to the mikvah six weeks after giving birth to my father, it was the middle of December. We can only imagine what it was like. After the difficult birth she had gone through, and the mikvah, very sadly, Sima Razel caught pneumonia and died. She left three little girls, besides her baby boy, my father, Zolmon Ellie. Her oldest daughter, Elka was about eight years old, Laya was five, and Fagle was about three.

[Photo:] A typical shtetl mikvah, Eastern Europe(ca. 1910)
The wooden tub, near the back wall, was for cleansing prior to entering the
actual mikvah, which was a small pool at the bottom of the stairs on the right
Photo courtesy of - http://yopera.com/ŻydziwprzedwojennejPolsce

It is a tradition among most *Ashkenazi*[21] Jews to honor people who were dear to them, who have died, by naming their children after them. We are almost superstitious about not naming babies for people who are still alive. My father and each of his sisters have a daughter who is named for their mother, Sima Razel. My cousins, Sylvia, Rosa, Razel, and I were all named for her. It is a common American custom of *Ashkenazi* Jews, to just use the initial letter of the person's Jewish

---

21 *Ashkenazi* ash ke nazi - adj. - Jews from Eastern Europe

name that they are honoring, when giving a baby an American name. Sometimes, as in my case, the first and middle names are reversed in the American name. The Jewish name, given to a girl, at her baby naming in the synagogue, or a boy at his *bris* (ritual circumcision) remains the same as the original. My cousin Sylvia's middle name is Rose and my name, Roslyn means rose, as our grandmother's name Razel means rose in Yiddish. My sister Bea, who was nine years old when I was born, chose Roslyn as my American name. Please don't tell anybody, but my American middle name is Sylvia.

Zolmon, only seven weeks old when his mother died, was sent to live with a wet nurse in Hlusk. The wet nurse was a poor woman who had lost her own baby. This often happened when mothers of new born babies died. They didn't have Similac baby formula. Zolmon's sister Fagel, only a few years older, was sent to live in Hlusk too, with Sima Razel's parents. Elka and Layah, my father's older sisters, stayed home with their father.

Mikhel had loved Sima Razel very much. But husbands and wives are only required to mourn through the first month after their spouse dies. When Sima Razel died, Mikhel had three young daughters and a brand new baby son. Before the year was over, Mikhel remarried. This time, the bride was a girl from Hlusk. Miasha was poor, plain looking and in her late twenties, an old maid. No one else would marry a widower with four children, especially when everyone in Hlusk knew he was still in love with his first wife, Sima Razel. From his nighttime dreams, he never stopped calling out for Sima Razel. But he was at that time, as I said, very well off.

When Zolmon was about two years old, Miasha gave birth to a baby boy who died in childbirth. Until that time, Zolmon had lived with his wet nurse in Hlusk. When Miasha's first born died, she took Zolmon home to Bobruisk and raised the toddler as her own. They became very close, and Zolmon always loved Miasha, as the mother he never knew. She became his mother and Zolmon would have done anything for her.
CB

❧ *Bobruisk* ☙

$Bobruisk$ (or Babruysk) was not a quiet little shtetl at the beginning of the 20th century. It was, and still is, one of the larger cities in Belarus, and dating back to before the middle of the 14th century, is one of its oldest cities. Located in the eastern part of Belarus, both Bobruisk and Hlusk are in the heavily forested Mahilyow Province. Bobruisk's main industry is logging, and it is the largest logging center in Belarus.

In addition to being a prominent trade center and logging industry hub, until World War II Bobruisk had been a major military base for the Russian Empire. The Bobruisk Fortress was constructed at the heart of the city by Czar Alexander I in 1810. Everyone in the city could hear the bell in the fortress tower ring out the hours of the day. With its massive stone walls and towers, it was the focal point of the city, and was one of the major fortresses of the western part of the Russian Empire. In its day, it housed thousands of Russian troops, and fought off Napoleon's army. During World War II, the occupying German forces turned it into a concentration camp and funeral pyre for 80,000 innocent people.

The Imperial Russian crown heads were always extremely xenophobic. That didn't make the Russian Empire a comfortable haven for the Jews. Like most of Europe's monarchs, the Czars believed that a homogenized populous was easier to govern. With the urging and complicity of the Russian Orthodox Church, they tried to convert all of Russia into one unified nation. Many of the

Russian regimes had tried to convert and Russify the Jews, but the Jewish communities refused to give up their beloved Torah and being Jewish.

There were Jewish people living in the Russian Steppes and the slopes of the Caucasus Mountains since the 5th century. The first record of Jews living in Belarus was in the city of Brest in 1388. Even though Jews lived in Russia and Eastern Europe for hundreds of years, they were always considered foreigners because they weren't Christians, and because they refused to convert and be baptized. Although lots of Jews spoke Russian, among themselves Jews spoke a different language; they spoke Yiddish. Unlike the rest of Europe, who observe the Sabbath on Sunday, the Jewish observance of the Sabbath is on Saturday. Jewish dietary laws kept them from eating the same food, especially meat, and the Jews had many other customs that were different as well. The Jewish people were resented for being clannish. In order to live according to the Torah, and to keep their own culture, the Jews remained together and were clannish. It prevented them from Russification and assimilating into Russian society. As a result, they were considered resident strangers in the land they had lived in for many generations. Although most never did anything disruptive or disloyal, until the end of the nineteenth century (when the labor movement and the illegal Zionist movement were created), and regardless of how they tried to prove their loyalty, Jews were always thought to be unpatriotic foreigners, and not to be trusted.

Russians not only didn't trust the Jews, they also blamed and made them scapegoats for every conceivable and inconceivable ill. In the Russians' collective worldview, all Jews were responsible for all of the problems of Russia. The unlearned *muzhiks* (mü-'zhēks Russian and Belarusian peasants), many of whom had no other source of information, were taught by many of their clergy that the Jews were evil. There is an old Slavic saying, "If the water in the sink is missing, it is because the Jews took it." This malicious and fallacious adage has always given the Russians, just like the Poles and most of Eastern Europe, the explanation for all of their problems, and in many areas still does. They, therefore, felt justified in treating the Jewish population badly, with higher taxes and harsh laws.

In most of Europe, Jews were not allowed to own land; so Jewish people didn't usually become farmers. Jews were restricted at various times from lots of other occupations as well. The Jewish people did the only thing left for them to do in order to earn a living. They became part of the merchant class, selling the things that they could import, or that guildsmen, or they themselves had made.

Catherine the Great, Czarina Catherine II, the Empress of all Russia, was very liberal in her attitude towards the Jews and Judaism. She knew the Jews didn't have any power and she recognized that they were a modest and quiet people; they weren't violent or aggressive. They were pious but weren't trying to convert anybody else to Judaism. Catherine the Great saw the Jewish population as what they were, a very industrious group, with many who were very good business men, but with most Jews just wanting to be left alone to scrape out a living, and to obey their Torah in addition to Russian laws.

The mercantile class from Moscow and Smolensk didn't like the competition that the Jewish merchants presented. In December of 1791, although she herself did not feel it was a good idea, Czarina Catherine II, never-the-less, allowed herself to be pushed into signing the edict creating the Pale of Settlement[22]. From the splendor and grandeur of her St. Petersburg Winter Palace, she decreed that the Jews of Russia only be allowed to live in the far fields of the western border of the Russian Imperial Empire. It restricted where most of the Jews of Russia could live. During that period, the Jews of Russia were about forty percent of the world's Jewish population. Thousands of people were deported from St. Petersburg and Moscow. From all over "mother" Russia, many in

---

[22] The word pale comes from the Latin word *palus*, meaning stake – specifically a stake used to mark boundaries. From this came the figurative meaning of boundary and eventually to mean border.

chains, Jews were forced to leave their homes and move to the area in western Russia known as The Pale of Settlement.

The Pale, as most people called it, was roughly 386,100 square miles (740,700 square kilometers) of territory, and grew to include twenty-five provinces on the western edge of the Russian Imperial Empire. It included the areas of White Russia (Byelorussia, now known as Belarus), most of Eastern Poland, Latvia, Lithuania, Bessarabia (Romania), the Crimea, and the Ukraine.

Things were not good for the Jews even in The Pale. The Pale of Settlement was 4% of Imperial Russia, but by 1910 it included five million Jews. More than 90% of the Jews of Russia were forced to reside in the poor conditions of the overcrowded cities and small towns in The Pale. The Pale of Settlement, a defined, self-governing area within Russia, was also regulated by laws that did not apply to the Russian Empire as a whole. In addition, there were laws that were much more restrictive within The Pale, that applied to the Jewish population, but not to the Christians. Jews were required to pay double taxes, and still had restrictions on their owning land. With few exceptions, they were not allowed entrance into Russian schools, thereby limiting their higher education. They were prevented from participating in many professions, forbidden to run taverns or sell liquor. The restriction against the sale of liquor by Jews was a severe hardship, because prior to the enactment of these laws, the making of liquor and the running of taverns had been a large Jewish industry.

There were Jewish merchants and factory owners that were well off; some were even wealthy, but the shtetl life of The Pale, offered only a very hard way of living for most of the Jewish population. Jews could not travel within Russia without an internal passport, but if they could get to a border, they were able to leave the country. Between 1881 and 1917, more than two million Jews emigrated, mostly to Western Europe, Palestine, and America.

Things were never quiet for Jews in Bobruisk, but it was especially hard at the end of the 19th and beginning of the 20th centuries, when things were extremely hard in all of Russia. The last

Czar, Nicholas Romanov II, instituted a campaign against the Jews that was historically one of the worst. His anti-Semitic restrictive decrees just never seemed to stop, and there were always new ones. To the Jews, it felt like the only purpose the government had was to make the Jewish people miserable. With the full knowledge and encouragement of the government, the Gentiles were instigated to riot against the Jews, and they didn't need too much encouragement in their ancient Judeophobia.

This was true even though at that time the Jews were about 60% of the population of Bobruisk. Whenever there were hardships in the Russian Empire, popular animosity toward the Jews made them an easy target to be the scapegoats for the government. They had all sorts of ways of singling out the Jewish population for unmerited harsh treatment. Their cruel and tragic, undisguised and deliberate use of pogroms was especially effective in redirecting the frustration of the *muzhiks,*[23] from the Czar to the Jews. The Czar's men would provide vodka and send instigators to incite the drunken muzhiks. Intoxicated by government-provided vodka, the drunken peasants committed bestial, unspeakable acts, ravishing Jewish women, and beating the men and destroying their property. Entire streets were destroyed. The mobs of muzhiks ruined synagogues, yeshivas, Jewish shops, and homes. They destroyed Torah scrolls, not realizing that the Torahs they desecrated were scrolls of the Old Testament, part of their own Bible. Nothing, and no one, in the Jewish population was safe.

The Imperial government would start pogroms, and when the violence got out of hand, they would bring the constables or Cossacks in to stop it. In reality, they used the Cossacks to start most of the pogroms, not just to stop them. The Cossacks pillaged and raped the shtetlach of the Pale at will. If the Jews of the shtetlachwere lucky to get warning, that the Cossacks were coming, the Jews would hide their wives and daughters from the Cossacks ruthless marauding presence, in fear that they would be raped. In one of the pogroms in Hlusk, My father's cousin, Miriam, was raped

---

[23] *muzhik - n. -* a Russian peasant

by Cossacks, in one of their pogroms in Hlusk. She was never the same after that. She used to walk around as though she was in a stupor.

[Photo:] Cossacks on the road, Eastern Europe (ca. 1915)
Photo courtesy of the Russian Military Museum/Russian cavalry

[Photo:] Cossacks leaving an Eastern European shtetl (ca. early 20th century)
Photo courtesy of the Russian Military Museum/Russian cavalry

Today, Cossack historians are attempting to rewrite history. They are trying to claim that they weren't responsible for the pogroms, but were the ones who were sent by the Russian government to stop the carnage. The Jewish people, who lived through the Cossacks' bestial raids, know the truth, and still talk about their cruel and inhuman invasions. I remember being awakened many times as a child by my mother screaming out from the nightmares of her sleep, shouting "The Cossacks are coming, the Cossacks are coming!!!!"

The Cossacks were fierce, militaristic communities living in the Steppe region of the Ukraine and southern Russia. The Imperial Russian army recruited them to the cavalry for their talents as the finest horseman in Eastern Europe, and because they were no strangers to fighting and guns. It is a Cossack tradition to put a rifle in a baby boy's hands to hold, before he can walk. The Cossacks hated the Bolsheviks, and they all hated Jews.

There were three major waves of pogroms against the Jews in the Pale: 1881-1884, 1903-1906, and in 1917-1921. The Jews of Bobruisk didn't escape these periods of devastating destruction or the wars. With the wars, the violent anti-Semitic attacks from the Russian people, and the unceasing poverty, who could blame the Jews for wanting to leave The Pale?

The Jewish people have been praying for a return to their homeland, Israel, for over 2,400 years. Even though there were always Jewish communities and Jews living in Palestine ever since the beginning of the Diaspora, when most of the Jews were driven out of their ancient home land of Israel, each yearat the Passover Seder table you can hear the annual reprise of their remembered Jewish dream with, "Next year in Jerusalem!" Some Jewish people say it more often. This wish for a return to the Holy Land isn't really relevant to the hardships of the Pale, or anywhere else that the Jewish people resided, but these cruel hardships did help to spur the Zionist movement. Zionism, as a reality, had been sweeping the Jewish world since before the end of the nineteenth century. In 1897, Jewish leaders met in Basel, Switzerland, where they held the first Zionist Congress, and organized the Zionist movement.

The organization of the Zionist movement saw the formation of emigration committees in most of the European cities that had large Jewish populations. They raised funds from the Rothchilds and other wealthy Jews to buy land in Israel. That land was offered for free to the Jews (mainly the Jews of Eastern Europe escaping the pogroms) who were willing to immigrate to what was then Palestine.

There were people from the Zionist centers in Minsk and Vilna who went all over Eastern Europe encouraging the Jews to become Zionists, and to move to Palestine, or at least to help others go and build the country. They organized groups and encouraged people to start learning how to speak Hebrew. One of these groups came to Bobruisk.

Mikhel's sister, Sima and her husband, Elitche Lubanoff, became Zionists. Elitche had become a Zionist, and then he convinced Sima to go to a Zionist meeting with him. Encouraged by his passion, and what she heard, she too became a Zionist. Zionism was against the law in Russia. So they didn't tell anyone when they went to the secret Zionist meetings. They couldn't wait for the day that they could save enough money to immigrate to Palestine.

The Zionists had come to Bobruisk, to offer that land for free to would-be settlers who could farm the land, especially people with sons. Sima and Elitche had some strong sons, and were offered land that had been paid for by the Rothchilds. The misery of Bobruisk had left Sima and Elitche no reason to stay in Bobruisk. They decided to accept the Zionists' offer and emigrate to Palestine. Not having any daughters, Sima invited her seventeen-year-old niece, Mikhel's daughter Layah, to go with them. Layah thought about it, but decided that she wanted to stay with her family. In 1917, Sima, Elitche, and their sons collected all that they had, and, in their horse and wagon, left their home in Bobruisk, Belarus forever. They told the family not to forget them, and to send them a letter once in a while.

In Bobruisk, the pioneers were told that if they could get to Odessa, there were Zionists there who helped people who wanted to move to Palestine. Most of the Zionists from The Pale that were headed for the Holy Land managed to travel by wagon, or train through all of the Ukraine until they got to Odessa, the Ukrainian port, on the Black Sea. In Odessa, they took a ship which sailed via Istanbul, and Beirut to the port of Jaffa, Palestine.

[Photo:] Jaffa, Palestine (ca. 1912)

Sima and Elitche Lubanoff and their boys struggled to get to Palestine, and they struggled to make a life when they got there. Life was reputed to be very hard in Palestine, but Sima and Elitche didn't really know how hard. The Lubanoffs settled in Kfar Tabor, on the land that they had been given from the Rothschild trust. Kfar Tabor is a village in northern Israel, at the foot of Mount Tabor. It is situated in the Lower Galilee, at the eastern end of the Jezreel Valley, about 17 kilometers (11 mi) west of Lake Kinneret (the Sea of Galilee). The fertile region is good grape country, and in addition to raising all sorts of other crops, the Lubanoffs became wine growers, and are partners in the Tabor Winery. My father's aunt Sima, and her husband Elitche had ten children. My family is now directly related to more than sixty families in Israel.

**[Photo:] Sima and Elitche Lubanoff (Mikhel Mnushkin's sister
& brother-in-law) Kfar Tabor, Israel (ca. 1955)**

Some of the ancient Jewish communities that still existed in the Arabic world during the 20th century were over 2,500 years old. Although Jews had lived in and were citizens of Arabic countries for many centuries, they were always second-class citizens. In the Arabic countries too, there were the pogroms and violence, and anti-Semitic restrictions and laws, until the Jews were expelled from most of the Arabic nations. The Jewish population was evicted under a resolution from the Arab League, who had determined that all Arab countries should throw the Jews out of their countries.

There were almost one million Jews, who were thrown out of their homes in the Arabic world, and forced to flee. I have a friend whose family was compelled to leave Baghdad in 1949. She was eight years old then. Her family were merchants, and they could trace their family tree in Baghdad back for more than a thousand years. I have another friend who was born in Cairo. His family lived in Egypt for many generations. Only a little boy in 1948, he still talks about how the police came and pushed them out of their home in the middle of the night. The police told them they had to leave Egypt with not much more than the clothes on their backs. My friend remembers barely making it through the desert, with very little food, until they came to the Israeli border. Thousands of the Jews who were forced to leave their homes in the Arabic world moved to Israel.

According to WOJAC, the World Organization of Jews from Arab Countries, Jewish property that was confiscated in the Arab countries would be valued at more than $400 billion today. They estimate that the Jewish-owned real-estate that they were forced to leave in the Arab nations is about 100,000 square kilometers (four times greater than the size of Israel).

On May 14, 1948, (5 Iyar, 5708 on the Jewish calendar) the resounding sound of *"Am Yisrael Chai!"* (the children of Israel live!), was heard around the world. This was the day, the United Nations' official announcement ended the British Mandate, and the independent Jewish State of Israel was reborn, on the land where the Kingdoms of Israel and Judah had been.

In 1949, about 600,000 Arabs voluntarily left the Palestinian areas that became Israel. These Palestinian refugees were told, by their Arabic leaders to leave, because there was going to be a war, and that after the war, they could return in triumph to take over all of Israel. The Arab League then passed a resolution that prohibited their member nations from giving these Palestinian Arab refugees citizenship in their countries.

It is more than sixty-five years later, the fighting over this small piece of ground hasn't ended yet. G_d willing, it will end soon.

After losing her first baby boy, and taking my father, Zolmon, home, Miasha and Mikhel had three more sons. Avraham was born on Tuesday, March 28, 1911. He was sickly as a child. As a result, Miasha always coddled and spoiled him. During one of the pogroms, Miasha, six months pregnant, lost another baby, a boy. He was stillborn.

Mikhel and his family lost everything in a long line of nightmares. The pogroms, the murderous riots, got so bad that they had to leave Bobruisk. The Yeshiva that Mikhel studied in had a massive fire, and most of it was burned down. Mikhel took his wife, Miasha and the children to live in Hlusk. Mikhel and Miasha both had family there. Miasha was pregnant again. After he settled his wife and children in Hlusk, Mikhel left. He wanted to build a better life for his family. He didn't want to go to Palestine because he thought they would have a better easier life in America. They had cousins in America, the "golden land"; so, that is where he went. He told Miasha that he would send for her and the children after he got settled there.

People in the family used to joke that Mikhel probably left Europe because he didn't like having two *schvigas*, (mothers-in-law), his first wife, Sima Razel's mother and Miasha's mother. But the truth is that they had no choice but to leave. The pogroms and the wars devastated the entire area known as The Pale, especially for Jews.

And then Muttel, the joker of the family, was born. It was about six months after his father, Mikhel had left.

Mikhel Mnushkin crossed the Atlantic on the S.S. Pennsylvania, out of Hamburg, Germany. There were 2,724 passengers; 162 were first class passengers, and 180 were in second class. Mikhel was one of the 2,382 men, women and children in third class, or what was really very fittingly called steerage, because they were treated no better than cattle. The S.S. Pennsylvania had a service speed of 13 knots. It docked in New York Harbor on January 5, 1912. Mikhel was about 39 years old. By the time he landed at Ellis Island, his name had been misspelled, and forever changed to Michael Mnuskin. He kept the name on his papers, but never called himself Michael Mnuskin. It was always Mikhel Mnushkin to anyone who knew him.

Passenger Record

First Name: *Michal*
Last Name: *Mnuskin*
Ethnicity: *Russia, Hebrew*
Last Place of Residence: *Glusk, Russia*
Date of Arrival: *January 05, 1912*
Age at Arrival: *39y*   Gender: *M*   Marital Status: *M*
        Ship of Travel: *Pennsylvania*
Port of Departure: *Hamburg*
Manifest Line Number: *0020*

**[Copy:] SS Pennsylvania's ship's manifest
listing for Michal Mnuskin (Mikhel Mnushkin)
Hamburg, Germany to NYC (ca. January 1912)**
Record courtesy of the Ellis Island Archives

Once in New York City, he went to his cousins, who were willing to help him. They had settled into a tenement on the lower east side of Manhattan. It was on Clinton Street near Grand Street. He lived there with them as a border for a long time.

Mikhel was not a tall man. He was naturally thin, with a slight stoop, from his years of leaning over his books, and then later leaning over a cutting table. He had a dark complexion and dark curly hair. With his cousins' urging and wanting to fit into his new world and look more like an American, he shaved his beard and cut off his earlocks.[24]   He kept a fashionable mustache. Although no longer financially well off, and no longer able to be a Torah scholar in a yeshiva, he was still a very religious man. He had shaved his beard when he came to America, but didn't go too much further in giving up his Jewish traditions and old ways.

---

[24] Earlocks (Yiddish: payess Hebrew: payot) : a lock of hair grown long in front of each ear worn by Ultra-Orthodox Jewish men obeying the biblical passage in Leviticus 19:27: "Ye shall not clip your hair at the temples; neither shalt thou mar the edges of your beard." 19: 28: "Ye shall not make any cuttings in your flesh for the dead, nor print any marks upon you: I am the LORD, your G_d." In other words they don't get tattooed either.

[Photo:] Michal Mnuskin (seated) formerly Mikhel Mnushkin
with two cousins, Lower East Side, Manhattan (ca. 1912)

When Mikhel Mnuskin was settled, and had saved enough money, he sent for his family. His oldest daughter, Elka, was already married. She and her husband Dovid and their three daughters, Shura, Rosa and baby Fanya, couldn't come on her father's papers. They had moved to Moscow, and weren't in Hlusk when the Germans came during World War II. We eventually lost track of them around 1949.But to my knowledge, they never left Russia.

When I was a little girl, my family used to send them packages. I remember going to the American Jewish Joint Distribution Committee, with my mother and my Aunt Lena to send the packages. My family did this until Elka asked that we stop. We received a letter from her telling the family that the packages from America caused them trouble with the Communists. Her letters used to come all blacked out in redacted silence, until they stopped coming at all. My parents hated the Communists, especially since they were afraid for Elka, Dovid, and the girls. My brother, Marty, tried to find Elka and her family through the Mormon database, but was unsuccessful. They had disappeared. It was like the world had just swallowed them up.

[Photo:] Elka (seated far right), Dovid Spielkoff and their
daughters Rosa, Shura and baby Fanya, Russia (ca. 1935)

Before the Russian Revolution, Russia was just as it had been in Poland at the beginning of the Polish – Russian War for Independence, when the Poles were declaring the birth of the Republic of Poland. At the beginning, the Polish leaders had promised the Jews of Poland equality. Once they had power, the first things they instituted were harsher laws and restrictions against the Jewish population than there were before. In Russia, the Bolshevik Revolutionaries promised equality and freedom for all under communism. The Jews had always received cruel treatment at the hands of the imperial Russian czars. At the beginning of the Russian Revolution, the Communists promised a better way of life in their new world order, without a class system. So, just as the Jewish people of Poland thought that they would have the promised equality under the new Polish government, before they were disappointed, Russian Jews also believed the campaign propaganda, that they would be equal citizens under a communist regime, and they too were deceived and disappointed. Lots of Jews joined the Revolution, and many of the Revolution's leaders were even Jewish. Unlike Poland, who only subjugated the Jews, the oppressive, secretive, Soviet Union under Premiere Joseph Stalin took away everyone's freedom. Although it was worse for the Jews, all citizens under the Soviet regime lost their rights of self-determination. A Russian government had finally managed to homogenize the population, not with the conversion of all to one religion, but with the almost complete eradication of all religions, and the loss of individual freedom. The Communists tried to destroy religion and traditions, and gave little in return other than empty promises.

When the Bolsheviks gained power, one of the Revolution's leaders, Vladimir Ilyich Lenin told the Premiere, Joseph Stalin who was an anti-Semite even though all three of his wives were Jewish, to leave the Jews alone. Lenin supposedly said, "Don't bother with them. Some will assimilate, some will intermarry and some will die off naturally. They will disappear as a race." In the atheistic Soviet Union, Lenin had declared anti-Semitism a state offense. Anti-Semitism never stopped, but was no longer openly sanctioned by the government, and the decree governing the Pale of Settlement was abolished. After the Russian Revolution in 1917, with the overthrow of the Czarist regime, it was hard for everyone, but it was worse for the Jews. Jews still had to prove their allegiance at every turn, even though most of them had, with little choice, abandoned their Jewish traditions, as the Christians had to abandon the church.

Here in America, my parents had two friends who were communists. This couple owned a grocery store and some houses that they rented out. My parents loved these people, in spite of their being communists. Always polite, my parents never said anything to them about being against communism. My parents wondered to each other, about these people who were here safe, earning a comfortable living, but complaining about the American government. My father used to ask my mother, rhetorically, knowing full well what the answer was, if they thought that they could be so prosperous with their houses and store under the Communists in Russia. ⚬

❧ *Bread for the Trip* ☙

When Miasha got the papers and money from Mikhel to go to America, she hurried to get ready to leave. She sold everything she could. They were almost ready to go, but she decided that it would be better to stay until after *Tisha B'av*. It was only another few days.

Tisha B'Av is the ninth day of the Jewish month of Av. On the Gregorian calendar, it occurs during July or the beginning of August. Tisha B'Av is the saddest day on the Jewish calendar, and it is a day of fasting and mourning. It is the day Jews commemorate most of their historical tragedies. Many coincidentally occurred on or about the Ninth day of Av, including the destruction of the first and second Holy Temples. The first Temple was destroyed by the Babylonians in 586 B.C.E. and the second Temple by the Romans in 70 C.E. The fall of Jerusalem in 70 C.E. and the destruction of Batar, the last independent Jewish city during the Roman period, are both remembered on Tisha B'av. In addition, during the Spanish Inquisition, the Catholic monarchy, Queen Isabella and King Ferdinand II issued their infamous Alhambra Decree ordering the expulsion of all Jews from every inch of the Spanish Kingdom by the end of July 1492. July 31, 1492 was on Tisha B'Av.

The three weeks before Tisha B'Av starts a period of mourning. The arks in synagogues are draped in black. Religious Jews observe the traditions of mourning like they would when a close relative dies. Tisha B'Av itself is a day of fasting. Just like on Yom Kippur, the Day of Atonement, from sundown to sundown the next day, not even a drop of water is supposed to pass their lips. As they do on Yom Kippur, religious Jews spend the day in synagogue praying. The Book of Lamentations is read, and prayers of mourning are said.

So Miasha decided it would be better to wait till after Tisha B'Av for them to start their journey to America. The day after the holy day, she decided to walk to the blacksmith. She had one cow left. Miasha had decided to go ask him if he knew anyone who might want to buy it.

[Photo:] A man going home after buying a cow,
East European shtetl (ca. 1918)

Miasha was very careful with the money and papers Mikhel had sent for them to go to America. She wasn't taking any chances with these precious things. She had hidden everything, all the money and the papers that Mikhail had sent. Miasha didn't tell anyone where she had put this treasure. She still had to go sell the cow. When Miasha left the house, to go to the barn to get the cow, no one knew that she had buried it all in the back of the big oven.

Miasha's mother was not willing to leave Hlusk to come to America, but she helped Miasha get ready to leave. While Miasha was gone, her mother made the food for their trip. Not knowingthat Miasha had hidden anything in the back of the oven, she made a casserole for them to take with them, and she baked two challahs. In a short time, everything was gone - all of the money and the papers literally went up in smoke. Now they were really penniless. They couldn't leave without money and the papers.

After they lost all of their money and their papers, Miasha didn't know what to do. She had to find another way to get money, just to feed them all. Hlusk was a small shtetl, and there was very little industry. Most people in the shtetlach lived from hand to mouth. Miasha knew how to make wine and brandy; so now desperate, she started making enough wine and brandy to sell, even though it wasn't legal to do this without the authority from the government. She had to be careful. She made blueberry wine, *schlivovitz* (plum wine), mead which is a honey beer. You make mead with honey, water and yeast.

There was a beautiful little church in Hlusk, and it had a wonderful organ. On Sundays, you could hear the organ playing from all over Hlusk. Miasha made the most money on Sundays and market days, when Hlusk was full of people. Her customers were the waggoneers, coachman and the Gentiles, who came to Hlusk on Sunday to trade their wares, and to go to church. Jews weren't allowed to sell liquor, but Miasha did it anyway. She was lucky she wasn't caught and sent to jail for this. She sold her wines by the glass, and for a few kopecks more, she would give them beans and meat, and maybe some tea or in summer a glass of *kvass*. Kvass is a drink that is something like lemonade; only it is made of stale sourdough rye bread. It doesn't sound good, but it is still popular in Russia and Ukraine. It is mildly alcoholic, but even children drink it. Kvass is thought to be a thirst quencher, a tonic for digestion, and, if downed after vodka, an antidote to a hangover.

Miasha kept the family all together, her two little boys Avraham and baby Muttel and Mikhel's children, Layah, Fagel and Zolmon. The children all went to school. The girls, Layah and Fagel, helped with the little boys, and all of the housework. Elka lived with her husband Dovid and their girls. They managed to scrape out a living and survived like this for quite a few years.

It was a hard life for all of them, but it was safer than in Bobruisk. Bobruisk was suffering. The anti-Semitic riots and the pogroms seemed to never stop. The Russians blamed the Jews for the Revolution. And they blamed the Jews in July 1918 for the murder of the Romanov family. The Cossacks came to Bobruisk and stirred up the Gentiles. Things always calmed down when the Cossacks left town.

The unrest eventually came to Hlusk too. Every Shabbos was quiet. Most of the people living in Hlusk were Jewish. The Gentiles from the surrounding farms didn't come to town until market day or Sunday, when they went to church. On Shabbos, all of the Jews were in shul. One quiet Shabbos morning, without any warning, the Cossacks came to Hlusk. They came into the shul. Of course it was full of people. Miasha sat with her mother, Layah and Fagel, and Elka and her little girls in the women's section, in the back, behind the curtain. Avraham and Muttel were sitting in the back of the men's section with their big brother Zolmon and Elka's husband Dovid. The Cossacks thundered up to the front. And without saying why, they started pushing the men around. They shot their rifles up into the ceiling of the shul. They heaved the Torahs on the floor and started killing the men. All of the men in the front row were killed. One man was slashed in the neck and decapitated by a crazy Cossack wielding a sickle. Other men were dragged out and tied to trees where they were whipped.

This was done purely because they were Jewish. When the Cossacks were finished having their fun, they got on their horses and left Hlusk just as they came.

My father's cousin, Yossel, was one of those men who were lashed to a tree. After the Cossacks had left them for dead, people cut the men down. Yossel's mother, my father's aunt Gittle, wrapped Yossel in wet bed sheets. She took him in a wagon to the hospital in Bobruisk. There they were able to save his life.

After this Miasha said, "Enough – no more! We are leaving." Miasha didn't know how they were going to get to America, or even where it was, but they were going. The Mnushkins weren't alone. Lots of other people left too. Elka and Dovid had a brand new baby girl, Shurya. They stayed, but eventually moved to Moscow. Laya said, to go to America they had to go to Warsaw first. Laya told them that she heard that Warsaw was about 614 kilometers (382 miles) from Hlusk, and a world away. How could they go without money or papers?

Miasha packed their things and got ready to leave. Miasha's mother never left, but this time my father, Zolmon, his two little brothers, Avraham and Muttel, and his older sisters, Layah and Fagel, all left Hlusk by Miasha pushing and coaxing, and her pure will power.

People weren't allowed to travel without travel permits, which the Mnushkins didn't have, and they didn't have the money to buy the permits, but they left Hlusk. To travel, you needed an interior travel pass - a passport (a *pravozhitelstuo*).This meant that the family needed six travel permits, which cost about 80 kopecks for each of them. They could pay off the police instead, but it might have cost as much as 25 rubles – a fortune. So they didn't want to meet the police anywhere on the trip because they would detain them, and possibly send them to jail. The Mnushkins tried to stay near the railroad, in order to follow the tracks so they wouldn't get lost. They went from one shtetl to the next, hoping to find Jews who would offer them food and a place to sleep, and would tell them how to go to the next shtetl.

They knew which houses belonged to Jews because of the *mezuzah* on the Jewish doors. According to Exodus, during the time when the ancient Hebrews were slaves in Egypt, the Hebrews marked their houses with lamb's blood, so that G_d would recognize a Jewish house, and pass over it during the plague of the killing of first-born sons. Thereafter, Jews have placed a mezuzah on the right side of their door frame as a remembrance of that time, and to remember to be good Jewish people. A mezuzah is a scroll of sacred parchment inscribed with a declaration of faith in God. A mezuzah is also a daily reminder, and a public declaration of Jewish identity and faith in G_d that he watches over us. The mezuzah is placed in a small decorative case. Jews kiss their fingers, then touch the mezuzah when passing.

The Mnushkins learned that Layah was right; the best thing to do was to get themselves to Warsaw. They heard that they could get help in Warsaw from HIAS.

The Mnushkins sneaked through borders, and hidwhenever they saw constables or their men. They had to be very careful because they didn't want to get caught and thrown in jail. The constables used to stop strangers in any village and ask to see their travel passes. Many times, the Mnushkins had to sneak over town borders, and sneak around the constable's men.

Once, the only way they could go was on the road that passed the constable's office, or through a small, but deep river. Zolmon was a strong swimmer, but no one else was. The water was icy and frigidly cold, but the Mnushkins had no choice. Miasha insisted; she told Zolmon, then about 17 years old, to get a log so they could swim across holding onto it. Zolmon found a small broken raft, at the side of the river. They used it to hold on to, so they could cross over. Miasha hung on to the raft and to Muttel. Fagel and Layah were each able to hold on. Avraham was not a good swimmer and not very strong. He lost his grip on the raft and started going under. Zolmon managed to grab his younger brother and help him across. If they had been in that water any longer, they would have frozen to death.

Once on the other side, they were wet and freezing cold, but they were alive.

The Mnushkins stopped at shtetlach and farmhouses along the way, wherever anyone would help them. Sometimes, good people who weren't Jewish helped them – gave them food, and a barn to sleep in. They wouldn't eat meat if it wasn't kosher. They only ate eggs, potatoes, bread, and vegetables when they were lucky to have that. When they were very lucky, Zolmon caught some fish. They passed fields that would have been full of rye, oats, barley, buckwheat in other seasons, but it was late fall and not picking season. The fields were empty. Jasmine, bluebells and roses that would have been there in another season were also gone. The fields were empty; the orchards were empty. There wasn't much growing. Living off the land was hard, and they starved. The only thing that kept them going was Miasha's determination and courage.

When Layah was a little girl, years before their journey, she had tripped and fallen. Not looking where she was going, Layah was running and tripped over a large tree root. She got up, but in a short time, her knee was swollen, and she couldn't walk. With no doctors to care for her broken knee and set it properly, it never seemed to heal. Layah could not straighten her knee, and it always hurt her just to walk. The pain of walking on it crippled Layah, and she always walked slowly, *schlepping* her broken knee. As always, Zolmon walked with Layah to make sure she was ok. He ran up ahead, and then ran back to Layah. Zolmon must have gone across Europe three times in distance doing this, but he didn't lose his sister.

The pastoral beauty of the landscapes they passed through, might have inspired poets, but the Mnushkins just wanted to get beyond each step they took. They went all through Belarus and Poland. As they went, it seemed that each day was colder, as winter was setting in. One time, they found a cave to sleep in, but mostly they slept out in fields or under trees. When they were lucky, they slept in good people's stables. Many nights they nearly froze to death sleeping outside. They went through Osiporichi, Slutsk,

Baranovish, Slonim, Volkovysk, Bialystok and a hundred other little shtetlach. Finally, they made it to Warsaw, and there they got help from HIAS.

It was in Warsaw that Fagel met Reuben. He was going to New York, America too. Fagel was very beautiful. She didn't remember her mother. She was only three years old when her mother died. People who knew Sima Razel always said that Fagel with her large blue eyes, white porcelain skin and long curls, looked just like her. Men were always chasing Fagel, but Reuben was the one who stole her heart. He wasn't rich, but he was very charming.

Miasha didn't object - a man; maybe he would be of some help. Fagel was already almost twenty years old. Miasha said both Layah and Fagel, should be married already. Fagel and Reuben were married by a rabbi that they met in the HIAS dining room. The Rabbi was also going with his wife and four children to America. He said that this is not the usual way for people to meet and make marriage arrangements. No matchmaker, no ufruf. But why should we keep two young people, who want to get married apart? Life is hard enough. They went outside. Four men held a tallis up over the rabbi and Reuben. Fagel marched around them seven times, the rabbi said the blessings and the prayers, Reuben smashed a glass with his foot, and they were married.

HIAS did help the Mnushkins go to America. They lent the Mnushkins the money for their shipstickets in steerage. The immigration laws of 1921 had changed things. People couldn't just move to America if they felt like it anymore. The American government had created quotas. Miasha and the Mnushkins could go and not worry about the quotas, because their father, Mikhel was already in America. But Reuben couldn't go with them. He had to wait his turn. It could take years. HIAS told Reuben, and many other Jews, that they should go to Havana, Cuba first. HIAS said that they would be able to go to America sooner from there. They didn't have quotas to America from Cuba. HIAS told them, to get shipstickets and that it would include the fare for the train. They said they could all go to Cherbourg, France, together. The Mnushkins would go to

America and Reuben could take a different ship to Cuba from France. HIAS told them that it was 1,605 km from Warsaw to Cherbourg (998 miles), and that they had to change trains in Paris.

After they got their shipstickets, Miasha wrote a letter to Mikhel telling him, that they were coming to America on the Cunard Line's R.M.S. Berengaria, and that it should land in New York at the end of January.   ∞

❧ *The R.M.S. Berengaria* ❧

Cherbourg was almost 1,000 miles from Warsaw. They took the train to Berlin, and rode from one end of Germany to the other. From there, the train went to France. They stopped in Paris, where they had to change trains. The train from Paris stopped at Evreux, Lisieux, Caen, Bayeux, and, then finally, in the port of Cherbourg.

At the Cherbourg docks, they boarded the Cunard Line's R.M.S. Berengaria. Following the directions of the sailors, Miasha, Layah and the boys, Zolmon, Avraham and Muttel, all went aboard. Fagel and Reuben lingered together on the dock, not wanting to separate but having no choice. Fagel was going with her family. She could go to America as an unmarried girl, because her father was there. She didn't tell the authorities that she was a married woman, because then they would not let her come as a member of her father's immediate family.

Finally, Fagel had to move forward with the crowd of passengers going up the ramp. People were carrying all they owned with them in heavy sacks, valises, and all kinds of bundles. Reuben promised he would come to her in America, no matter what; he would find a way. Fagel went aboard ship, not wanting Reuben to see her cry. Looking down from where she was standing on deck, she could barely see him waving good-by to her from the cold wet platform. Fagel watched, as the ship pulled away from the European mainland. She knew that she would never see Europe again. As

Cherbourg grew smaller and smaller in the distance, she wondered when she would see her husband, her Reuben, again. She didn't know it yet, but she was carrying his baby with her in her belly.

The R.M.S. Berengaria was a very beautiful, luxurious steamship. Flagship of the Cunard Line, she was the best they had to offer. The ship was huge, sitting there at the frosty dock. It was the size of a very large building. There were many very wealthy people traveling on that ship. It had every luxury you could imagine, and quite a few that you couldn't. They had a room for exercising, a fancy room just to smoke in, and they even had a swimming pool. There was an orchestra that played music when the meals were served by uniformed waiters, and in the afternoon at tea. In the evening, the perfumed, coiffed ladies waltzed with their elegantly dressed gentlemen to the sounds of Strauss. They even had picture postcards showing how beautiful the ship was.

[Cunard Line Picture Post Card:] R.M.S. Berengaria, on board the
Winter Garden Restaurant (ca. 1923)
The Mnuskin family came to America in steerage, on this ship in 1923.
Photo courtesy of the U.S. Naval Historical Center

[Cunard Line Picture Post Card:] R.M.S. Berengaria, on board
Pompeian swimming pool (ca. 1923)
The Mnuskin family came to America in steerage, on this ship in 1923.
Photo courtesy of the U.S. Naval Historical Center

But the Mnushkins never saw any of that. They had tickets for the steerage section of the ship. The very crowded steerage section was the lowest area of the ship, where the only music they heard was that of the ship's engines.

The deck of the R.M.S. Berengaria's steerage was full of people, and freight, and baggage, and who knew what else. There were Jews in long scraggly beards, along with the poor of every nationality, from all corners of Europe, all traveling to a hopefully better life in the "golden land." The sounds of people speaking in every European dialect and language from Albanian to Yiddish, were heard over the sounds of the ship's whistle. There were sailors shouting orders, and babies crying, mothers screaming to their children to stay close. There were people trying to sneak on board without tickets. The poor emigrant passengers were all *schlepping* their baggage, and everything they owned, their family photographs, candlesticks, old pots, pans and carpet bags. They had wicker suitcases tied up with rope, and valises stuffed with anything they could drag with them. They were tripping and stumbling over their things, and other people's things. Sailors led them down narrow steps to the lowest levels of the ship, where they were shown to their bunks.

[Photo:] Typical outside steerage deck on an ocean liner steamship (ca. 1925)
Photo courtesy of the U.S. Naval Historical Center

Steerage, with over 900 passengers, was divided up into three sections. Men traveling alone were at the very front, and women traveling alone were at the far rear. The largest section was in the middle and designated for families. Everyone was supposed to sleep in bunks that were double tiers of very small cots, with one cot jammed right next to the other, cot-to-cot. Steerage passengers had no real place to put any of their things, except in that six foot by 30 inches of bunk space. Mattresses and pillows were filled with dried seaweed and straw, not like the goose down pillows of the upper decks. The immigrants in steerage had only cold salt water to wash with, and after a few days at sea, the poorly washed wooden floor reeked of vomit. In this same space, down the middle of the floor, there were tables and benches lined up. This is where the steerage passengers who were well enough to eat were doled out their meals. There were American laws that said the immigrant passengers in steerage destined for the United States were entitled to at least 1½ navy rations per day. The food was awful - mainly watery potato soup and herring; not the tea and scones with clotted cream served on porcelain and silver to the sound of violins, as shown in the postcards of the R.M.S. Berengaria's Winter Garden Restaurant. But the passengers in steerage didn't know about the fineries of the upper decks. They just knew that they were very uncomfortable.

Looking at steerage, you couldn't be sure how a person could breathe, sleep and have any privacy in such a crowded, cramped, stinking hole. Only your worst enemies should have such a trip. But all of these immigrants thought the same thing – this wasn't forever. If they lived through it, they could bear it, for the journey to America and a better life than the one they left in the old country. They were bound for the "golden land."

The passengers were all very excited. As soon as they were shown to their bunks, they put their stuff down, and started looking around, talking to the other passengers, asking questions in this strange place in the belly of the ship.

Miasha, Layah and Fagel were trying to get comfortable. Muttel was running around looking into everything he could. Zolmon was talking to the steward asking him, how long it would be till they got to England, the next stop. Avraham went and lay down in his bunk. This was not usual for him, but he was tired, and he soon fell asleep. It was surprising that anyone could sleep through so much tumult. You could hear the ship's whistle blow as they set sail. They were on their way. An Italian man started playing an accordion.

The R.M.S. Berengaria was crossing the English Channel. The first and only stop before they landed in America was just across the channel in Southampton, England. But before the R.M.S. Berengaria got to England, the woman on the cot next to Avraham noticed he was sick. Her little boy tried to play with him, and Avraham wouldn't talk to him. Even with all that was going on around him, Avraham slept. When the little boy pushed Avraham, he turned over, and the boy's mother could see Avraham's face was all red. In all the noise and hoo-ha, nobody from the family had realized. The woman started shouting in a loud voice; asking what was wrong with him. Avraham looked like he was all hot, and his face was very red, like he had a fever. Before anyone knew what was going on, a doctor was there. He wasn't a doctor who came to help and make Avraham well. He was there, telling Miasha that Avraham was being taken off the ship in Southampton, England. The doctor told her that they were not allowed to keep him on board the ship, where he could make everyone else sick. The Mnushkins had hardly even gotten comfortable. Miasha had no time to ask where they were being taken, or where she was going to go with no money and now an obviously sick child. What about the rest of the family? She had to leave with Avraham. No time to think of what to do. No time to even say a real good-by to the others. Miasha told them to stay and go to America. Layah, Fagle, Zolmon and little Muttel watched terrified, as the sailors demanded that Miasha take Avraham and get off the ship. Before they could say no, Miasha and Avraham were gone.

Layah, Fagle, Zolmon and little Muttel stayed on the R.M.S. Berengaria. They didn't know where Miasha and Avraham were being taken, or if they would ever see them again. Zolmon asked the steward if he knew where they were being taken. The steward seemed to understand Zolmon's Yiddish and answered, "Atlantic Park, in England." "Where is that?" "It is in England," the steward answered Zolmon. Zolmon wondered where England was, but didn't ask any more questions of the busy man, because he could barely understand him anyway.

The ocean crossing was miserable. It was winter, so it was very cold, and the sea was rough. The steerage passengers prayed that they would land safely. Like a lot of the other passengers, Layah and Fagel were seasick. Steerage smelled so bad from all of the vomiting that the only place to get a bit of fresh air was up on the freezing cold deck. Fagel didn't know it, but she was pregnant. She spent the whole time throwing up and not just in the morning. Layah was so seasick that she never left her bunk. After Miasha and Avraham had been taken away, only G_d knows where, the other four Mnushkins stayed very close together. Nobody had to tell ten-year-old Muttel not to disappear. He stayed close to them unlike his usual way of going off while satisfying his curiosity of every little new thing. They didn't know where Miasha and Avraham were, or what was wrong with Avraham, but none of them could wait to get off that ship.

Layah, Fagle, Zolmon and Muttel finally landed in America on Saturday, January 27, 1923, a Shabbos. After a long while, they were taken by ferry, with the more than 900 other steerage passengers, to Ellis Island. It was a short trip from where they had docked in New York, but it took quite a few hours to unload the R.M.S. Berengaria, and then load the ferries.

Once on Ellis Island, they were split up. Layah 23 and Fagel 21 were sent to the women's quarters. Zolmon and Muttel went to the men's section on the other side. Layah told Zolmon not to let Muttel out of his sight, as though there was a possibility that he would.

Zolmon was seventeen years old, and just as scared as everyone else. Seventeen, he was almost a man. He was ashamed to show how frightened he felt, so as usual he put on his smiling brave face, and told Muttel not to worry, and that they were going to be all right. But they weren't all right; their mother and brother had been taken and missing for more than a week. They didn't know where they were, or if they would ever see them again. Now Zolmon and Muttel were supposedly in America, but separated from their sisters, in this strange place. They could see America in the distance, but they weren't there yet.

Zolmon and Muttel were reunited with Layah and Fagel in the Ellis Island dining room, when they were given food for the first time in many hours.

Some Hungarian woman noticed that Layah was limping. As always, Layah couldn't straighten her knee. Trying to be informative, the woman told Layah that they would probably throw her out and deport her. She would have to go back to Europe, because they don't want cripples in America. Then, another woman said that if her family would promise to support her, they might let her stay.

Layah became terrified that they would send her back. When she told the others what the women had said, Zolmon said that he was strong, and could work. He would promise them that he would take care of her. Fagel said, "And papa will come and tell them he will support you."

They were told to sit in the big hall, and wait their turns to be inspected and examined with everyone else. When it was finally their turn, they were called to go up to the official. Layah tried to make like she didn't have a limp, and Zolmon walked beside her to help her. It didn't work. The officials could see that Layah couldn't walk without limping. They chalked her jacket with the mark of the big **L** for lame. Layah started crying; she had already heard that they designated cripples with that mark, and then deported them. The doctors looked at her knee, and didn't see anything, but they could see that she walked with a limp. She didn't tell them that it still hurt her to walk. She admitted that she had broken her knee in a fall. The inspectors agreed to let Layah stay if her father came and promised to support her. Fagel, Zolmon and Muttel passed the medical examinations, and they were ready to go. Not that they would know where to go. They couldn't leave until their father came and got them. The Ellis Island officials sent Mikhel a telegram, telling him to come get his family.

Mikhel Mnuskin was expecting them. Miasha had sent him a letter from Warsaw, telling him that they would be coming on the R.M.S. Berengaria at the end of January, and now here they were. He was very excited to finally be seeing his family. He hadn't seen them since 1912 - eleven years. Mikhel had never seen his youngest son, Muttel, before. He was born after Mikhel had left to go to America. Mikhel went and took his children to where he lived on the Lower East Side of Manhattan. The first thing his children told him was about what happened to Miasha and Avraham. Their father did not know what to do, or how to find them. He did not know who to ask. Mikhel said for now, we will go home. He reassured them. He said, "We will find someone to help us find them. The rabbi will know what to do, and who to ask." In his heart, Mikhel didn't believe it. Heartbroken, he believed that his wife and son were lost to them forever. &

ⅎ *Fresh Off the Boat* ⅚

Mikhel brought his four children to where he lived in the filthy, decrepit, dark tenement on Clinton Street. He had taken this apartment after getting the letter from Miasha, telling him that they were coming to America. Before this, he lived as a border, sleeping on a couch in a friend's front room.

The next day, Mikhel went to work. Before he left, he told his newly arrived family that if they went out, they shouldn't go too far and get lost. The four new immigrants, no longer the Mnushkins, but now the Mnuskins, went walking around their new neighborhood. They looked at all of the people, and wondered how they were going to fit into this new world. They were all naturally friendly, especially Zolmon and Muttel. The four talked to the other people in the building, and the people on their street. They didn't have to tell anyone that they had just come from Europe. People knew, just from looking at them, that they were greenhorns, and fresh off the boat from Ellis Island.

One woman from the second floor told them that they would have to sign ten-year-old Muttel up for school, or they would get into trouble. Children had to go to school in America, but it was free. They asked her, where the school was. She said that it was not far, and motioned up the street.

Zolmon, Laya and Fagel, all grown-ups now, their childhoods long gone, knew they would have to find work. The four walked around the Lower East Side, exploring their new home.

They had never seen a Chinese person before that day. He had a long braid hanging down his back, like some girls wore, but most girls wore two braids. The Chinese man had what looked like a *yarmulke*[25] on his head, but he didn't look Jewish. He was talking very fast, yelling at another man. It seemed like he wanted him to pay him for something. He scared Fagel. She grabbed Muttel and said, "Let's walk. We should keep a good distance from him to us."

In New York, there was something different happening on every corner. Every time they turned a corner, they saw something interesting. On one block, there was a juggler, right there in the street, with people standing around watching him. On another block, there was a woman singing for coins. The streets were full of people, and stores, and peddlers, all busy doing something. There was a small boy kicking a can up the middle of the street, until a horse and wagon came. Then the boy ran to the side. There was a man playing a fiddle, with his violin case open on the sidewalk, ready for donations.

Not that day, but a few days later, when they were walking down the street, they saw an organ grinder with a monkey. An organ grinder was a man, maybe a Gypsy that walked around the streets, with a box that played music. He turned the handle, and music came out of the box. The monkey was dressed in a little hat and a jacket. The monkey danced around begging for money, holding a tin cup in his outreached hand. And that was the first time they had ever seen a monkey.

The Lower East Side was a crazy quilt of people, mostly Jews from every country in Europe. It seemed like they were all selling something. There were carts that were full of all kinds of stuff.

---

[25] *yarmulke* yahr' mul keh *n.* – Yiddish, [*kepah* - Hebrew] the skullcap head covering worn by Jewish men and some women during religious rituals, and by Orthodox Jewish men at all times

Peddlers were selling pots and pans, and clothing, fresh vegetables, whatever you needed they had. There were stores and shops lining both sides of the streets. There were stores that sold clothing, and there were the dressmaker shops, shoemakers and watchmakers. And there were the stores with food, kosher butchers, chicken markets, bakeries, delicatessen stores, dairy stores, and appetizing stores. They had foods there from all over the world.

Most of the people they saw were speaking Yiddish, but lots of people were speaking other languages. Zolmon, Laya, Fagel and even Muttel could read and write in Yiddish and read the prayer book in Hebrew. After crossing half of Europe, and meeting all the different people on the ship, all four of them seemed to be able to say more than a word or two, and get along in about five different languages: Yiddish of course, some Russian and Polish, a little German, a bit of Hungarian, but almost no English.

When Mikhel came home, they told him what the woman on the second floor said about Muttel going to school. Their father said yes, they had to take Muttel and sign him up in the school. Everyone thought that was wonderful, except Muttel. Mikhel told them that they could go to school too. In America, they had English classes for grown-ups at night, and they were also free. What a wonderful country.

But the first thing the three older Mnuskins had to do was find jobs. They thought that they might be able to find jobs working in the shops. The next morning, they took Muttel and signed him up for school. Then Laya, Fagel and Zolmon started going into the stores and asking for work. Very pretty Fagel found a job first, working as a salesgirl in a bakery. Fagel's success gave Zolmon and Laya courage. They kept looking, asking everyone they met if they knew of some place that needed help. Two days later, someone told Laya, there was a help wanted sign in the window of a dry goods store. She went there, and talked them into giving her the job.

Zolmon found a job as a helper in the fresh fish market. He was a strong boy, so they used him to carry in the crates. He swept the saw dust floors, and put down new saw dust. The fish market kept him busy. Zolmon worked in the fish market for about a month, when he heard about a better job. Mr. Bergman, from the 3rd floor in the building where they lived, heard that he was looking for a job. He didn't know that Zolmon had already found one. Mr. Bergman stopped him on the stairs. He said, "Hey kid I heard you need a job. My boss needs help. It's a job as a house painter's assistant." When Zolmon told him that he already had a job, Mr. Bergman said, "Don't be a *schmuck*. You don't owe them anything. Take the better job. Here is the address. Go tell Solomon, the boss, that I sent you."

Zolmon was a good, honest kid. He didn't know what to do. He didn't want to do anything to spoil his reputation. Zolmon just got the job at the fish market. So, he asked his boss, Yaakov, the fish market owner, what to do. Yaakov said, "Number one, you are not a slave by me. I don't own you. This is a free country. You can do what you want. I wouldn't want to keep a nice young man like you from getting ahead. And number two, you didn't get the other job yet. If you do get that job making more money, go and be well. I wouldn't think less of you. If you don't get it, I'll still keep you here. You are a good, hard working and honest kid. But next time, don't be so nice. Next time, get the job first, and then tell the first boss. Another boss, not like me, would just fire you on the spot for being so good."

So Zolmon went and asked for and got the job as a painter's assistant. In the new job, he made more money working for a man named Solomon. His new boss told Zolmon that he liked his cheerful way, and he always trusted men named Zolmon, because that was his Jewish name too.   ೞ

❧ *Atlantic Park* ☙

*W*hen Miasha and Avraham were taken off the ship, Avraham was too sick to think about anything. Miasha was quietly trembling with fear. She did not know where they were being taken, or what was going to happen to them. She didn't understand what the man who had forced them off the ship was saying. She only knew he was leading them off the ship, and then off the dock. There were a few other passengers, as well, that he was taking away. There was an Italian man and his wife and one other passenger, a man who was alone. He was a short man who might have been Austrian. Miasha didn't know why the other passengers were there. These bewildered former ship's passengers were all boarded onto a wagon to maybe G_d knew where, but they didn't.

Terrified, Miasha silently worried about what was wrong with Avraham, and if he was going to be ok; now she could see he was very sick. She had no money, and didn't know what she was going to do, or how she was going to take care of her very sick child. She didn't know how she could feed them, or where they would stay in this foreign place. Miasha didn't know what was happening to her other children. She feared for them, and wondered if they would get to America. She struggled not to think about the possibility of never seeing her youngest, little Muttel, and her family again - would they be ok?

Eventually, Miasha, Avraham and the other passengers taken off the ship were taken to somewhere outside of the city of Southampton, where the ship had docked. Without any further protest, they were driven to a very large building, and the wagon driver motioned them to get down out of the wagon.

They were taken inside. Once there, someone spoke to Miasha in Yiddish, when they realized that was her language. People seemed to speak to the other discharged passengers in their language as well. They were told to show their papers, their shipstickets. They were taken to be bathed, like it or not, and their baggage was taken to be disinfected and deloused. Because Avraham was sick, they took Miasha and her young son to the infirmary instead. It was a large room with many beds, but very clean and bright, and there were nurses taking care of the patients. There, a doctor and nurse examined Avraham. Someone explained to Miasha in Yiddish that Avraham had scarlet fever. He had the telltale rash. The doctor said that it was very bad, and that he could die. They told her that they would do their best to take care of him, and try to make him well. Miasha could see that they were nice people, and were trying to help her. Miasha said that she didn't have money to pay them. They told her that it was paid for by the Cunard shipping company, as part of her passage. These kind people told Miasha that she and her son would be able to go to America on another ship, when Avraham was well, but until then they would be taken care of there. They told her that she wouldn't have to pay anything extra. It was all part of her passage fare.

When Avraham fell asleep, they took Miasha to a room for women with children, and showed her where her bed was. She didn't know it, and it wouldn't have meant anything to her if she did, but they were at Atlantic Park, a refugee center and transit camp in Eastleigh, England. Eastleigh is a village just north of Southampton. During World War I, Atlantic Park had been an American airbase, and the building they were in used to be an airplane hangar. The airbase used to house about 4,000 American airmen. After the war, it was converted into a center for refugees trying to emigrate from all over Europe. Today, it is the site of the Southampton International Airport.

After World War I, there were an enormous number of refugees from all over Europe, but mainly Jews from Russia. Since before the turn of the century, the United States had become a haven for the Jews running away from the anti-Semitic violence, and dire poverty of Eastern Europe. By the end of the 1800s, more than two million Jews had landed on American shores. In 1921 alone, 520,000 people fleeing war torn Europe had passed "Lady Liberty", with her welcoming outstretched torch, on their way through the New York harbor. They crowded into the big cities of America, mainly New York. Now the United States didn't want any more immigrants, or anything foreign from Eastern or Southern Europe. These people were no longer welcome. The United States started changing their immigration policies and laws, and changed the quotas. Lots of people who didn't have relatives in the United States were not allowed to leave Ellis Island to immigrate to the U.S. and were sent back to Europe. Hundreds of them were sent to or detained at Atlantic Park.

They weren't wanted in America, and the British didn't want any more poor immigrants to stay and become part of the English landscape either. The United States demanded that the shipping lines do something with these refugees until they could be placed somewhere. The shipping lines were making so much money transporting their human livestock cargo that they didn't want to do anything that might stop or lessen this enterprise. So, in 1921, the Cunard, White Star, Oceanic and Canadian Pacific shipping lines joined forces, and set up the Atlantic Park Hostel Company to house these poor people temporarily. The shipping companies agreed to support and pay for the refugees until they got to where they could live permanently.

The former airplane hangars were turned into the Atlantic Park Hostel. There were dormitories, kitchens and dining rooms, social rooms, and the infirmary, a school, a church and a synagogue. The Atlantic Park Hostel was originally meant for trans-migrants changing ships or people who had been deported back to Europe with no place to go, but it grew into what was almost like a small town. When Miasha and Avraham landed at Atlantic Park, there were close to a thousand people living there. During the time, that Atlantic Park was a refugee camp, many thousands of people had been interned there.

**[Photo:] The Atlantic Park dining room, Atlantic Park Hostel,
Southhampton, England (ca. 1923)
Miasha and Avraham Mnuskin were interned at Atlantic Park in 1923**
Photo courtesy of the Southhampton Public Library, UK

The refugees were meant to be there a short time, but some of these unfortunate people were at Atlantic Park for as long as seven years, waiting to emigrate. They had nowhere to go after America changed their policy. They were from all over Europe but a large percentage were poor Yiddish speaking, Jews from Russia. Many of these stateless paupers, unwanted people, refugees to nowhere, were there for so long, waiting to move on, that they started living almost normal lives. The Atlantic Park detainees weren't earning a living, but it cost them nothing to live at Atlantic Park. Some of the immigrants started having social card games and playing chess. Some of them played ball. There were a couple of football teams. They put on shows and the children attended the Atlantic Park school. Some even went into the town of Eastleigh and took part in the annual carnival.

Miasha and Avraham weren't involved with any of this. Avraham was too sick and Miasha stayed at his side almost every minute. He had fever and chills, and was throwing up. His throat was very sore. He couldn't keep down most of the soft food they gave him. He was bright red from the rash that covered him. The rash was like sand, rough sand, and it itched. His face was red too except for around his mouth, which remained white.

More than a week passed like this, until Avraham started feeling better. He got up and asked for something to eat. He was hungry. The doctor told Miasha the worst was over, Avraham was going to be ok. They were going to be able to go to America. They wouldn't be kept back by quotas, like a lot of the others, because they had family in America already. Miasha had written a letter to Mikhel telling him what had happened, and where she and Avraham were. And she wanted to know if the other children had gotten there all right.

After a few weeks, Avraham seemed like he was all better. He was tired but was able to leave the infirmary. Miasha started asking about the ships, and how they could take a ship to America. They told her they would get them on a ship soon. Miasha and Avraham were happy. They were going to be with the family in their new home. They got a letter from Mikhel that the other children had gotten to New York, and everything there was ok.

About a week later, before they could board another ship, Avraham started complaining that he had a headache. Again, he looked red, and Miasha saw that he had a fever. She panicked that the scarlet fever was back. Miasha immediately took him to the infirmary. She trusted them to make him well.

The doctor examined Avraham. He said it wasn't scarlet fever this time, but a worse complication of it – rheumatic fever. Within two days, all of Avraham's joints were swollen and hurt. His breathing was short, and his chest hurt him. Avraham was only twelve years old. He hadn't been bar mitzvahed yet. He was too young to die, but he was very sick. Miasha knew lots of people died from scarlet fever, and lots of people died from rheumatic fever. She prayed her son would get well.

It took about another month for Avraham to get better, but little by little, he did. The doctor told Miasha that he was going to be ok. The doctor also said, that Avraham now had a rheumatic heart, and he would have to be careful, and take good care of himself for the rest of his life. Miasha never stopped *tsittering*[26] over Avraham – he shouldn't get sick again, G_d forbid.

Eventually, they were taken to a ship in Southampton. It was just before Passover. Miasha knew they would be on the ship for Passover, but she didn't care. When they told her that she and Avraham could go, and that he was well enough, she said ok. She wasn't waiting for anything if she could help it. Avraham, too, said, "Let's go. I'll be ok." Miasha sent her husband, Mikhel a letter telling him that they were coming to America. Then they got ready to leave Atlantic Park.

The ship that Miasha and Avraham took was the SS Aquitania. During World War I, the Aquitania was a British troop transfer ship. But now she had 3,230 paying passengers, 619 in first

---

[26] **tsitter** **tsit' ter** (rhymes with twitter) Yiddish verb; **tsittering** means: worrying, shaking or trembling with fear, afraid

class, and 616 in second class. The first and second-class sections weren't as beautiful as they were on the SS Berengaria. It didn't matter to Miasha and Avraham. They were in steerage with 1,995 other people. To them it didn't matter what first and second class were like. Besides, they were happy to be really leaving Europe.

There was a so-called Passover Seder in steerage for the Jewish passengers. The food wasn't any better than it was when it wasn't Passover, but they did have matzo and they read the story of Passover and said the traditional blessings.

The SS Aquitania was 45,647 tons, and had a service speed of 23 knots. They crossed the Atlantic and arrived in New York harbor on Friday, April 6, 1923, just before Shabbos on the sixth day of Passover. ❧

໒ာ *Americans Now* ອຊ

𝓜iasha's letter telling Mikhel that they were coming didn't arrive until two days after the Aquitania landed in New York Harbor. So, Mikhel was happily surprised when the telegram from Ellis Island came to tell him that his wife and son were there. They were all happy and excited to have Miasha and Avraham there with them. Muttel was very fast to tell Avraham that he was going to have to go to school. Like his mother, whose name was changed to Mary, Avraham's name had been changed at Ellis Island to the now Americanized Abraham. The Ellis Island officials told him that in America, people would probably call him Abe. He liked it. Twelve-year-old Abe, took on his new name happily. In New York, the neighborhood boys started calling him Abie (Abe' bEE). He liked that too, and Abie stuck with him. No more Europe, no more old country. He was all better, and he was going to be an American with an American name.

Zolmon, Laya, Fagel and Muttel's first names had not been changed at Ellis Island. Abie said it was time for all of them to become Americans, and he talked them all into giving themselves new names, in their new country. He said they didn't want anyone to think they were "greenhorns", did they? He seemed to learn that word fast. They all did want to become modern, like Americans. They each thought about it.

So, Zolmon shaved his blond beard, he didn't have much of a beard anyway. And he changed his name to Solomon, like most men whose Hebrew name is Zolmon. When he went to work, he told his boss he had taken an American name, and from now on to call him Solomon. His boss said, "You can't be Solomon. We can't have two Solomons." His boss laughed, "Somebody will think you are the boss. Why don't you call yourself Sam; that's your initials?" S A M were his initials for Solomon Alex Mnuskin. He didn't like it, but he wasn't going to argue with his boss. Sam stuck. He was called Sam from then on, even after he went to a different job.

Laya thought about it. She liked the way Lena sounded. Fagel took the name Fanny, but it didn't seem to stick. Everyone still called her Fagel. Fagel really didn't ever tell anyone to call her Fanny. She wanted to be American, but she didn't want to change too much. She was waiting for her husband, Reuben, to come. Fagel didn't want to change so much that he wouldn't know her. Little Muttel became Max, and more often Maxie. Miasha remained Miasha. She told her family, that her name had been Miasha all of her life, and she wasn't changing it.

Miasha stayed home to take care of Abie and Max. She did all the cooking and cleaning for all of them. Miasha was a great cook. Her mother had taught her, and she taught her girls.

To make some money, Miasha took in other people's children to watch while their mothers were working in sweatshops. She always had two or three kids that she took care of during the day, besides Abie and Max.

Abe and Max went to school, and with each day they became more American. After school, they went to the *cheder* (children's Hebrew school) to practice for their bar mitzvahs. When they could, the boys played ball. Sometimes, they played at the Henry Street Settlement House with the other kids from the neighborhood. Usually, they went to the nearby Seward Park.

Sam, Lena and Fagel worked during the day, and went to school at night to learn English, and to become real American citizens.

During the summertime, on the days that they weren't working, when it was so hot you could fry an egg on the sidewalk, Sam and some of his friends would swim off the piers at the East River. It was dangerous, but cooled them off on a hot day.

Fagel realized she was pregnant. She was happy that her baby would be born in America. She only wished her Reuben was here with them. The baby was born at the end of September; the first Mnuskin born in America. She was a beautiful little girl, and looked just like Fagel. Fagel gave her the Jewish name of Sima Razel after her mother. They called her Razelleh (rAz′ e leh) the affectionate form of Razel.

Fagel had worked at the bakery until the baby was born. After the first year, Fagel weaned her baby daughter. Miasha took care of the baby and Fagel got her old job back at the bakery. They were happy to have her. She was friendly and all of their customers liked Fagel. The Mnuskins were making a life for themselves in America.   ෙ

❧ *The Doughboy* ❧

*L*aya, now Lena, was born in 1900. When they landed in New York, she was already 23 years old. Fagel was younger but already a married lady; Lena was still single. She wanted to meet somebody nice and get married. In this country, she knew she didn't have to have a matchmaker or a dowry. She was very friendly and liked people, but was shy with the boys. Lena knew a lot of young people met at the dances they had in the social clubs. But she wasn't going dancing with her lame leg.

Her friend Yetta told her that she should look more American, and not like a greenhorn. Yetta talked Lena into buying a dress that was more modern, and talked her into putting on make-up. Lena's face broke out, and she never tried putting on make-up again. Modesty and wanting to hide her crippled leg, Lena didn't lift her hem to the flapper length at the knee. But she did like the new shorter dresses and shortened her hem to mid-calf.

It was autumn of 1925 when their cousin, Celia said that her husband Max had a nice friend who might be a good match for her. His name was Louie and he was a house painter. Celia and Max Shikoff were sweet people. Lena trusted them to know a good person when they met one. Celia told Lena she would tell Max to bring Louie for Shabbos dinner, and that she should come so she could meet him. Lena agreed.

Celia, Max and their four children had just moved to the Bronx. They lived on Jennings Street. Celia told Lena how to take the El to the Freemen Street Station and which way to walk from there.

They had stopped being strictly observant of the Shabbos rules soon after they came to America; so Lena didn't think about not traveling on Shabbos. Lena got off from work early on Fridays. The store where she worked, like most stores on the Lower East Side, closed early on Fridays so they could get home before Shabbos.

Fagel suggested that Lena come to the bakery where she worked, and she would get her a cake to bring to Celia. So, Lena did that. Fagel gave her a fresh baked chocolate babka, and she put it in a box tied up with string. Fagel had told the other women there where her sister Lena was going. They gushed over her and wished her well. One of the women said, "You don't have make-up on. It wouldn't hurt you to put on a little make-up, a little powder, and rouge on your white cheeks – at least some lipstick." Lena said no, no, but relented to their pleas for her to put on just some lipstick.

Lena wasn't hopeful. She kept thinking that nobody who was that good would want a cripple. But she took the train up to the Bronx, and got off at the Freeman Street station. She walked up Freeman Street the way that Celia told her to, turned right for one block, and then made a left turn on Jennings Street. The apartment building they lived in was at the end of the block.

Once she was there, Celia said to come in; Louie had just come too. You may have both taken the same train. Louie lives on the Lower East Side too.

Louie Levine was tall with dark hair and a small mustache. When he said hello, his face broke into a big smile. He was not just a nice man, he was also a very handsome man. Lena didn't expect that. It didn't intimidate her. She figured that he would see her walk and not want to know her. Why would a handsome man like him, who could have lots of pretty girls with two good legs, want her? Assuming that all was lost, she wasn't the shy Lena she was with other men, because she was sure it didn't matter. She relaxed and was her usual friendly, bubbly self. Lena was just like she would have been with her cousins if Louie weren't there.

Louie was a house painter, like her brother Sam. She asked Louie if he knew her brother Sam, but he said, "No, there are a lot of house painters in New York." Louie liked Lena, and didn't care about her limp. He had been a doughboy in the army, and had seen lots of nice people get injured and crippled. It didn't matter to him.

Louis Levine was born Lazer Levine on February 7, 1898, in Bialystok, Poland. He was the first boy born in his family after seven girls. They had four more children after him, to make eleven children altogether. The Levine family immigrated to New York in 1910 when Louie was 12 years old. The Levines also found themselves living on the Lower East Side.

The world exploded in Europe on June 28, 1914, with the assassination of Archduke Franz Ferdinand of Austria, heir to the Austro-Hungarian throne, and his wife, Sophie. They were shot by a Bosnian-Serb, while riding in an open topped car on tour in Sarajevo. Austria-Hungary retaliated against Serbia, and before anyone knew it, all of Europe was on fire with World War I. Germany declared war on Russia and France, and Britain declared war on Germany. World War I wasn't really caused by the assassination. It was caused by the usual reasons men and countries go to war - greed and power. The economic, imperialistic, territorial rivalries among Germany, Austria-Hungary, Russia, Great Britain and France caused this war.

The Brits were singing the words to the very popular war song, "IT'S A LONG WAY TO TIPPARY". It boosted their spirits, while the killing continued far away on the continent.

Promising neutrality in the war, and to keep the United States out of it, in 1916 American President, Woodrow Wilson won re-election to the White House. He campaigned and won with the slogans: "He kept us out of the war" and "America first". Less than six months later, on April 6, 1917, he urged the US Congress to enter "The War to End All Wars", and declared war on Germany. This was just after a German sub deliberately sunk the British non-militant ship the S.S. Lusitania. Congress agreed, and America entered the war. The whole country sang "OVER THERE", the war song written by George M. Cohan. It became very popular. Singing and hearing this song made people feel patriotic. It made them want to support the far away war in Europe.

Most Jews in America thought highly of Woodrow Wilson, and trusted him. If they were citizens, they voted for him. This was not just because he was a Democrat, but mainly because Wilson, the son of a Christian minister, had appointed a Jewish man, Louis D. Brandeis, to the Supreme Court.

Brandeis, a contributor to the liberal wing of the Democratic Party, was noted for his writing on the benefits of competition in business and his opposition to monopolies. President Wilson, believing that the government must be a moral force for the betterment of society, had a lot in common with Brandeis. There were a lot of anti-Semitic people who didn't want Wilson to appoint Brandeis to the highest court in the country, especially if they didn't agree with him on the issues. But Wilson stood firm. He said that he didn't know anyone more qualified to be a Supreme Court Justice than Louis Brandeis. It was 1916 when President Woodrow Wilson made history by appointing the first Jew to the Supreme Court bench.

Then in 1917, he publicly called for the wide support of the United Jewish Relief Campaign because they were raising funds for European War relief.

When the United States declared war on Germany, the U.S. had a standing army of 127,500 men. General John J. Pershing, known as "Black Jack" Pershing was designated the Supreme Commander of the American army in France. Pershing immediately realized that they didn't have enough troops, and asked Wilson to send more men.

On May 18, 1917, President Wilson signed the Selective Service Act. It authorized him to create a draft. It was the job of the Selective Service System to pick the men to be drafted into the military service. All men had to register for the draft, even immigrants. At first, only men between the ages of 21 to 31 had to register for the draft. After September 12, 1918, they were taking men 18 through 45. These men got orders from the War Department to present themselves at their local draft board and be prepared for roll call.

[Photo:] English class for World War I immigrant American soldiers using *National Geographic Magazine* to teach (ca. 1917)
Photo courtesy of the U.S. National Archives

Louie volunteered. He was nineteen. He didn't wait to be drafted. Who would want to go back to Europe? To a war? He had seen enough of Europe to last a lifetime; but he went. He became an American when he came to this country when he was twelve years old, and his country was at war.

He went to basic training and became a Doughboy. "Doughboy" was the nickname for America's soldiers during World War I. Most authorities are in disagreement as to where that name originated, but that is what they called the soldiers. U.S. Army Private Louis Levine wasn't alone. Jewish soldiers have served in all of America's wars. There were nearly half a million other immigrants, and more than 4 million American troops who were sent to fight in World War I. The Army had men serving who had been born in 46 different countries. This group had to be made into a cohesive unit. The military had to rethink their training programs in order to teach these men how to get along and pull together. They needed to be able to talk to each other, and understand orders, or it would be dangerous. The Army had to allow these men to keep their own cultures, or they might not be cooperative. They had to do this while making these men patriotic to the United States. The Army instituted all sorts of new programs to prepare these young recruits to become soldiers. One of the most important programs was teaching the young immigrants as much English as possible before they left for the front so they could understand each other and work as a team.

In the tough 13 weeks of basic training at boot camp, the boys and men were turned into soldiers. From "REVEILLE" to the sound of "TAPS" at night, in rain, sun or snow, they were taught to stand stone faced at attention, how to march in step and in line, how to salute, and who was who in rank. They had sergeants telling them how high to jump, and when to come down. These men were trained in hand to hand combat, how to shoot a rifle, throwing grenades, and how to crawl around on the ground, so that they didn't get blown up. From sun, up to sundown, they did physical exercises, maneuver drills, and hiked for miles with heavy packs on their backs. They got used to the sound of gunfire, were taught how to take care of their weapons, and how to live in a combat zone. The Army turned them all into what were called "the Doughboys." Most of them were sent to Europe to lick Kaiser Bill, and make the world safe for democracy.

The Army had all sorts of training programs besides English and basic training. They trained Louie to do mainly two things. They taught him to be a cook and they trained him to be a lineman. As a lineman, he was one of the men who would go ahead of the others in the fields to fix or put up the telegraph lines. And when he wasn't up a pole stringing wire, he was one of his unit's cooks.

Although it was very dangerous to go ahead of the rest of the company, never knowing that there wasn't a troop of Germans coming, the linemen also had a little more freedom. In camp, there were many hours and sometimes days, when they had to wait. They waited for orders from above, they waited for supplies, they waited to hear what the reconnaissance guys had to say; mainly they just waited, often not knowing what for. The linemen weren't as confined to spend the long, lonely hours in camp just waiting. Louie was never afraid of heights and climbing up those poles made him feel free. It was better than sitting there just waiting in camp or in a foxhole. He could look down on the world beneath him and feel a brief rush of freedom.

Louie was sent to fight in France with the Allied powers. Like the other soldiers, far from home and lonely, he looked for other things to do, when he wasn't stringing lines or fighting. A lot of soldiers would go to church when they were near one, even if they weren't religious. It was a way of meeting people and socializing. On Friday nights or Saturday mornings if Louie was near a shul, he would go in for the service. The French Jews were always very nice to the Jewish American soldiers who came. As is customary with strangers who come to a service, the congregants welcomed him, and someone would always invite him to their home for a Shabbos meal.

One Friday, while stringing wire, he found himself in a little German village right on the French, German border. He saw there was a shul, and people were going in for the Friday night service. He went in, but no one came over to welcome him. They got quiet when they saw him - an American soldier. This was World War I and these Jewish people were good Germans. He didn't mean to frighten them, but just the sight of him, an American soldier, alarmed them. No one welcomed him, and no one offered him dinner with their family. After saying the prayers, he quietly left.

Not far from that German village, Louie was in a foxhole with his buddy Carmine, when they were caught in a bombing assault. It buried them alive. Louie was able to dig them out, but found his pal Carmine had been hurt. His buddy didn't make it. Carmine died a few hours later.

Louie was awarded the Victory Medal, and was one of the lucky ones who came home alive and not crippled. By the end of "The Great War", there were more than 40 million military and civilian casualties. It ended on June 28, 1919, with the signing of the Treaty of Versailles.

**[Photo:] Doughboy, U. S. Army Private Louis Levine,
wearing his Victory Medal (ca. 1918)**

Now Louie was home. Trained as a telegraph lineman, he thought he had it made. He knew he had a good job waiting for him with the New York Telephone and Telegraph Company. They paid good money for trained linemen, and they were always looking for men. Louie was very surprised when he went down there to ask for a job, and they said no. They point blank told him they didn't hire anyone with a name like Levine. They didn't want Jews.

Louie got a job as a painter. Not everyone wanted to go up and paint the outside of buildings on those little wooden platforms, even though the pay was much better than for regular painters. Always unafraid of heights, he was a natural for the scaffolds.

He was working, and wanted to settle down with a wife and family. When his friend Max offered to introduce him to his wife's cousin, Louie said yes.

They finished Celia's chicken dinner, and ate the babka that Lena had brought. They all sat drinking hot tea with lemon, sipping it through the sugar cube they held between their teeth. At the end of the evening, both Lena and Louie said thank you and left for the train. They both lived on the Lower East Side, so it was natural for them to take the train together. When they got off the train, Louie surprised Lena when he asked if he could walk her home. She thought he was just being a gentleman, but she said yes. She was again surprised when they got to Clinton Street. He said that he had had a very nice time and asked if he could see her again.

Lena and Louie were married, not long after, on October 17, 1925. They were happy together and always singing. Lena gave birth to a beautiful, baby girl on November 19, 1926. They named her Sima Razel too, but called her Sylvia Rose, Sylvie for short.

When Lena's father, Mikhel, saw Louie's father at the baby naming, he of course said mazel tov to him. Louie's father asked, "Is this one your first grandchild?" Mikhel proudly told him, "No, I have another granddaughter here, and three more granddaughters from my oldest daughter, Elka. They are still in Russia; they should live and be well. All together it's now five, thank G_d." Louie's father said, "Some big shot! So, what! I have 35 other grandchildren." ✣

ഔ *Minford Place* ൦

Not long after, Max and Celia moved from the Lower East Side up to the Bronx, they tried to convince everyone they knew to move to the Bronx. Max told Mikhel that they would be better off in the Bronx. Max said, "They have much bigger, nicer apartments for less money in the East Bronx. There, the apartments are newer and lighter, more fresh air. It is not so crowded there. Your family is growing. It would be better for the children. You would have to take the train to work but you should move to the Bronx. Also, they say that there are more Jews in the Bronx than anywhere else in this country. They even call it the Jewish borough.[27] You'll feel more at home there." So Mikhel and Miasha did move. With Celia's help, they found an apartment at 1425 Charlotte Street, right near the Jennings Street market.

---

[27] "The Jewish borough"- according to the Bronx County Clerk's Office, in 1930, more than 50 percent of the population in the Bronx was Jewish - mostly centered in the South Bronx and the Grand Concourse. In the 1960s the Jews moved to the suburbs, and many Jews who were retired moved to Florida. The Bronx then became a borough full of other immigrants.

[Photo:] Typical, Bronx tenement neighborhood block (ca. 1930s)
Photo courtesy of the NYC Public Library Photograph Collection

It was mostly a poor Jewish immigrant neighborhood, like the Lower East Side, only newer. The brick buildings in the Bronx were still tenements, but were much bigger and much taller than the brownstone tenements in the Manhattan neighborhood they had left. Most of the apartment buildings were six stories high. They couldn't build them taller than six stories without putting in an elevator, and these buildings were all walk-ups. A lot of the Bronx streets were like brick walls. Buildings started at one corner of the block, and continued one right after the other to the end of the block. The cement sidewalks were laid to the edge of the cobblestone or asphalt roads, leaving no room for grass and trees.

Jennings Street, from what used to be called Wilkins Avenue, and is now called Louis Nine Boulevard, to the Southern Boulevard El, was the hub of the neighborhood. It was a market street with lots of stores. They had kosher butcher shops, a kosher bakery, a fresh vegetable market, a dairy, a fish store, and a live chicken market that was kosher, of course. There was a dry goods store on the corner of Jennings and Charlotte Streets and a barber shop two stores down from that. There was a big shul right there on Minford Place, half a block from Jennings Street.

The apartments in the Bronx were also bigger, newer and brighter than they were on the Lower East Side, even if you did have to walk up all of those stairs. When you had bundles, it was a long walk for those who lived on the upper floors. Most of the taller buildings had dumbwaiters in the apartments to get rid of the garbage, so that at least you didn't have to drag that downstairs. You opened the little door in the wall, and put your bag of garbage on a board that was attached to ropes. Then you pulled the rope to lower the garbage to the cellar, where the super took it away for collection.

They had iceboxes for the food, and sinks in the kitchen with hot and cold running water. These buildings had gas ranges for cooking that you had to light with a match, instead of wood stoves, like the homes on the Lower East Side. The apartments were heated with steam that came up from the coal-burning furnace in the cellar.

The steam was piped up to iron radiators that were painted silver. There was a silver radiator in almost every room. Each apartment had its own bathroom in the apartment with a toilet. The toilet had a chain that went up to a water box that was sitting up near the ceiling. When you were finished, you pulled the chain, and water came down into the toilet through a pipe and washed everything away through another pipe in the floor. The bathrooms also had a sink and a footed bathtub with a shower with hot and cold running water. The apartments had electric lights. Everything was very modern, even for poor people.

Lena and Louie moved to Brooklyn. Louie had bought a candy store there with his sister Dora and her husband Dave.

Reuben still wasn't able to come from Cuba, so Fagel and Razel still lived with Mikhel, Miasha and the boys, Sam, Abie and Max. Miasha still took care of little Razel, so Fagel could go to work. When they moved to the Bronx, Fagel looked for and found a job on Jennings Street so she wouldn't have to schlep back and forth on the train every day to her job at the bakery on the Lower East Side. Her new job was working at the bakery around the corner at the Jennings Street market. It wasn't just easier; she saved money too, because she didn't have to pay the nickel carfare each way; Fagel could walk there.

Abie and Max went to school, and Sam went to work and to school at night. Max Shikoff took them to his shul, the Minford Place Shul. The family settled into the Bronx neighborhood.

Mikhel was very learned in the Torah. He quickly became one of the leaders of the Minford Place Shul. Now an empty lot, the very large and once famous Minford Place Shul was founded in 1894. It was at 1424 Minford Place, near the corner of the first block from Jennings Street, where Minford Place and Charlotte Street ended at the Jennings Street market. When I was a little girl, I used to go up to sit with my mother and Bubby Miasha in the women's section of the balcony during the Rosh Hashanah and Yom Kippur services. The whole family was there. I thought that synagogue was enormous, and the most beautiful building I had ever been in. It had magnificent stained-glass windows.

Having a beautiful voice, and knowing many of the cantorial pieces, Mikhel would frequently act as the cantor, but I never heard him sing. He got very sick and died in 1928, before my parents met. Mikhel was having very bad stomach pains. Friends took him to the hospital and they did an emergency operation. He did not recover.

The chevra kadisha came and took care of him. Mikhel Mnuskin was laid out on the floor with candles all around him. He was buried in a plain pine coffin built with wooden nails, just as Jewish law requires. The family were members of the Hlusk Society. The Hlusk Society was a group from the old country, people who had all come from Hlusk. It was like lots of other groups from the old country that were organized by people who came to America and wanted to keep in touch with other people from their shtetl. They had meetings and visited with each other every once in a while. They collected money to send to Israel in order to get the Hlusk Yizkor book published and for the Hadassah Hospital in Jerusalem. But, mostly, they arranged for their members to have a Jewish burial. The Hlusk Society members all paid into a Jewish cemetery, the Baron Hirsch Cemetery on Staten Island. When the time came, their families wouldn't have to worry about where to put them. There weren't many people at Mikhel Mnuskin's funeral because the cemetery was all the way out on Staten Island. It was a hardship for people to take off from work, and schlep all the way out there. Just his family and the rabbi went.

The Mnuskin family went from the Bronx, all the way down to the southern end of Manhattan on the subway, where they took the ferry out to Staten Island. Sam went with the coffin on the horse and wagon. The Baron Hirsh Cemetery is an old Jewish cemetery at the northern end of Staten Island. Some of the gravestones have photographs of the person whose grave it is. Like many people from Hlusk who were members of the Hlusk Society, it became the Mnuskin family cemetery. My grandfather, Mikhel Mnuskin was the first member of the family to be buried in America.

On May 5, 1929 Lena had another baby girl. They named her Minnie for Mikhel. When 18-year-old, very modern Abie heard that, he said, "What are you kidding? You can't name my niece Minnie! All of the *yentas* in the neighborhood are named Minnie." Lena and Lou thought about it for a couple of weeks. As they thought about it, their new baby girl didn't really have a name. Then Lena took the baby to the doctor for a checkup. The doctor and the nurse asked what her name was and Lena said she wasn't sure yet. She and her husband had named her Minnie but her brother had talked her out of that name. The nurse said, "It is the month of May. Why not name your baby Mae? That is a lovely name." Mae grew up to be a very pretty girl, and tall like her father. She was happy not to be called Minnie. She has three children - two boys, Tyler and Miles, and the youngest a girl named Heidi. Mae had to have a daughter of her own to tease her mother by calling her Minnie Mae.   ❧

℘ *News From Cuba* ℘

*F*agel usually sent a letter to Reuben and received one back about once a week, frequently more often. They had been writing like this since they had parted in Cherbourg. By the end of 1928, Reuben was still in Cuba. He had found a job there, was saving his money, and waiting till he could come to be with her and Razel. One time a week passed, and then a second week passed, and there was no letter from Reuben. After the third week without a letter, Fagel became frantic. She thought she was going to lose her mind if she didn't find out what was wrong. Was Reuben hurt? Was he, G_d forbid, killed? Was he sick? These thoughts kept going through her head, and worse thoughts; thoughts that were too terrible to even think.

Finally, a letter did come. It wasn't Reuben's handwriting. It said that he was sick. He had caught malaria - the scourge of Cuba, and nearly died. The letter told Fagel that he was getting better, and hoped that he would be completely well soon. It said that a good friend was kind enough to write the letter for him because he was still too weak.

Fagel worried about Reuben so far away from her, but also wondered about the friend who had written the letter. Anyone could see, that it was written in a very fine hand by a woman.

Fagel was still working in the bakery on Jennings Street. One day a lady, a customer, came into the bakery. In talking to the salesgirl that was helping her, she mentioned that she and her family had just emigrated there from Cuba. When the salesgirl heard that the woman had come from Cuba, she right away called Fagel over to meet her. Fagel hoping to hear good news about Reuben, of course, asked if she knew him. The customer said yes. She knew him. Not knowing that Fagel was his wife, she told Fagel that he was living with some woman on the same street that she and her family had lived on in Havana. The customer said that she knew that he had had malaria, and that his landlady had nursed him back to health.

I don't know if it was true or not. For all anyone knew it was a different Reuben. A lot of men are named Reuben, and too many people to count had malaria. Maybe this woman, the customer, was wrong and she wasn't talking about Fagel's husband. Anyway, Fagel was very upset. Nobody could convince her that it wasn't her Reuben that the bakery customer was talking about. And no one could calm her down. Was it the shame or did she love Reuben so much? She drank a glass of poison when she heard of the affair.

Her brother Sam worked night and day to pay for Fagel's medical bills at the hospital. Despite all the efforts to save her, after almost six months, Fagel died. Fagel was buried at the Baron Hirsch Cemetery on Staten Island, not far from her father. She was too young to be there.

People who knew Fagel's mother said that Fagel was as beautiful as her mother, and that her little girl, Razel looked just like them. They all had the same long, almost blond hair that flowed down their backs in waves, and they had big beautiful, blue eyes and pink cheeks that stood out on their porcelain white skin. Everyone had always admired Fagel's and little Razel's beauty, and especially their hair.

In a very sad way, Fagel was lucky; she never knew about her little girl, Razel. No one had the heart to tell her. While Fagel was in the hospital, Bubby Miasha took care of Razel as she always had. One day, she left Razel with a neighbor's young daughter. She took the El train to go visit Fagel in the hospital. The young babysitter prepared lunch for them. While cooking, she caused a small fire. Little Razel went near the range, her beautiful long hair caught fire, and she died. She too was buried, too young, at the Baron Hirsch Cemetery, waiting for her mother to soon be put in the ground next to her.   ଔ

✍ *The Goody-Goody Greenhorn* ✍

$\mathcal{M}$y father, Sam, a very friendly man was always laughing and telling jokes. Unless they gave him reason to think otherwise, he always thought the best of people. His positive outlook kept him from thinking about the past or unpleasantness. Truly a cock-eyed optimist, Sam always looked forward to things working out well, and looked back on the experiences of his life through rose-colored glasses of remembrance. He only talked about the good times; I never heard about the hardships he lived through from him. Other people told me what the family had gone through. I don't know if he wanted to spare me, or if he just wanted to put those times out of his mind; knowing my father; probably both. He would always talk about how much better the fruits and vegetables were in Russia, and that they used to eat them fresh and ripened from the garden. When his sister, Lena would hear him say that kind of thing, she would say, "What food? We starved most of the time! Sam, you only remember the good times."

Sam was a very honest, hardworking, traditional man. He never drank except a little wine at religious observances. He never gambled or went out with other women. Sam didn't even go out with "loose women" before he got married. He always worked very hard, and before he married, he, of course, lived with his mother, Miasha, and his family, and gave Miasha most of his money. His younger brothers, Abie and Max, used to make fun of him for being such a goody-goody and a greenhorn. I guess he embarrassed them with his old fashioned conservative ways. Sam never forgot that his real name was Mnushkin, and he always pronounced it that way. His brothers, Abie and Max couldn't forget Europe and their former name fast enough. They became Americans named Mnuskin as soon as they got here.

Sam was six years older than Abe and eight years older than Max. Abie and Max were just little kids when they came to America. All Max and Abie wanted was to be real Americans, have a better life, and a good time. Miasha had heard that you could make a good living as a woman's hair stylist, at that time called a beautician. You just had to go to school for it. When they were old enough, she encouraged Abie and Max to go do this. Just teenagers, they took the money Miasha gave them to go to school to become beauticians, and gambled most of it away playing craps up on the roof in the next building. It was a long time after that they learned the values in hard work.

A friend had taught Sam how to drive a car. Sam loved driving. He found a good deal he could afford on an old Hudson, and bought it. He loved driving that car. Sam taught Abie and Max to drive, as well as all of his friends.   ೞ

℘ *Golden Age of Jewish Boxing* ℘

*I*n talking about this book, my father told me that his brother Max had wanted to be a boxer – unimaginable to me. A Jewish boxer? Uncle Maxie? Most Jews are unaggressive, conservative, sober, non-violent people. Not that they would hesitate to open up a big mouth, to give as good as they get in words; they would do that. But I still couldn't imagine a boxer coming out of a Jewish home, and absolutely not my uncle Max. Not a big man, Max must have been a lightweight. He was a gentle, generous man, with a great sense of humor. In my life, I don't remember him even raising his voice, let alone hitting anybody. Then again, nobody wanted to spend their lives bent over a sewing machine working in a sweatshop, if they didn't have to.

When Max was old enough to work, Sam had gotten him a job working as a painter's assistant and then later a painter, just as he had gotten Abie a job painting two years before. Max hated it. Abie and Max both did. They were always scheming on how to find a better way to make a living.

One Saturday, Abe's friend Moe wanted them to go with him to the Bronx Coliseum to see the fights. The West Farms area of the Bronx was not far. The Bronx Coliseum was at 177th Street and Devoe Avenue, next to the Starlight Amusement Park. They had boxing matches and other sporting events there. The best fights were at the Garden - Madison Square Garden, when it was down on Eighth Ave. and 50th Street in Manhattan. The Garden was only a few years old then. Sometimes they had a really big match at Yankee Stadium, but the Bronx Coliseum wasn't small potatoes either. They had some major contenders there too. Max enjoyed seeing that first fight, especially when he heard how much money the boxers were making. Even the lousy boxers were getting more than he made in a week's wages, for just a few rounds in the ring.

It didn't take much for him to become a fan. Max started listening to the fights on the radio. He loved to hear the rapid fire, "tobaccoed – out", gravelly voice of the announcer, screaming the blow-by-blow accounts of a fight. Max could picture him standing there in his tuxedo, announcing each fight, yelling into his megaphone. There they were, two young men, strangers before they got on that canvas floor, now trying to knock the living daylights out of each other. Max loved the excitement. And the more he thought about it, the more he thought he would become one of those men.

Actually, as hard as it is for me to believe, because not just my Uncle Max, but none of the Jewish men I have ever met would seem to be a likely candidate for this, but during the years between 1900 and 1940, there were more than 30,000 Jewish prizefighters and 22 Jewish major contenders. Those years were considered "The Golden Age of Jewish Boxing."

Determined to pursue this career, Max started going to the gym. At first, he just hung around watching; then he started working out. He bought a pair of trunks with a Jewish Star emblazoned on the leg, like other Jewish boxers proudly wore. Max found that he was strong, fast, and had a will power that matched his iron fists.

He did this in secret. Max knew his mother wouldn't like it; she would be very upset if she knew. So, he didn't tell her. Only his brothers, Abie and Sam, knew his plan to become a prizefighter. He made them promise not to tell their mother, and not to tell anyone else, so she wouldn't find out. Neither of his brothers wanted her to worry, so his secret was safe with them.

He figured that he would tell her, if he had to, when he was rich and famous. Max could just imagine what she would have said had she found out. "What you think, you're a *shtarker* (a strong guy)? You will get killed. The *trumbeniks* (street thugs) fight –not nice Jewish boys. You are not from the fighters." But he also knew that even a young kid could make more money in a match that was only a few rounds than anybody laboring all week in some sweatshop or swinging a paint brush. Like a lot of poor immigrants, Max decided to become a prizefighter. He thought that would be his road to easier riches.

My father told me that Max became a pretty good boxer. He even won a couple of small matches. He never fought at the place that he dreamed of where every prizefighter wanted to box, Madison Square Garden, or even better Yankee Stadium. Max hated the mouth guard. He felt like he couldn't breathe with that damn thing on. He used to put it in, and then spit it out. Max could never find a place for it in his mouth. This was in the days when boxers weren't forced to wear the mouth protectors. The trouble was, Max had a bad habit, when he was boxing, of sticking his tongue out of the right side of his mouth. His career didn't last long. He kept saying, just one more purse, one more purse, but wisely Max stopped boxing before he got hurt. He decided that he needed his tongue. My father said, he was very proud of Max, and grateful that he decided to throw away his gloves.

Sometimes, Abie or Max would borrow the car from Sam, and go take a couple of girls from the neighborhood out for a ride. They were real studs. They both went out with a lot of girls.

Abie was very handsome. He looked a lot like the movie star, Gilbert Roland. The girls were always chasing him. At 31, Abe was still very good-looking, and the girls were still chasing him. This wasn't new. What was new was that there was this one cute redhead, Dottie, who caught his attention. She was a girl from the neighborhood. Dottie worked as a bookkeeper in an office. She didn't like Abie, the smart aleck, and wouldn't give him the time of day. Of course, he was smitten. Abie and Dottie got married in 1943, and had four beautiful daughters, Michelle, Lynn, Brenda and Paulette.

Max, with his stylish mustache, was very charming and funny. The girls liked him too, and he liked them. Once, Max got "syph." He knew he had the first symptom. Max found the telltale sign, a sore on his penis. He ran to a doctor to get a Wasserman test. Everybody knew about the telltale sore. People were running to doctors for the test if they found any little pimple near their genitals, but Max really had syphilis. He had to go through the very painful treatments. This was before the widespread use of penicillin. In those days, the cure for syphilis was neosalvarsan, an arsenic compound that was injected locally into a vein in the penis. The treatments were very painful and very expensive. Max was lucky; some people had severe side effects of nausea, vomiting, abdominal pain, and diarrhea. He threw up a bit, but it wasn't as bad as some people had it.

Max didn't get married until he was 36, when he married his girlfriend Pauline. Bubby Miasha was not happy about his marrying her. Pauley, as everyone called her, was a divorced woman with two kids. This was 1948, long before the sexual revolution and women's liberation. Divorce was considered scandalous, and all girls were supposed to be virgins on their wedding night. Most men didn't want to marry a "loose woman", and, certainly, no man's family wanted him to.

Miasha said, "What do you need with a divorced woman, and somebody else's children, to this bargain? What do you need to raise somebody else's kids for? Besides, you practically live with her already; why marry her? Who buys the cow when they get the milk for free? You are a good-looking fella. Go get a young girl and have children of your own."

Max said, "Pauley made a mistake when she married that *mamzer*,[28] that *trumbanick*. So, she made a mistake! She is still a good woman, Ma, and I love her. We are getting married."

Miasha screamed at him, "Good – *shmood*! You are *meshuggah, nisht klug*[29]! It's a *shandah*[30]!"

Probably, the best thing that ever happened to Max was his marrying Pauley. He settled down and had a family. He became a father to her two boys, Ronny and Jerry. When they were almost grown, Ronny and Jerry asked Max to adopt them legally, and he did. He loved those boys, and they loved him. They weren't married long, when Pauley gave birth to another boy. Max named his new son after his father, Mikhel, and they called the baby, Michael, and more often Mikey. Miasha got over being mad, especially when Michael was born. As I remember, Max and Pauley were always happy together - always laughing.

Max did stay out of the sweatshops, and didn't last as a painter. He and Abie bought a taxi and became New York City taxi drivers. It was very hard work but at least they were their own boss and didn't have to take orders from someone else. ₧

---

[28] *mamzer* mam' zer n.- bastard; illegitimate child

[29] *Meshuggah, nisht klug* meshug'gah• nisht •klug - Yiddish phrase - crazy not smart
Meshuggah - crazy; nisht - not; *klug* - smart

[30] *shandah* shan'dah n. – something that is shameful, a shame

[Photo:] Pauley & Max Mnuskin's wedding
left to right: Pauley, Max, Miasha, Abe (best man), Abe's wife
Dottie, and Abe & Dottie's little girl Michelle (1947)

∞ *Times Were Hard* ∞

I'm not sure, but I think that Lena and Louie had their candy store in Flatbush. I know it was in one of the Jewish neighborhoods in Brooklyn. I was never there, because it was long before I was born. It looked like most candy stores in New York at that time. It had a glass showcase on the left, just as you came in, that held the penny candy. It was stocked with Double-Bubble Gum, the newly invented bubble gum. Children weren't the only ones who loved to make bubbles with that gum; everybody did. They also had all sorts of hard candies, licorice, and chocolate. They kept boxes of cigars in there, too.

On the right side, when you first came into the store, there was a wooden newspaper and magazine rack. Right after the candy case, there was a long marble counter with high, backless stools. This was the soda fountain. At the front end of the counter, sat a small display box of packages of Sen-Sen (the original breath mint).

They sold ice cream from scoops, ice cream sodas, and glasses of seltzer, at the counter. There was a malted mixer there. And, of course, they sold everybody's favorite - egg creams. There wasn't a candy store in New York City that didn't serve egg creams. Egg cream is really an odd name for a sweet chocolate soda that is full of fizz, but doesn't have any eggs or any cream. You put a couple of spoonsful of Fox's U-Bet Chocolate Syrup in the bottom of a soda glass. And it had to be Fox's, that's it; no other chocolate syrup tasted the same. Then, you poured 1/2 cup of cold milk in and the rest is just seltzer. Stir it fast and you have New York's famous egg cream. You gulped this thirst-quencher down fast; otherwise the fizz went flat.

In the back of the candy store, there was a public telephone. Like in most candy stores, before people had their own phones, the phone in the candy store was the neighborhood's phone. People called each other there, and the owners kept messages for their customers. Sometimes, the store owner would send one of the kids who were always hanging around, to go tell somebody that they had a call. People waited around for expected phone calls, and just because there wasn't much else to do in the neighborhood – no TV then. The local candy stores were the local hangouts in the poorer neighborhoods of New York City. Mostly, you found unemployed men from the neighborhood who had nothing else to do and the teenagers. Poor women always had something to do. They took care of the children (some upwards of 10 kids), made the meals, cleaned the house, and did the laundry. The candy store was like a meeting place. They almost couldn't help it, but the neighborhood *yentas* used to pass along all of the day's gossip. The candy store was where you went to get a glass of seltzer, the newspaper, and the neighborhood news. It was where people heard all the latest gossip and the *yentas* chatted it up. It was *"yenta tell-a-benda* central."

Louie's store was open long hours, usually until 10:00 o'clock at night. All four of them, Louie, Lena, Louie's sister Dora, and her husband Dave, used to take turns working in the store. The two women worked in the mornings, and the men worked all day into the evening hours. They worked hard, standing on their feet most of the time. But even so, they never did well in that Brooklyn store. The candy store was not really in a wonderful spot. You had to be in a busy place for a candy store to do a good business, and theirs wasn't. They owed a lot of money on the loan they had taken to open the store, and, then, the "Great" Depression hit, and things got really bad. The shelves were bare because they didn't have the money to stock them. They closed the store, and Lou went back to painting. He was always able to get a job painting the outside of buildings, because not everyone wanted to go up on the scaffolds.

Cost of Living 1930
U.S. Bureau of Labor Statistics

yearly inflation rate - 2.8%
average cost of new house - $7,145.00
1 gallon of gas - 10 ¢
house rent - $15.00 per month
a loaf of bread - 9 ¢
one lb. of hamburger meat - 13 ¢
Pontiac car - $745.00
average wages per week - $37.00
average wages per year - $1,970.00

Lena and Louie decided to move up to the Bronx, to be closer to Lena's family. Lena figured she would get a job working in a store, and Miasha would watch the kids, five-year-old Sylvie and two-year-old Mae, while she worked.

Before Lena could get a job, she was in trouble. Her knee was hurting her much more than usual. Was it from *schlepping* all of that stuff up and down the stairs in the move, and from chasing after the girls? Who knows? Her knee always hurt. It had never really healed, and now it was so swollen her knee looked like a grapefruit.

Louie took her to Montefiore Hospital on the other side of the Bronx. They said that she had tuberculosis of the knee, and, if it spread, she could die. They opened her knee and cut out what was infected. The doctors put Lena in a full leg cast, and told her and Louie that she would have to stay in that cast till it healed, and that it could take a very long time.

Louie had free health care for himself because he was a vet, but not for his family. He had to pay for the hospital. His mother told him to leave that cripple, and her girls in the Bronx, and come live with her. Lou got mad, and wouldn't even listen to her. Leave his family, his wife, his girls? Was she mishuggah?

Miasha took care of his girls, and he worked harder to pay the hospital bills. Miasha was already watching Shima's little girl, Edith. Shima was a neighbor, whose husband had died. She worked in a sweatshop to support herself and Edith. She paid Miasha to take care of Edith. Shima and Edith became close friends, like members of the family. When Lena went to the hospital, Miasha took care of Sylvie and Mae, as well as Edith. They lived in the next building, on Charlotte Street. Lou would bring the girls in the morning, before he went to work. Miasha would take Sylvie and Edith, both about five years old, to school. She and two-year-old Mae would go home, and Miasha would spend the day cooking and washing for the family. Louie, who had been taught to cook by the Army, never failed to roll up his sleeves and help in the kitchen.

When he could, Lou would go to the hospital to see his Lena. The nurses could hear them singing, from down the hall. The hospital kept Lena in that full leg cast for most of the two and a half years that she was there, but she didn't die.   ও

**[Photo:] Lena and Louie Levine holding their first grandchild,
Sylvia's daughter, Carole, at the Bronx Zoo (ca. 1950)**

288

[Photo:] Sylvia Levine, 22 (seated) & Mae Levine, 19
(Lena and Louie Levine's daughters)
at Cousin Dorothy Shikoff's wedding, Bronx, NY (ca. 1948)

꧁ *A Yankee Born* ꧂

Marty was my parents', Frieda and Sam's, first-born and everyone's favorite. He was born on April 28, 1933, and he, too, was named after my father's father, Mikhel. Frieda never knew Sam's father; he had died before she had met Sam. Marty was the first Mnuskin boy born in America. The first grandson on both sides, and as anyone will tell you, boys were special and held in a higher place of esteem than the rest of us. Bubby Miasha adored him; he was named after her husband Mikhel. Lena's younger daughter, four-year-old, Mae was also named after Mikhel, but that was different. She was a girl.

Lena was still in the hospital for her knee, and Bubba Miasha was taking care of Sylvia, Mae and Edith. Abie and Max still lived with Miasha on Charlotte Street. Sam and Frieda hadn't moved into their new apartment around the corner yet, so they brought the new baby, Martin home to Charlotte Street. This was a full house.

Seven-year-old Sylvia and Uncle Max had just come in. Sylvia was showing off her new shoes that Uncle Max had just bought for her, when Sam and Frieda walked in. They just came home from the hospital with the new baby boy. Everyone was very excited to see him.

Starting with Abraham, Jews have been circumcising their sons for thousands of years. Martin was a very healthy baby, so in keeping with the ancient Jewish, sacred covenant with G_d, as commanded in Genesis, he had a *bris*[31]. It was on May 5, when he was eight days old. This was a wonderful event. It happened to be four-year-old Mae's birthday. She was there, but the party wasn't for her. Her older sister, Sylvie, and Edith were both in school.

It was a Friday morning, but almost everyone came. Shima couldn't take off from work; so she wasn't there. It was the height of the depression and not everyone had work. Those that did have work took off if they could to come and be at the *bris* and celebrate.

The family came. The men put on their *yarmulkes* when they walked in. Frieda's father, Barney, and Disha came all the way up from Brooklyn. Barney was a very proud zaidy. Martin was his second grandchild. Hasha had given birth to Clara the year before, but this was different because Martin was a boy. Barney brought his friends Mendel and Tuvia and Tuvia's wife Blooma to the bris. Barney knew Tuvia from the Lower East Side, from before Tuvia had brought Blooma over from Europe. Now, Tuvia and Blooma lived right there on Charlotte Street. They, too, had moved up to the Bronx. Tuvia brought his violin with him.

Hasha and Nathan also came to the bris with their one-year-old baby girl, Clara. She was just learning how to walk. Miasha, Abie and Max were all there, of course. Celia and Max Shikoff came. Lena was still in the hospital, but Louie was there. Friends, neighbors and people from the Minford Place Shul came. Such a happy occasion, who doesn't want to go to a bris?

When everyone was there crammed into the little apartment, the ritual passing of the baby boy began. Everyone was quiet as they watched. The members of the family who were chosen to perform this ritual, of course thought it an honor. Frieda and Sam decided who to ask to do the passing, the day before the bris. Frieda presented her baby boy to the first person, her sister Hasha. The first person who has the honor of being given the baby by the mother is always a woman who will have children or more children.

---

[31] *bris- n. -* the Jewish ritual male circumcision with the removal of the foreskin; a commandment in Judaism usually performed on the 8th day of a male child's life or upon conversion to Judaism.

Hasha took him from Frieda, and brought the baby to the second person, Abie. The second person, who is given the honor of taking the boy is usually a man. He, too, is generally someone who will one day have children. Abie very carefully handed the baby to Frieda's father, Barney. The third person is usually the baby boy's grandfather. Barney carefully, but with a quiet joy, sat down with his precious, baby grandson in his lap. As expected, they were seated in the traditional empty chair that was left for Elijah. It is called the Throne of Elijah. The *mohel* (the man trained to perform a circumcision), then took the baby from the very proud grandfather, and placed him on the table. When the circumcision was finished, the mohel and the rabbi said the blessings. The rabbi said the blessing for wine, and everyone took a sip from their glass. The mohel put a few drops in the baby's mouth to quiet his screaming. Then the mohel handed the crying baby to his father, Sam. Sam cradled his son in his arms, as the mohel announced the name that Frieda and Sam had chosen for their son - Mikhel ben Zolmon Ellie. The mohel recited more prayers and then Sam proudly handed his crying baby son back to his smiling brother. Abie took him and handed him back to Hasha, who gave him back to his concerned mother. Frieda went into the bedroom to nurse and comfort her baby, and to look for herself at what they had done to him. Hasha came in to be with her, and to nurse her baby girl, Clara. They smiled as they heard the mohel yell "Mazel Tov!" And then everybody joyously yelled "Mazel Tov!"

Prohibition, the 18th Amendment to the Constitution, wouldn't be repealed for another seven months. So, Prohibition or no Prohibition, they had gotten a bottle of schnapps especially for the bris, from Leo the neighborhood bootlegger. The day before the big day, Abe went to him. When Leo heard it was for the bris, he gave him a special price. At the bris, they poured a little schnapps into everyone's glass. Then everyone raised their glasses and yelled "L'chaim!"

Miasha hustled everyone over to the table. She worked hard to make this feast for her first grandson's bris. She made blintzes, and a noodle pudding with farmer cheese and raisins. The other women all brought food, too. It was a dairy meal so, of course, there wasn't any meat. There were bagels, lox and cream cheese, herring, a honey cake and a sponge cake. So, of course, they ate lunch. Then Tuvia took out his fiddle; it was a celebration. He played the klezmer music from the shtetl and everybody's favorites, "MY BLUE HEAVEN" and "AIN'T SHE SWEET."

On Sunday, May 28th Marty was 31 days old. Being a first-born Jewish boy, he had to be redeemed. In biblical times, the first-born boy was either redeemed for five silver coins, or his life was dedicated to working for the Temple. Observant Jews still perform this ceremony today. The ceremony is called a *pidyon haben* (pid' yon ha ben'). This ceremony is always performed by a *Kohen*[32] (a Jewish high priest). Lena's husband Louie happened to be a Kohen and he was very happy to do it.

The baby boy is placed on a pillow surrounded by riches, in hope that the way he starts his life will be the way it continues. The women all loaned Frieda any jewelry they had, especially gold.

A pidyon haben is done during a festive meal. So, Frieda and Miasha cooked. Other women brought food too. They set the table for a feast. Again, the whole family was there.

Sam proudly presented his squiggling son to Louie on the pillow. As tradition dictates, Sam said to Louie in Hebrew, "My Jewish wife has borne to me this first-born son." The Kohen responded to Sam, in Hebrew, with the ancient question, "What would you prefer to have, your first-born son, or the five silver coins which you are obligated to give me for the redemption of your son?"

---

[32] Kohen, KO' hen, Kohanim (pl.) *n.* - men who were chosen to be the High Priests in the Holy Temple, and are the direct decedents of Moses' brother Aaron. Aaron, and his direct male descendants, were chosen by G_d to be the *Kohanim* (Exodus 28:1-4) this as an "everlasting office." During the 40 years that the Jews wandered in the desert, and in the Holy Temple in Jerusalem, until its destruction, the *Kohanim* were the High Priests. They performed the ritual sacrifices. During religious services the Kohens have the honor of being called up to the Torah before anyone else. Their lineage has been passed down from father to son for five thousand years. In modern times DNA has proven that this blood line still exists.

Sam answered, his baby boy. So, the Kohen took the five silver coins that Solomon gave him. Then Louie gave them the coins back as a gift to them, from him, to the baby. The Kohen said a blessing for the baby, and wished him a good long life. He then said a blessing for the wine. Everyone had a sip of wine and then yelled Mazel tov! Louie was asked to do the honor of saying the blessing on the challah bread and then they ate. Again, they raised their glasses with a little of Leo's schnapps and said L'chaim! Tuvia took out his fiddle; it was another celebration.

Two years later, my sister Bea was born. She was named in the synagogue for Frieda's mother, Chaiya Bailya. There were no special celebrations for her birth. Sam went to synagogue to name her, and that was that. It was nothing with nothing.   ☙

ஓ *One Bottle of Milk* ∞

My family was never rich. To tell the truth, they were really very poor. But when I was born, we weren't as poor as they all were during the "Great Depression." Nothing great about it! Things must have been unimaginably difficult for them all. By 1933, almost 25% of the United States was without a way of earning a living. It seemed that the whole country was out of work, and the rest were just hanging on. My father, Sam, was one of the millions of people who were out of work. Sam and Frieda had absolutely no money. My brother Marty and my sister Bea were both born during the height of the depression. Having babies just made things that much harder for my parents. This was before the days of unemployment benefits and welfare; there was nothing like Food Stamps. There were bread lines and soup kitchens. A lot of people in this country were literally, for real, starving. Most of the good men of the country who were having trouble finding work were feeling ashamed, and blaming themselves for not being able to feed their families and pay the rent. People were putting their children in orphanages so the children would at least have food. There were people who became homeless when they could no longer pay the rent. Thousands of them set up places to live in the streets. They built shanty towns of temporary houses that they made out of scrap wood, scrap metal, cardboard, crates, found bricks, and anything they could scavenger up to make shelters for themselves and their children. Most people were blaming the Republican President, Herbert Hoover, for the country's nightmarish economy, and for not doing more to help them. So, it wasn't a stretch for the public to call the shanty towns of the homeless "Hoovervilles" in his honor. There were Hoovervilles in all of the big cities across the country. In New York City, there were quite a few Hoovervilles. There was one in Central Park, and, as they told us in the Broadway musical "Annie", there was even one under the 59th Street Bridge.

On the radio, Ted Lewis was singing and his band played, "In A Shanty, In Old Shanty Town." Ted Lewis, born Theodore Leopold Friedman, was known as "Mr. Entertainment." Jews were proud of him, because he was one of them. During the 1920s and 30s, he was very popular with everyone, second only to Paul Whitman. People in the Ted Lewis audience always heard him yell out his famous catchphrase, "Is everybody happy?" Bing Crosby sang the heartfelt "Brother, Can You Spare a Dime." Another very popular crooner, Rudy Vallee and his group The Connecticut Yankees, sang the song "Life Is Just a Bowl of Cherries". People liked that happy song because it cheered them up, even though life to many wasn't a bowl of cherries, just the pits.

One business that didn't seem to be having trouble was the liquor business. Prohibition was started in 1920. By the end of the decade, you still couldn't sell liquor legally, but the gangsters were having a wonderful time, making money hand over fist. Their saloons, called speakeasies, and blind pigs, and gin mills were illegally selling booze they served in teacups.

The blind pigs, or gin mills, were just dives. These were the bars for the poor working man who wanted a drink and a place to hang out. Some had gambling, and striptease acts, and what not in the back. Some of the better speakeasies had well-dressed ladies with short dresses and bobbed hair who were paid to sit with the clientele, and to make the gentlemen "happy". There were nightclubs with gambling, craps and poker in the back, and jazz in the front. Men came with nice girls, too. The speakeasies were mainly for the rich. Yes, there were those who were rich during the Depression. The rich got richer, and the poor got poorer, just like always, only more so.

My parents and my Bubby Miasha were hard working honest people. They never had anything to do with this. Besides, who had money for such things? My family never even drank, except a little schnapps on special occasions, and some wine on Shabbos and Passover. But Bubby Miasha thought she knew a good business when she saw one. She started talking about starting up a little business making bathtub gin and wine. Not a big business, just enough to help out. She knew how because that was how she made money in Hlusk before they left. She still always made wine and *slivovitz*, (prune brandy) just for the family. That wasn't illegal. Who could mind a little prune brandy that she kept in a jar. And you couldn't have Passover without grape wine. She was a very law abiding woman, but she was also very courageous. She said in Yiddish, "Desperate times sometimes make people take desperate measures. And it wasn't legal for Jews to do it in Russia, either." Sam said, "Mama, this is not Russia. Here, they won't kill us if they catch us, but we could go to prison. And they will catch us. You can't do this." So Miasha talked about it occasionally, but didn't actually start her own bathtub gin business.

Frieda talked about not having money for food and being unable to feed them, because Sam couldn't find work. Nobody could find work. The only good thing was that they weren't homeless, and nobody was trying to kill them, like when they were in Europe.

Both Frieda and Sam had been involved in the birth of the labor unions. Frieda started working in a factory sweatshop when she first came to this country when she was eleven years old. Sam went to work as a painter's helper as a kid when he came over from Europe. They both lived and worked through the historically horrible conditions that demanded the creation of unions. Both Frieda and Sam were right there in the thick of it, when bosses were hiring thugs to beat up on the workers who wanted to start unions. At different times and places, they had each walked the infamously dangerous picket lines. They were familiar with the union busting scabs wielding clubs, who had been hired especially to beat up strikers. Bosses hired scabs to prevent the unions from gaining power for the poor workers who just wanted a decent way of earning a living.

Sam always complained about the unions. He said that in some unions the officials were very corrupt, real racketeers, crooks. But he remembered the days when there were no unions. He was often heard saying, "The unions are a big disappointment, with the gangsters running them. The unions have become terrible institutions, and the only thing worse than the unions, was not having them at all. But what is worse than the worst thing of all is not having a job and any work."

Sam, a hard worker, never stopped looking for a job. When there was work, he would wake up and leave the house about five in the morning to get out to the suburbs, where they were building new houses. That was where the jobs were. He would come home after a long day, and collapse in his chair. He always looked tired, but that didn't stop him from making jokes. But that was when there was work.

Frieda never forgot the freezing cold, snowy day that she was walking in the street crying, not wanting to go home, because she didn't have the money to buy milk for her babies. She had just gone to the grocery store to buy milk. She put the milk on the counter, and asked the grocer to please put it on her bill. He said that he was sorry. But they already owed him so much money, that he couldn't keep letting her take stuff, until they paid at least part of what they already owed him. Frieda told him that she didn't have any money just then, that they would pay him, as soon as they could. Her husband would find work soon, but he had to let her have the milk. She didn't have any milk in the house for her two little ones. They would starve. What should she do? He said he was sorry, but everyone was in the same trouble. He had to be able to feed his own children.

Frieda knew what it was like to starve. It was one thing for her to starve; it was a whole other thing to not be able to feed her babies. That was unendurable. Frieda left crying, and not knowing what to do, or which way to go. She couldn't go home without milk for her little ones, Bea and Marty. She wasn't going to let them starve. Frieda walked for many blocks, not even knowing where she was going. As Frieda was walking and crying in the snow-covered street, she saw two bottles of milk. They were just sitting on a stoop, in front of a house. A milkman had delivered them. An honest woman, Frieda only took one of the bottles of milk home to give to her children. She left the other bottle of milk, sitting where she found it.

Then things got worse. That winter, 1936, Hasha became very sick and died. Frieda was really crushed. She took a lot of the photos she had of Hasha, her brother Hunia, and her mother and in a fit of rage tore them all up. Frieda said if she couldn't have the real people in her life, she didn't need cold, hard pieces of paper.

Hasha's baby daughter, Clara was about three years old. Clara lived with Frieda and Sam for a while, but it was very hard for them. Sam said that they were having trouble feeding their kids, they couldn't take on another child. He said, "Clara has Nathan, her father, and Nathan has a mother. They should take care of his daughter, not us."

Nathan said that he couldn't take care of Clara. He didn't know how to take care of a three-year-old little girl, and he didn't have any money, either. His mother wouldn't take the three-year-old little girl in.

Frieda, angry with Nathan and the world, answered Sam with what she often said about other men, not her husband, the Yiddish cliché: *"The totta ge try ven de mama de by."* Translated it means, "Fathers care and are caring for their children, when the father is with their mother." My mother didn't think this about my father. She was talking about Nathan, but she was angry with Sam for not helping her take care of Clara.

Frieda always mourned Hasha, and felt the pain of losing her sister. But also, she never stopped feeling the stabs of guilt from letting her sister down, by not being able to take care of her little girl. When Frieda was ten years old, and their mother had died, Hasha had raised her and did everything to take care of her, just like Hasha had promised their mother she would. Hasha had become Frieda's mother and father. It broke Frieda's heart to fail Hasha and her daughter Clara. Nathan placed Clara in an orphanage in Queens. She had food there and was safe. Clara lived there until she was about ten when Nathan remarried. Frieda never forgave herself, or her husband Sam.

Clara grew up to be a very sweet and capable, good woman. She worked in a hospital as the billing administrator. She married a wonderful man named Alan Putzer and has two children Howard and Debbie, and two grandchildren, Adam and Dana.

**[Photo:] Alan, Howard, Clara and baby Debra Putzer –
Howard's birthday party (ca. 1962)**

When Sam didn't have work, he always went looking for a job at the union hall. He would go to the union hall every day to look for work and to hear what was happening. During the Depression, he rarely got any work. There just wasn't any work to get. What there was in the union hall were a lot of other men standing around, waiting for somebody to say something positive. And there were always men there, sitting around playing cards for money, not just for fun. Sam always liked playing cards, especially pinochle. He was very good at card games, and could basically count the cards. Today, casinos throw people out who they believe are counting cards. It isn't dishonest; this ability just gives the card player who can do this an enormous advantage. Sam was an honest, hardworking man who didn't approve of any gambling. He thought a penny-ante game of pinochle once in a while with friends, just for fun, was one thing, but gambling was a whole other story that he didn't want to be part of.

One day, when he had no work, and they had very little money, he sat down at one of the card tables. When he stopped playing, he had won enough money to feed his family for a while. After that, Sam sat down at the card tables every time he went to the union hall to find work, and couldn't get any. Sometimes, he took his little boy, Marty with him, to give his wife Frieda a break with the new baby, Bea. Marty played with the other little kids who were there with their fathers. Marty remembers that they never left until his father had won enough money to buy food for the family. When Sam finally did get work, he didn't gamble.

The gambling money was a help, but it wasn't a living. When Frieda heard about the Home Relief program, she told Sam that she was going to sign them up. Sam said, "I'm a strong man, and I'm able to work if I can find a job. How can we take charity?" In spite Sam's pride, Frieda went and stood on the very long line and signed up for and was given Home Relief. She also signed Miasha up for the program. That made things a little better.

In 1932, everyone was still blaming the Republican president, Herbert Hoover, for the mess the country was in. Jobless men used to turn their pockets out of their pants to show that they were empty. These pockets were nicknamed Hoover flags. That year Democrat Franklin Delano Roosevelt ran for president. He defeated the very unpopular Hoover. In his campaign, Roosevelt claimed, that he would end the Depression. FDR promised "A New Deal for the Forgotten Man." His campaign song, "Happy Days Are Here Again" was heard across the country. Trying to be an optimist, he kept a reminder on his desk - a small sign that said: "Let unconquerable gladness dwell." Roosevelt gave the people hope for a better future. They were feeling better already, and they loved him.

On Election Day, November 8, 1932, Franklin Delano Roosevelt was elected the 32nd president of the United States in a landslide. He started out by trying to keep his promises. He tried to put people back to work with all sorts of work programs that he bullied through Congress. The government started public works projects with the TVA and the WPA, putting up government buildings, and building needed roads and dams.

Sam stood on line for hours to get a job painting government offices. Uncle Louie got a job planting trees at the newly built Bronx Court House, over near Yankee Stadium.

By the end of 1933, you could hear the voice of Ginger Rogers on the radio, singing out "WE'RE IN THE MONEY." The country wasn't in the money yet, but people were feeling more optimistic. The veil of gloom had been lifted.

Another reason everyone's spirits were lifted was that FDR signed the repeal of the hated Eighteenth Amendment, and the prohibition of alcohol was ended. You could buy a drink to drown your sorrows or celebrate, and not worry about getting arrested.

World War I was supposed to be the war to end all wars; obviously, it didn't. In Europe, there was another world war going on - World War II. The news from Europe was not good. To tell you the truth, I can't write about this. As I've already told you, Hitler succeeded in his demonic path of destruction too well, before his ultimate defeat, for me to be able to write about it. I frankly find it too painful. Besides, there are many books out there, that can enlighten you about this far better than I can. The war involved the mobilization of over 100 million people in 50 countries, making it the most widespread war in the history of the world. The estimated casualties were upwards of 60 million people; G_d only knows how many people were injured, how many were made homeless refugees. Two world wars, and all I can say is – **For what?**

The Depression seemed to end even before America entered World War II. With Europe at war, American industrialists were making and selling everything Europe needed. These industrialists were making fortunes, and there were more jobs for the working man.

With a little more money in their pockets, the country wanted to forget their troubles, and to forget about war. Among other forms of fun, America went to the movies. Talking pictures - the talkies as they were known, were still in their infancy. And money or no money, the public managed to flock to the escapist entertainment. They enjoyed being scared with movies like *King Kong*, and laughing at the Marx Brothers in *Duck Soup*. The movie *My Man Godfrey* with the very popular William Powell and Carole Lombard, was a comedy about a man who lost all of his money in the 1929 stock market crash and ended up a butler. Movies about the wealthy were very popular. People liked seeing how high society and "the other side" lived, imagining themselves in their shoes, if they ever won the Irish sweepstakes. These were the movies that ordinary people wanted to live in. Despite his dislike of serious gambling, every occasionally, my father bought an Irish sweepstakes ticket in the hope that he would win. Unfortunately, he never did.

It was about 1940, when one morning Marty woke up not feeling well. Frieda decided to let her seven-year-old son stay in bed, and took her little girl, Bea to kindergarten. When she came back, she could see that Marty had a fever. His face was all red, and he had a sore throat. Frieda knew what it was. She had seen it too many times before. She got her neighbor, Mrs. Jacobson, to go to the corner candy store to phone up Dr. Breakstone, the family doctor, and ask him to come. Frieda knew Marty had scarlet fever. She didn't need Dr. Breakstone to tell her. Frieda was outwardly calm, but inside she was terrified. Dr. Breakstone came. He examined Marty, and told Frieda not to worry. He said that they would do the best they could for him, and that Marty would be ok. Bea was at kindergarten when the doctor came, and my father had found a job, and was working. Dr. Breakstone put a quarantine sign on the door. He told Frieda that nobody could leave or be allowed back into the apartment until Marty was well. The house was under quarantine.

Sam took Bea to stay with Bubba Disha and Zaidy Barney. He couldn't take her to Bubba Miasha, who lived around the corner, because they were afraid that Lena's kids would catch scarlet fever if Bea got sick. During the day, Sam went to work. Sam stayed at his mother's house to be near Frieda and Marty so he could bring them what his wife asked for. Frieda couldn't leave their apartment, so Sam had to bring her what she and Marty needed. Like everyone else in the Bronx who wanted to talk to someone in an apartment building, Sam would go to their building, and stand on the sidewalk, yelling up to Frieda to come to the window. None of them had such an extravagance as a phone then. Frieda would lean out of an open window, and shout down to her husband, telling him how Marty was doing, and to tell him what she needed. Sam would bring her groceries, and leave it at the apartment door. He kept his distance, and stayed on the other side of the hall when Frieda opened the door. He wanted to give her a hug, but didn't. He had to be careful not to catch scarlet fever – what would happen to his family if he got sick and died? He didn't want to even think about it.

Bea was about five years old. Bubba Disha scared Bea. When the little girl woke up in the middle of the night to go to the bathroom. Disha wanted Bea to use the chamber pot, but Bea didn't know how to use a chamber pot; they had a toilet at home. But that wasn't why Bea was upset. Bea started screaming in terror, when she saw Disha - Disha looked like a ghostly witch. Disha was wearing a long white night gown, and her hair, that was usually pinned up in a bun, was hanging down to her shoulders in a scraggly, gray messiness. But the worst part was that Disha's cheeks were sunken into her head, because she had taken out her false teeth. Five-year-old Bea didn't know that people could take their teeth out, and had never seen Disha look like that before. A week and a half later, Marty got well, thank G_d. He didn't die. Sam got Bea, and they went home.   ❧

[Photo:] Marty Mnuskin's Bar Mitzvah 1946

❧ *Jennings Street* ❧

Our family was poor, but we kids didn't know it till we were adults. My parents were always giving charity to the people they called poor. We always had food and clothes and a place to live. We were members of what are called the working poor and everyone we knew was in the same boat.

When I was born, we lived at 800 Jennings Street. It was the building on the south-eastern corner of Jennings and Chisholm Streets. At the other corner of the block was Bristow Street. That was where Wolf's candy store was. Half way down the block on our side of the street there was a synagogue, but we didn't go to that one. We went to the Minford Place Shul with the rest of the family. Our apartment building, a red brick structure, was a five story walk up. We lived on the third floor in a five room, corner apartment. There was a living room, three bedrooms and a small eat-in kitchen. We had our own bathroom in the apartment with a toilet, a sink and a footed bathtub that had a shower. Above the tub ran a silver colored pipe that went up almost to the ceiling and then went around in a large ring holding up the shower curtain.

The apartment had electric lights and an electric doorbell. The kitchen had a gas range that usually but not always lit without need of a match and a real refrigerator, not an icebox. There was a dumbwaiter in the kitchen that we put our garbage in and then pulled the ropes to send the garbage down to the bowels of the building in the cellar.

My parents had taken the smallest, darkest bedroom for themselves. It had one tiny window looking out into the alley between our building and the one next door. From this window, you couldn't see anything but the red brick wall from the adjacent building. My parents both always gave us the best they could, even better than they gave themselves. Marty had his own room with a window looking out onto Chisholm Street. Bea and I shared the large corner room with two windows and two beds.

Standing at the walls under the window sill in each room, were large steam radiators that were painted silver. In the winter, they got hot and when the landlord paid for sufficient coal kept the apartment warm. The steam was made by the coal furnace that was in the cellar. Coal was delivered every week or so by the big coal truck. The coal was sent flying down a shoot through the iron doors that were in the sidewalk in front of the building. There was a mountain of coal down in the basement and to heat the whole building the super used to shovel the coal from the mountain into the furnace.

When I was about six years old, I had gotten the chicken pox during the coldest week of the year. Again, for the tenth time that winter there wasn't any heat in the building. I was in bed buried under the covers even though I had a high fever. My family was walking around in the apartment with their winter coats, gloves, scarves and hats on. You could actually see your breath in the apartment when you spoke. This time my mother didn't just call the landlord to complain; she called the New York City Board of Health.

The building used to be owned by kindly Mr. Friezel. He liked my father very much and whenever my father was short on the rent or needed money, Mr. Friezel would hire him to do some painting in one of his buildings. But Mr. Friezel was old and his son had sold the building and all of Mr. Friezel's properties. The new landlord, Mrs. Sumner was milking the building for every penny. There was never enough coal to heat the building or for hot water. She was a rather stout woman with a mouth that was an ugly gash in the middle of her dour, arrogant face. My mother used to call her a *mahkeshaife* (mock' ke shA fe – a mean woman, a bitch).

The Board of Health was so overwhelmed with complaints from all parts of the city that they didn't always do anything about most of the complaints they received. But this time they actually sent an inspector because there was a very sick child - me. They made Mrs. Sumner fix the boiler and give more heat.

My mother was not an aggressive woman and never started up with anyone but when Mrs. Sumner came and threatened to throw us out if we didn't stop making trouble, my mother shoved her out of the apartment. Mrs. Sumner nearly fell down the hallway stairs. We never had trouble with her again. It was never too smart to start up with my mother and when she was 95 it still wasn't smart.

Even, when I was a little girl I knew my mother had had a hard life. I rarely seemed able to disagree with her on anything she said and not feel badly afterward. I not only wouldn't want to risk her anger, I didn't want to do anything to disappoint her or worse say anything that would have hurt her feelings.

When I was a schoolgirl, we wore skirts and dresses to school. Girls were not allowed to wear pants to school. Pants were men's and boys' clothing. When I went outside during the cold winter months, my mother would force me to wear these ugly pants called leggings. They were thick woolen pants with suspenders. They were the same kind of pants that toddlers wore for snowsuits. I was even expected to wear them when I walked to school. I wore a dress underneath these pants and took them off with my coat when I got there. I thought they made me look like a baby and I didn't want to wear them. Bea didn't have to wear leggings. I couldn't argue with my mother over things like that. She said that I couldn't go outside without them because I would catch pneumonia. Rather than argue with her I would just put them on. When I got downstairs to the ground floor I would go behind the staircase, take off the hated leggings and hide them behind the staircase. I then walked to school freezing but happy. When I came home I would put the leggings on before I went upstairs. Luckily for me I never got caught.

I can still remember worrying about what my mother would have had to say if she found out that my brother, Marty had taught me to eat cracklings (pork rinds) that he bought at Wolf's candy store. Boy, were they delicious! I must have been about five years old and had never tasted anything like that before in my short life. We were kosher and that was the first time I ever experienced disobeying my mother or breaking the Jewish dietary laws. Cracklings are not only not kosher, but it is meat from a pig and unthinkable to eat, absolutely forbidden. Marty told me not to tell anybody because it was trafe (trAfe – not kosher). And I never told anyone until now.

Marty is eleven years older than me; I was always his baby. I have always adored him and would have kept any of his secrets even when I was five. He used to ride me around with him on his bicycle. He bought that English racer bike with his own money. Marty worked unloading trucks after school at Charlie's Fruit and Vegetable Market. He worked very hard to buy that bike and to buy other things too.

There was a knock on the door one day in the middle of the week. My mother opened the door and there were two men standing there with a washing machine. They asked, "Does Freida Mnuskin live here?" My mother said, "Yes, but what is this?" One of the men said "Mrs., it's your washing machine. Where do you want us to put it?" Freida got upset and started shouting at the delivery man, "This is not for me! I didn't buy that thing! What are you doing here? You are in the wrong place. We can't afford such a thing, please take it back. I can't pay you for it." Then Marty walked in behind the men. He said that he had bought it for her, that he had worked at Charlie's Fruit and Vegetable Market and had saved all the money to buy it for her. He was seventeen then. He had watched her scrub our clothes on an old washboard in the bathtub and thought this would be better. Marty knew what a hard life my mother had had. At seventeen, he wanted to do what he could to make it easier for her.

That washing machine did make it easier to do the wash but it didn't do anything for ironing. They hadn't invented the steam iron yet and Freida still ironed clothes like everyone else by moistening them slightly by sprinkling the clothes with a bottle of water. The bottle was from soda pop and she had put small holes in the cap with a nail like most people did.

When Bea was promoted from the sixth grade to junior high school, Bubby Miasha asked her what she would like for a gift. Bea told her that she would really like to have a camera. Bubby Miasha gave her the money to get a little Kodak Brownie. After that, it seemed like Bea was always taking pictures. The first picture she wanted to take was of us. That camera did not have a flash so you couldn't take pictures in the house, but it was sunny that day so we went outside. Bea took pictures of Bubby Miasha, my mother, Marty and me.

[Photo:] (Left to right) Marty, Bubby Miasha, Frieda and Rozzie (me)
standing next to Wolf's Candy Store, on corner of
Bristow and Jennings Streets, the Bronx (ca. 1947)
Photographer: Bea - first picture she ever took with her Kodak Brownie
camera, that was a gift from Bubby Miasha for graduating
from public school

There was always music in our house. When we had company, somebody would suddenly start singing usually Yiddish songs and everyone would join in. But even when we didn't have company my parents used to sing along to the Yiddish songs or the songs of Al Jolson on the records they played on the phonograph or heard on the radio. When Bea was a teenager she played Rosemary Clooney's record, "Come on To My House" and Doris Day's "How Much Is That Doggie in The Window" Bea and Marty both loved to listen to Bing Crosby and Frank Sinatra and the Dorsey brothers. Marty taught himself to play a harmonica and it was always fun to listen to him play.

In 1949, despite all the opposition to the bill, Harry Truman signed the minimum wage law raising the wage from 40 cents to 75 cents an hour. This affected 22 million people whose wages were increased.

Cost of Living 1949
U.S. Bureau of Labor Statistics

General Motors car: $1,750
NYC subway or bus ride: 5¢
gasoline: 27 ¢/gallon
house: $14,500
bread: 14 ¢/loaf
milk: 82 ¢/gallon
postage stamp: 3¢
average annual salary: $3,800
minimum wage: 75 ¢ per hour

I was a little girl in 1948 when my parents got us our own telephone that was in our apartment. In my Aunt Lena's apartment building on Charlotte Street there was a pay telephone on the third-floor landing in the public stairway. My aunt and uncle's apartment was on the fifth floor. When the telephone rang someone, who lived on the third floor would answer it. They would shout out the name of the people the call was for, and frequently who was calling, and what they wanted. Sometimes they even made a comment that rang with sarcastic wit. My cousins Sylvia or Mae would go running down the stairs when they heard their names called out. Everyone knew everyone else's business. But our apartment building didn't have a public phone so my parents got one for us right there in our apartment.

All telephones had party lines, which meant that you shared your phone line with other people. You were lucky if it was only one other person or family. The other people who shared the line were strangers but you had the same telephone number. All the phone numbers started with a word prefix only using the first two letters of the word. Ours was SEdgewick. There was a system where you answered the phone when it rang the number of rings that was designated for you. You weren't supposed to pick it up and listen when it was a different number of rings because that call wasn't for you and you would hear what the other people were saying. In the beginning, we didn't get many calls. Who was going to call us? Nobody had telephones. I used to sit near the telephone just watching it and waiting for it to ring. If it rang I would pick it up and listen with my hand over the mouthpiece even when I knew it wasn't for us. I knew all of the other party's business. Sometimes they realized that I was listening and would yell at me to hang up. Then I did hang up. I laughed. They didn't scare me because I never saw who belonged to these anonymous voices. They were just voices like on the radio.

Later that same year we got a 16" television. It was a Magnavox and it had the largest screen made. Like all televisions in New York City then it only had seven channels; channel 2, 4, 5, 7, 9, 11 and 13 and they could only broadcast in black and white. Televisions used to take a while to warm up when you turned them on. But we weren't impatient because we didn't know that it would ever be different. The day that television was delivered was a day I will never forget. I was so happy and couldn't wait to watch our very own television. I didn't have to watch on my friend Bobby Tellis' set anymore. I could watch ours. Anyway, since I had caught whooping cough, even though I didn't have it anymore, Mrs. Tellis, Bobby's mother was scared he would catch it so she wouldn't let him play with me.

My mother, father and sister Bea were discussing where to put the just delivered television, so that you could see it from every chair in the living room. Marty and his friend George Rosatti walked into the house and went into Marty's room. Nobody paid them much attention, not with the brand-new television to set up. They had after all a very big decision to make. My mother, father and Bea had to figure out how to rearrange all of the furniture in the living room, so the now most important item in the house could be seen from the sofa and every chair in the room. It had to be a place of honor not just practicality. After moving everything around the room three times, they were sufficiently satisfied with where they had chosen to put the television. About a very long half hour later, they plugged it in and we finally sat down to watch. I couldn't wait. But that was when the strange noises started coming out of Marty's room. We could hear what sounded like people talking. It sounded like my mother's, father's and Bea's voices. The whole discussion of where to put the brand-new television was coming out of Marty's room, like on the radio; only it couldn't be coming from the radio. It was like some kind of strange magic. What was happening???? We all squeezed into Marty's room where Marty and George were laughing. They showed us a very peculiar thing. It was a big box with two large spools of wire going around and around on top. This contraption could copy sound, voices and even music and then play it back. George had gotten this box somewhere and then sold it to Marty. That was always a fun machine until the wires got tangled up like yarn but not as easily untangled as yarn. We were already one of the first families around to have a television set. A television and then the wire sound recorder; what an unbelievable, splendid day!

Bubby Miasha, then an old lady who barely spoke English and never really Americanized in any way, could not understand the technology of this new invention of a radio with a picture. At first, she walked around the television trying to figure out what made it work. She used to enjoy watching television with us but could never understand how the same people were in our little box that was in my uncle Abe's little box, and that there were so many people in there.

The program I couldn't wait to watch was *Howdy Doody*, the children's puppet show. Everyone else in my family couldn't wait for Tuesday night; that was *Uncle Miltie* night. On Tuesday night at 8 o'clock if you had a television it was tuned to NBC to watch *The Milton Berle Show*. When the show started in 1947, Life Magazine reported that there were only 136,000 homes in the country that had a television; by 1956 there were 30 million. Tuesday nights anyone who had a television set was on their living room sofa watching "Uncle Miltie" do his funny antics and shtick. He charmed the country with his ridiculous costumes, outlandish sight gags, slapstick and silly props. It was not an unusual thing for him to walk on stage and into our homes through the TV screen wearing an awful dress and carrying a toilet plunger. All the famous show business stars wanted to make guest appearances on that show from Frank Sinatra and Tallulah Bankhead to Berle's friends, Lucille Ball and Desi Arnaz. He gave himself the name "Uncle Miltie" and that stuck because he was like a beloved member of everyone's family spending every Tuesday night with us.

It was an expected thing that on Tuesday nights my Aunt Lena and Uncle Louie would come over to watch and laugh with us at "Uncle Miltie". They didn't have a television. Milton Berle was born Mendal Berlinger in 1908. It never failed that someone in the room, usually Aunt Lena would bring up the fact that Berle was Jewish, like nobody else in the room knew. American Jews were proud and surprised that the whole country was watching "Uncle Miltie" on their televisions even though he was Jewish.

One of our absolutely not-to-be-missed favorite shows was a half-hour comedic drama called "The Goldbergs". This show should not be confused with the ABC television show called "The Goldbergs" created by Adam Goldberg in 2013. The original program "The Goldbergs" was always broadcasted as a live show. It started in 1929 on the radio before it moved to the small screen. It was the first domestic situation comedy on television. "The Goldbergs" wasn't always about funny themes but it was always about the every-day, would be "real life" experiences of an ordinary family living in a tenement in the Bronx. What made it unusual was that the family was Jewish. "Uncle Miltie" wasn't portraying a Jewish man; Milton Berle just happened to be a Jew. "The Goldbergs" were actually portraying a Jewish family. Who would think that anybody would care about a poor JEWISH family living in a tenement in the Bronx? But the country somehow did.

Molly Goldberg, the main character was a stereotypical "Jewish mother". She even reminded me of my mother. She may have bought the dresses she wore in the same store in the Bronx where my mother and aunts bought theirs. They looked the same. Mrs. Goldberg made you feel right at home. Molly was a bighearted, loving *budinsky* with her finger in everyone's business, especially her families. She was a real yenta but not in a mean way. The show would start with Molly Goldberg leaning out the window in the real-life mode of tenement communication to talk to her neighbor, Mrs. Bloom who lived across the air shaft from her. Molly would shout, "Yoo hoo, Mrs. Bloom...." Molly would tell Mrs. Bloom all of her latest news and problems.

Every episode of the show was produced, written and directed by Gertrude Berg, the actor who played Molly. The writing, acting and cast were wonderful. Menashe Skulnick, a well-known comedian from the Yiddish theater was a member of the cast. This show was very real and very Jewish and despite that it was very popular. We lived in a tenement in the Bronx and we could relate to the Goldbergs. But Jewish or not the American public could also relate to this ordinary family who had if not the same kind of lives, had the same kind of troubles that most ordinary families had. We never missed seeing "The Goldbergs".

Sometimes on Sundays, especially when it was warm out, we would take a trip to my favorite place in the world. Where we lived on Jennings Street, it was only a few blocks to Southern Boulevard. We would walk down to Southern Boulevard and either walk up the stairs at the Freeman Street Station to the El train or if the bus was there we would take it north all the way up Southern Boulevard to the Bronx Zoo. The Bronx Zoo is one of the largest zoos in the world. Everywhere you look in the Bronx Zoo there is something exotic to see. The monkeys, the ape always fanning himself with lettuce, the sea lions swimming around in their pool. At feeding time people bought fish and threw it to the sea lions to catch. I loved the zoo. My parents once let me go for an elephant ride. I still collect elephant and monkey *tchotchkes*.   ❧

℘ *Wheat Germ and Waffles* ℘

The most important thing to my mother was food and not just any food. I mean good, wholesome food. When I was growing up, it seemed like she spent most of her time in the kitchen cooking. She loved food and she loved to cook. And if she didn't see you eat, that meant that you hadn't. Hungry or not you were going to eat what she had cooked. My mother always said, to encourage our eating, that the food was good; she had made it herself. That meant she knew what she had put in the pot was of the best quality because she had prepared it herself. She hadn't left the cooking and the selection of the ingredients to someone else's hands. The food my mother cooked was unlike, in her mind, the food one could buy outside of the house that might not only be *trafe* (not kosher), G_d forbid, but even worse to her, not fresh or wholesome. In fact, meat that is not fresh isn't kosher. My mother thought it was very important that food be fresh because it made for healthier eating. Being healthy was a paramount consideration. And she believed that having good food made you healthier. My mother and my Bubby Miasha both used to say, "If you have your health you have everything."

When I was a little girl and we lived on Jennings Street I used to go food shopping with my mother almost every other day so she could buy fresh food. We used to walk the three blocks down the hill and across Wilkins Avenue to the Jennings Street market.

On the left side of the street was Charlie's Fruit and Vegetable Store. Not only was the store filled to capacity with open containers full of produce but they also had open wooden crates standing outside in front of the store that were filled with fresh fruit and vegetables. The overflowing crates looked like a small wind would make it all go tumbling on to the cobblestone road we called the gutter.

A bit further down the block was Jake's Pickles. That was where Jake and his wife used to sell the vegetables they pickled. Nothing more than an outdoor stand, just an alley between two buildings, Jake's Pickle Stand was famous in the Bronx. Anyone who had ever tasted Jake's pickles even once judged them to be the best pickled vegetables in the world. People who moved away from the neighborhood still came back to buy Jake's pickled vegetables. My family still talks about them. I haven't had Jake's pickles since I was seven years old but I can still remember their delicious taste. He had big wooden barrels filled to the brim with sour green tomatoes, sour peppers, sauerkraut and pickles, half-sour and very sour. Jake and his wife worked hard preparing and selling their vegetables, standing outside in all kinds of weather with nothing more than a canvass awning to keep the weather out. Jake's wife always had an angry look on her face like she too had been pickled. No one ever knew her name. Everyone just called her Jake's wife.

Actually, I don't remember ever seeing either one of them ever smile. They were two little Jewish East European immigrants with a very strange way of doing business because Jake was very picky about who he was willing to sell to. But it didn't stop the customers from lining up in front of their barrels. In those days, a most vendors sold things unpackaged and you had to bring your own containers with you. Jake sold the pickles loose. You had to bring your own jars. And if Jake didn't like your jar, if it was too big or too small or he just didn't like the way you asked him for pickles, he wouldn't sell to you. Never mind that you just stood on the long line for twenty minutes waiting your turn for him to serve you. His manner was just as famous as his pickles because you never knew when you got on his line if you were getting what you wanted or leaving empty-handed and everyone knew this.

I was always a friendly little girl and Jake liked me. My mother used to give me the jar and the money and told me what to ask for. She would stand over on the side like she didn't know me. Not only did the people on line seeing me with my jar push me up to the front of the line, just to be nice to a little girl, but Jake always gave me more than I asked for. He would fill my jar and give me a small pickle in my hand.

Across the street there was a live kosher chicken market where my mother bought chicken. It was a narrow store with wooden counters and a wooden floor. Like most food stores the floors were covered with saw dust to absorb any spills or wetness. In the back, there was a chicken plucker. He plucked the feathers off and cleaned the chickens for you. His counter was next to the Dutch door that opened up to where the live chickens were kept in the yard behind the store. My mother didn't buy chicken breasts or drumsticks wrapped in plastic like you do today in a supermarket. She used to buy chickens that were alive and still walking, feathers and all. She would look out the open-top half of the Dutch door and pick out the one she wanted. It was cheaper to buy a chicken that had already been slaughtered but she knew if she bought a live one it was fresher. She saved money by cleaning the chickens herself instead of paying the chicken plucker to do it.

Next to the chicken market was the bakery where my mother bought bread. That is where she got the dark round pumpernickel, seeded rye breads and bagels we loved. On Fridays if she didn't bake the challahs herself she bought them there. The bakery was filled with the aromas from the freshly baked bobkas, cakes and breads. I liked their very large black and white cookies but my favorite was their charlotte ruse. I never see them anywhere today. A charlotte ruse is a delicious, round little piece of sponge cake that sits in a white cardboard cup with a scalloped rim. It is topped with real swirled whipped cream and a bright red maraschino cherry. Occasionally my mother would buy one for us and we would share it while walking in the street.

Next to the bakery there was a large market, with a lot of different vendors inside. They had a kosher butcher in there where my mother bought meat and an appetizing counter on the other side of the market. Staring back at you through the glass window of their counter that separated you from their selection of appetizing foods were the stacks of golden smoked white fish. From that counter, they sold whatever you could ask for from an appetizing store. A kosher appetizing store is a lot like a gourmet deli only they don't sell any meat. A kosher appetizing store sells smoked fish, like white fish, sturgeon and lox, herring prepared in different ways. Like most appetizing stores the appetizing counter in the Jennings Street market sold herrings that were prepared every which way you can think of. They had schmaltz herring, pickled herring, herring in cream sauce, herring in wine sauce. They carried all kinds of salads and also sold dairy, a wide variety of cheeses. The easiest way to describe a kosher appetizing store is to say that they sell what you eat with a bagel.

And halva, they all seem to have different kinds of candies and sweets, especially my favorite candy - halva. I may be mistaken about its origin, but I believe that halva is one of the oldest known confections in the world dating back to 3000 B.C. and was originally from Arabia. The recipes vary greatly from place to place as it is eaten everywhere from the Horn of Africa to the mountains of Nepal and everywhere in between. In some parts of the world halva was thought to have aphrodisiacal effects and to promote fertility. The kinds of halva you find in a Jewish appetizing store are logs or large round cakes made of crushed sesame seeds cemented together with honey. Sometimes whole pistachios or other nuts are mixed in and some are covered in chocolate. I've heard sesame halvah derided as tasting like sweetened pressed sawdust, but I love it.

Behr's Dairy counter was in that market next to the appetizing counter. Mr. Behr stood behind his counter carefully spooning out the sour cream and pot cheese himself that you asked for. He had all sorts of cheeses, cream cheese, Swiss cheese, and the farmer cheese my father liked. He used to cut off the amount of cheese or butter that you wanted from a long bar and wrap it in wax paper for you to take home. Mr. Behr also had cakes and cookies that were dairy cakes. Behr's dairy was where the chocolate seven-layer log cake came from that we liked to eat with a glass of milk as an afternoon snack. We couldn't eat that kind of cake as a dessert after dinner because it was made with cream and at most of our dinners my mother cooked some kind of meat or chicken. It isn't kosher to eat milk and meat at the same time or during the same meal.

The Daitch Dairy was down that same block. My mother liked buying butter from them and sour cream and they had the best cream cheese but my father didn't like their farmer cheese. He preferred the farmer cheese that Mr. Behr sold. The Daitch Dairy was a modern, brightly lit store with a ceramic tile floor. And it was less expensive than Behr's dairy. They didn't have someone serving you from a counter. They had prepackaged cheeses and butter that you helped yourself to from a refrigerated showcase. After you picked out what you wanted you brought it up to a cashier who took your money and put it all in a paper bag that they supplied. This was a more modern store than any of the other stores that we shopped at. My mother carried all the groceries home in her oilcloth shopping bag that she always brought with her.

Usually my mother bought chicken on Thursdays to prepare for Friday night's Shabbos diner. She used to clean the chicken as soon as we got home. On those days, I stayed outside to play because when my mother was cleaning a chicken the whole house would smell of chicken innards and burning feathers. She would cut the chicken open and take the innards out. Except for the liver, the innards and feathers were thrown out. Sometimes there were little unborn eggs inside the chicken. My mother put them aside in the refrigerator to cook in the chicken soup.

When my mother finished cleaning the chicken she cut out the fat that was inside the chicken and made *schmaltz*. Schmaltz is rendered chicken or goose fat. She would put the yellow mass of fat and some cut-up chicken skin in a little pot with some chopped onions and rendered it down until it was liquid. The small pieces of cut up skin became fried and are called *gribbeness*. These tasty little bits of fried chicken skin are a lot like (G_d forgive me), cracklings - fried pork rinds, only better. My mother, like most Jewish cooks, used the *schmaltz* as shortening for cooking anything that was to be eaten with meat. The taste of food that is made with *schmaltz* is indescribably delicious. When my mother finished making the *schmaltz* we would dip a small piece of pumpernickel in the fresh warm liquid and eat it. It sounds awful but it is delicious.

I think my mother's love of food and cooking came from her love of taking care of people and cooking was also a creative outlet for her. If you asked her how she made a particular dish, she would tell you she made it with love. Maybe too it was because she knew hunger and knew that malnutrition caused illness. Whatever the reason she sure could cook.

My mother made most things from scratch. We spent long afternoons shelling peas and peeling carrots and other vegetables, a large portion of this being eaten raw on the spot as we worked. My mother never believed in food that came already prepared and overly processed. I don't think I knew what canned vegetables tasted like until I was about ten, except for Heinz baked beans. We had baked beans when we occasionally had frankfurters and the beans had to be Heinz. I think Heinz baked beans were the only kosher canned baked beans sold at the time.

Even though she was way ahead of her time, it seemed natural for my mother to believe every word that the nutritionist, Dr. Carlton Frederics was saying on his radio show. She easily accepted his teachings that food and vitamins and eating healthy food could make people healthier. Bubby Miasha had taught my mother how to cook when my parents first got married. My mother and Bubby Miasha both believed and often repeated the old Yiddish proverb, "What we put in our mouths we find in our bones" (*"Vus me laykt in der tzainer me gefint in de bainer."*) It rhymes in Yiddish. In other words good food made you healthy.

And both my mother and grandmother objected to the dieting crazes to be thinner. With sarcasm, my mother would say, "Skinny, *shminny*!" or "Diets, *shmyitz*! They'll make themselves sick, then they'll be happy." My mother gave instructions to do everything in moderation including eating when she would say, "Anything you do too much is no good and if you do it too little it is also no good. You need to eat good food to be healthy. And those skinny, mini models don't look normal or healthy."

On Dr. Frederics' say so, my mother started sneaking wheat germ and only G_d, Dr. Fredericks and my mother knew what else into our food. She had to sneak it in because most things didn't taste as good with these new and unfamiliar ingredients. Dr. Carlton Fredericks and my mother took it one step further. They believed that not only neglecting to put healthy food in our mouths was important but what we ate that was bad for us was equally important. Long before the rest of America ever heard about cholesterol, on Dr. Fredericks say so, my mother completely stopped using *schmaltz* and switched to using only vegetable oil. Not only did she throw the chicken fat out with the innards and feathers she now had to buy and pay for vegetable oil. This was not just more expensive but was also a Jewish epicurean hardship because if you have ever tasted a dish that was prepared with schmaltz you would not be too satisfied with the substitution.

As an adult, when I wanted any of her recipes, I had to actually be at my mother's apron strings watching and writing down everything she did. My mother and Bubby Miasha cooked in the ancient way of adding ingredients by remembering how and what and how much to put in. I had to calculate her measurements of the ingredients because she measured everything by her experienced eye. She would say, "Who needs to measure? You need to taste it and feel it, after a while you know how much is right." She would laugh at herself and say she cooked by "a *shiss* and a *giss*". To *giss* is to pour something wet and to *shiss* is to pour something dry, like flour.

Despite the wheat germ and lack of *schmaltz*, my mother was the best cook in the whole family. *Knishes* and *kugel, kreplach, blintzes, kasha* every dish you could think of. Some dishes only my mother and father would eat. My brother, sister and I wouldn't touch some of them – like *petcha*. *Petcha* are jellied calves' feet, too foreign looking for my palette. Or pickled calves' tongues - *feh!* The sight of that would make me run out of the kitchen.

My favorite food was waffles. That was because my mother making waffles meant it was a party; the house was full of people when my mother made waffles. My mother liked to feed all of our friends and both my mother and father always welcomed all of them. My parents were both very friendly people. When our friends came over to our house, my father would say, "Fradal let's bring out the waffle iron." My mother used to say if her children were home in her house with their friends, she knew where we were and she didn't have to worry about us. She happily welcomed and fed our friends. It made our friends want to be at our house.

My sister Bea, Marty and I all had friends of every nationality and race. Our neighborhood was multicultural and multiracial before they coined those terms. My best friend was an African American girl named Judy. She was in my first-grade class. Judy's parents both worked at Bronx hospital. As I remember, they came from Jamaica before Judy was born. Judy and her family lived across the street from us.

I met Judy the first day of school when we were in the first grade. My mother had taken me to school. It was too far for me to walk by myself or even with friends. I went to Public School #54 on Freeman Street, about three blocks from where we lived. Freeman Street is a major street and there was too much traffic for me to cross the street by myself.

As we were walking my mother had given me a piece of candy like she always did on my first day of school, even though it was the first thing in the morning after breakfast. While walking, we met Judy and her mother. Even though Judy and her family lived across, the street we didn't know them. My mother asked Judy's mother if she could offer Judy a piece of candy. She told them that it is a Jewish tradition to give children candy on the first day of school to remind them that learning is sweet. Judy's mother said that would be ok. Judy and I were both very happy to find out that we were in the same first grade class with our teacher, Mrs. Myers.

It was the 1950s - we were in the middle of what was called "The Red Scare" and later called the "Cold War". Russia, technically called the Soviet Union, was trying to convert the whole world to communism. After World War I and then World War II we had the Korean War. The Korean War was the war to stop communism from taking over all of Asia. It was the war of containment, the war to prevent what was called the domino theory. This war was caused by fear. The fear that if Korea fell to the communists all of Asia would fall into communist hands. The "pundits" said it would be like a row of standing dominoes: the first one falling, pushing the rest down and tumbling country after another country into the communist bloc. The real reason was as always, money and power. The Korean War was technically not a war, but a conflict. The U.S. government termed it a United Nations' police action so they wouldn't have to call it a war. For the U.S. to be at war, there had to be a declaration of war by Congress. But Congress never voted on this war. With more than half million Koreans dead, I am sure that the Korean people thought that enough Korean people had died, when the world invaded their country and turned it upside down, to call it a war.

The Russians had already done a test explosion of their first atomic bomb. People were scared. Americans thought we might have an atomic war with Russia. The world knew about how we had destroyed Hiroshima and Nagasaki by dropping the atomic bombs on them, but the general public did not yet know a lot about the dangers of radiation and fallout.

The government decided that the basements were still supposed to be shelters if we were attacked just like they were during World War II. Most of the "shelter" signs had never been taken down. They were still up showing people where the shelters were. They weren't airtight so I don't know what good they thought they were going to do if the Russians dropped an atomic bomb on us. Nobody thought that they would use old-fashioned butterfly bombs or daisy-cutters if they attacked us. There were people who even started building their own shelters, storing food and bottles of water in underground, airtight, cement bunkers. They thought that would save them if the Russians attacked us.

We kids didn't know what to think that first week of school when Mrs. Myers gave us these ugly beaded metal chains to wear around our necks. The chains had metal tags that Mrs. Myers called dog tags. She said that soldiers in the army wore them and that if anything bad ever happened to us or if we got lost, people would know where our parents were. The dog tags already had our name, address, our date of birth, our parents' names and the name of our school already pressed into them. Mrs. Myers said we were supposed to wear the dog tags all the time. She didn't say and we kids didn't know that the real reason we had to wear those dog tags was so people would know who we were if we were killed.

Mrs. Myers taught us, like all the teachers in the New York City schools were teaching their classes, not only what to do in a fire drill, but what to do in the duck and cover drills. The duck and cover drills were like fire drills only we didn't go outside like we did during the fire drills. Mrs. Myers told us that if she or any teacher ever yelled "duck and cover" or if the fire bell kept ringing without stopping we were supposed to drop down, facing away from the windows and crawl under our desks. She said we should put our hands over our heads and keep our eyes closed tight until she said we could come out.

The air-raid drills weren't the only thing that scared us. Mrs. Myers our teacher was rather frightening herself. She was a middle-aged, heavy-set woman with dark hair and dark eyes and she used to make us do what she said by being very mean. When someone did something she didn't like Mrs. Myers would just come over and grab them by the shoulder and just about turn their arm out of its socket. She never did it to Judy or me; mainly she did it to the boys. My mother came to school one day to bring me my forgotten lunch bag. When she walked into the classroom, she saw Mrs. Myers attempting to tear a boy's shoulder off. My mother, never considering the prudence in restraint, told Mrs. Myers to stop it. She told my teacher that it was not right to hurt a child like that and she said it right in front of the whole class. All the kids knew my mother was right and we all silently cheered. My mother went and told the principal about what she had seen Mrs. Myers do to that boy. He offered to change my class. At that time, it was the end of June and only two weeks left to the school year, so I stayed.

Besides Judy, I also used to play with Carmen and her little sister. They lived with their mother in the basement apartment next to the super's apartment in our building. Carmen's mother like my mother was always cooking and taught me to love fried plantains. Carmen and her family were from Puerto Rico and were teaching me to speak Spanish. I learned to count to ten and to be able to say hello, but could never understand what they were saying. They spoke so fast, I never got the gist of it.   ❧

℠ *The Smelly Pot* Ⅎ

❁he only time I remember Bubba Disha, my mother's step mother, ever coming to visit us was when I was sick with whooping cough. Disha came to read the wax. She had to *schlep* all the way from Brooklyn on the El, up to our apartment in the Bronx. I suppose she must have been to the Bronx at other times too, like my brother's bar mitzvah or something, but I don't remember those times.

Except for her father, my mother's entire immediate family had died young. Each of them had been struck down by some kind of illness much too soon. As a result, you couldn't sneeze in our house without my mother getting very upset, and fearing the worst. Being sick and getting over it was not something my mother ever took for granted. Sometimes, when we had a little cold, or some minor ailment, the only thing we would want was to be sick in peace, and suffer through it; but that was not possible. Like it or not, my mother would torture us with remedies and kind care. You could absolutely not succeed at saying no thank you, to my mother. We all learned to hide minor ailments as well as we could, and sometimes big ones. We didn't want her to worry, and we didn't want to be tortured with her kindness. It kept us from ever becoming whiners. Whooping cough being a very serious disease, my mother wasn't fooling around. She was doing absolutely everything the doctor said, plus. My mother was not going to allow whooping cough to get me, her youngest.

I must have been about four years old and I can still remember Bubba Disha coming that day. My father was working, and my sister and brother were at school. Nobody was home when Bubba Disha arrived, except my mother and me.

Bubba Disha took the pot that my mother handed her and heated up some stuff on the stove. It really stunk very badly. When it was heating, this stuff smelled up the whole house. It was the wax. I know because I can still remember the smell. I didn't know what Bubba Disha was doing. I just watched her wondering what she was cooking, and what was going on, not realizing that it had anything to do with me. Then, my mother and Disha sat me down in a chair at the kitchen table, without telling me why. My mother told me to just be quiet and sit still. She said this wasn't going to hurt me. Standing behind me, Disha held the small, smelly pot over my head. While saying words I didn't understand, she swirled the melted liquid wax around in the pot. It didn't touch even one hair on my head. But I was terrified as I sat there silently unable to see what was going on above me. Interested only in what was in that pot, neither of them told me what was going to happen next or what to expect. Bubba Disha looked in the pot, studying what she saw. She told my mother what she saw about me in the designs made in the melted wax, and what it meant. She was reading my future in the waxy swirls. Unfortunately, I don't remember what she said; I was too frightened to listen. She must have told my mother that I wasn't going to die from whooping cough because my mother seemed very pleased. Then Bubba Disha pleased with herself and me, took her coat, kissed us good-by, and went back to Brooklyn.

When my mother (Frieda), and her sister Hasha first came to America, they lived with their father and Bubba Disha on Cherry St. and Jackson Ave, on the Lower East Side of Manhattan. But then Bubba Disha found a better place for the four of them in Brownsville, Brooklyn. They moved around a lot because Disha was always finding a better, cheaper place for them to live.

After my mother got married, Bubba Disha and my zaidy, Barney, moved to a smaller apartment in Brownsville, on Sutter Avenue. That is where I remember visiting them. We used to go on the El all the way out to Brownsville to visit Bubba Disha and my zaidy. I can still remember their building on Sutter Ave. Their apartment was on the first floor of a small two-story row house, all the way in the back of the building. It was down a long, dark hallway on the left side of the staircase. I never went up that staircase, and I don't know who lived there.

You entered my grandparent's apartment right into the front room. On the right, there was a huge wood-burning stove that took up almost the whole wall. They not only cooked on it, but it was the source of heat for their two-room apartment. Stacked on the left of the stove was the large pile of wood. In the corner, they had an icebox. On the other wall, they had a footed bathtub, right there in the front room.

To go to the toilet, as in lots of poor tenements of the time, you had to leave the apartment, and walk down to the end of the hall to the bathroom. That bathroom was a windowless, smelly, dark closet of a room. I hated having to use it. To flush the toilet, you pulled the wooden knob on a long rusty chain that was attached to a large box of water near the ceiling. My zaidy and Bubba Disha shared the bathroom with the Chinese man who lived next door. My father said that his apartment smelled like opium. Bubba Disha and my zaidy had a small bedroom in the back of their apartment. There was a chamber pot under the iron bed that they used at night, so that they wouldn't have to go out to the hall in their bed clothes during the night.

I don't really remember my mother's father very well. I was little when he died, but my sister Bea remembers him always telling stories. She and my brother Marty both remember our zaidy very fondly. They describe him as a sweet, gentle man who was always patient with them.

[Photo:] Frieda Mnuskin (right) and her father, Barney Levine
standing on the stoop in front of the building where he
and his wife Disha lived on Sutter Ave. in Brooklyn
Photographer: Bea Mnuskin with her Brownie camera (ca. 1947)

Marty told me he remembers that when he was little he sometimes rode with my grandfather up on his horse drawn wagon. Once in a while, he took Marty for a ride with him as he rode through the streets of Brooklyn peddling and salvaging old metal stuff. People often paid him to dismantle their things, and take them away. It was a special treat for Marty when our zaidy had to take the horse and wagon out, and took Marty with him for the ride. Zaidy Barney said Marty could help him. Our grandfather, Barney, was about 60, and Marty was about 10 years old when they used to ride together, and Marty thought Zaidy Barney was a very old man.

When my grandfather heard that Marty had learned to fish from the other boys at the Crotona Park Lake near our house in the Bronx, he started taking him to fish at the piers in Canarsie. Marty and our grandfather would walk up to the El, and take the train all the way down to the end of the line, near the Bay. Marty, always impatient, said that he would put his fishing line in, and then take it out, and wonder why there wasn't a fish on his hook. But our grandfather was always patient, and he told Marty that he had to wait.

Bubba Disha died in 1949. She never had any children of her own, just some nieces, her brothers' children, and us. My mother's father used to come and visit us after Bubba Disha died. Many times, my parents asked him to live with us, but he didn't want to. In his senility, and being hard of hearing, he thought my mother was trying to poison him, and wouldn't eat with us. He had overheard my mother tell my father that my grandfather shouldn't eat cakebecause he had diabetes and it would poison him.

My grandfather moved himself into an old age home in Coney Island, right near the boardwalk. Before it was converted into a rest home for seniors, it was the Half Moon Hotel. My mother was very upset, and really angry, because it was so far for us to visit him on the other end of Brooklyn, and he did this without talking it over with her. She wanted him to live with us, or at least somewhere close by in the Bronx. I loved going to see him in Coney Island because it was right near the beach. I could understand why he wanted to live there.

It was August 10, 1955, I was little, and he was in his seventies when he died. My parents would not allow me to go to the funeral. They told me, that funerals were not for children. The whole family went, my older brother Marty, then about twenty-one, and my sister Bea 19 went, but my parents wouldn't take me. Trying to shelter me, they made me go to school that day. I wondered for a long time, but just could not imagine, what went on at funerals that I couldn't see.   ❧

₨ *The Coughing* ₧

*A*fter having whooping cough, coughing seemed to just be a normal part of life for me. I didn't die and I wasn't contagious anymore, but I did cough a lot, and frequently I had a lot of trouble breathing. The doctor just didn't seem to know what to do about it.

Whenever it snowed, my mother had a problem. She wouldn't really let me go outside to play for very long because she thought the cold made me cough more. Sometimes, my mother would bring a bucket full of snow into the house, and let me sit at the open fire escape window sill, to play with the snow that way. I didn't get as cold and wet that way as I did playing with the snow in the street. I could see the other kids playing outside on the other side of the street. They were having snowball fights and building snow men, laughing and having fun. My mother didn't think it was good for me to get cold and wet. I used to beg and she would relent and take me outside for a little while. Sometimes the cold did make me cough but I thought it was worth it. I didn't care; the snow and playing with the other kids was fun.

Once, when I caught a cold with a sore throat, my mother gave me what she said her great-grandfather, Hershel the doctor used as a cure for a sore throat and a cold - a *guggle-muggle*. My family's version of a *guggle-muggle* is hot milk, honey, a splash of whiskey, and a raw egg yolk. Yuck! I can still remember what it tastes like. I hated it so much, but worse it seemed to make me cough even more. I was glad my mother never made me drink that again.

**[Photo:] Rozzie and Frieda Mnuskin, Jennings Street,
the Bronx (ca. 1948)
Photographer: Bea with her Brownie camera**

Dr. Breakstone, our family doctor was a very kind little man. I remember him well with his big mustache, sitting behind his desk, always wearing a brown suit. But he didn't seem to know what to do about my coughing. My parents believed in turning the world upside down if necessary in search of the way to help their children. When Dr. Breakstone didn't seem to know the answers to how to help me stop coughing, my mother started asking other people.

It was my Uncle Max's idea that it was probably the cold weather that made me congested and cough. Max thought that I might stop coughing if we lived in a warmer climate like Miami,

Florida. Uncle Max said that Miami was beautiful and a much better place to live anyway.

My mother was easy to persuade. She always loved the sun and the beach. My father, blond haired with blue eyes and very fair skin, hated being in the sun. He could almost literally get sunburned by looking out the window. But he could be persuaded to move to Miami if I stopped coughing there and it did sound like a lovely place to live. Max made it sound like paradise. My parents decided that maybe Max was right. Even though it was a terrible financial hardship for my parents, my mother took me to Miami that winter to see if I would stop coughing there. My parents had decided that my mother should take me there to see if the warmer climate would help. If I felt better in the warm Miami sun shine, they would move us all to Florida.

Bea was about sixteen then. She had saved up quite a bit of money, and she offered it to my parents to help them pay for the trip to Florida. My parents gratefully took the money and bought airplane tickets for me and my mother to go to Miami.

My mother had cousins who went to Florida for the winter. She wrote to them and they said we could stay with them until we got settled.

So, my mother and I went on our very first airplane ride. Those were the days when it was still exciting to see airplanes fly off. LaGuardia Airport had an observation deck on the roof for people to watch the planes take off and land. The passengers walked out on the tarmac and up a staircase that was rolled over to board the plane. People seeing passengers off would go up to the roof to catch their last glimpse, and watch as their loved ones boarded, and to wave good-by to them.

My mother found a tiny, furnished two-room apartment for us near Collins Avenue, in Miami. It was not far from the beach. After we moved in, she enrolled me in school. My mother was planning to stay about three months just till the winter was over. My parents thought that would be enough time to see if it made a difference in my breathing, and if I stopped coughing.

My parents had a hard time paying for this move so my mother started looking for a job. She hadn't worked in quite a few years, not since before I was born, but that didn't stop her from getting a job. She was walking out of the kosher butcher shop when she saw a help-wanted sign in a kosher-style deli on the street. The sign said they needed a kosher style cook. She went in, and talked the owner into hiring her. I don't know what would make my mother think that she could cook in a restaurant just because she was a good cook in her own kitchen. She hadn't ever cooked in a restaurant before. She didn't even eat in restaurants that often. Who had money for such things, and most restaurants aren't kosher anyway. But none of this stopped her. Despite her tiny size, my mother was a very gutsy woman. She never accepted the idea that she couldn't do something she wanted to do. With sheer chutzpah, and nothing more, when the owner of the restaurant asked her what experience she had before, she told him, "You'll be the first and I promise you won't be sorry. And if you don't like my food after one day, so you won't pay me. What have you got to lose?" He needed a cook badly so he did hire her for the day. As she said, he felt he had nothing to lose.

He did like her cooking. He loved it. She made roasted chickens, chicken soup and *kugels*. A *kugel* is a deep-dish casserole usually made of potatoes and onions or noodles. The customers were licking their fingers. The trouble was that the chickens he gave her to roast weren't really fresh, and she didn't want to cook them. She thought they should be thrown out. Actually, they were too old to be kosher. Food is required to be fresh in order to be kosher, but this deli wasn't kosher. It just served kosher-style food. The restaurant owner told her that they didn't throw anything out and that she should cook them. So, she cooked the chickens a long time and put in so many spices that it disguised the taste. He did pay her and wanted to hire her permanently. Feeling guilty about feeding people what she thought was garbage she never went back.

She then found a job in an ad in the newspaper, working at a luggage factory sewing leather bags. She still hadn't forgotten how to sew on a sewing machine. Sewing that thick leather was hard work but the pay wasn't bad.

My mother loved Florida and so did I. The weather was beautiful but very hot. Thinking that I would be more comfortable with shorter hair, my mother convinced me to get a haircut because of the heat. I had long hair and when it wasn't in two long braids I could sit on it. She took me to a beauty parlor where I was the one sitting in the chair for the first time in my life. I was about seven years old and that was my first real haircut.

My mother always wanted to see things that were unfamiliar to her. She loved going to places that she had never been to before. So, when I wasn't in school, and my mother wasn't working, we went all over Miami together. The first time we went into the city of Miami, I asked my mother if she knew where it was and how to get there. She answered me the same way she always did. "Don't worry there is always somebody to ask. If my sister, Hasha and I could find America, then we can find anything. You too, Rozzie, you can do anything anyone else can do. You just have to try. Don't be afraid."

We took a bus into the city. It went over the bridge called a causeway. My mother and I spent a wonderful day looking around. When we came back, the bus was crowded. We got the last two seats. At the next stop a little old woman with groceries got on the bus. I immediately got up to give her my seat, just like I always saw my parents do. I was surprised, when the old woman and my mother both insisted that I sit down. My mother also motioned me to be quiet. The old woman was a black lady, and this was the 1950s. She couldn't take a seat from a white girl without causing trouble. Neither she nor my mother wanted trouble. When we got off the bus, my mother tried to explain the meanness of the South to me. But I didn't understand any of it. All I knew was that for some reason black people were treated differently from other people in Florida. They were treated like they weren't nice people. I didn't know about segregation in the South with white only bathrooms, lunch counters and even white only water fountains. And I didn't know why any of this was the way it was.

Those were the days when black people were called Negroes or colored in "polite" conversation. Even in New York the word Negro was frequently whispered like it was a secret that nobody could notice if someone was black. But I didn't know that, and I didn't understand. My best friend Judy was a black girl. In my mind, Judy was a nice girl and her family weren't Jewish, but they were nice people. I couldn't understand why anybody would want to be separate from Judy and her family. My brother, Marty's friend Roy was from Jamaica; he was black. He was always fun and very funny. I didn't understand what made them different and my mother couldn't tell me why. She just said, "There are a lot of mean people in the world".

The day after our ride on the bus, when I went to school I realized that there weren't any black kids in my class or anywhere in that school. My mother told me it was a "white only" school and only white children could go there.

The following weekend I had another shock. I found out, for the first time in my short life, that there were people who didn't like Jewish people either for some reason. We were at the beach with my mother's cousins. I told them about there not being any black kids in my school, and what had happened on the bus. They weren't surprised. The cousins started talking about some of the big hotels in Florida not allowing Jews to stay there. They were saying that some of the hotels even had signs outside, right there in front saying "NO JEWS ALLOWED".

But what really made me feel like crying was when my mother's cousin Alkonie, from Halifax, Canada, said that Arthur Godfrey owned one of those hotels, the Kenilworth Hotel on the other side of Miami. There were some hotels that had signs saying no Jews but they said it in code, "select clientele" or "Gentile clientele". They didn't bother to say no Negroes; that was a given. The Kenilworth was one of the hotels that had a sign right there out in front, that left no room for misunderstanding. Its sign read "NO DOGS AND NO JEWS ALLOWED".

Arthur Godfrey was a big TV star, with his own show, a variety show. I used to see him on television, everybody did. His show was very popular. I didn't really watch his show, it was for grownups, but my parents did. It was called "Arthur Godfrey Time". His nickname was The Old Redhead, because he supposedly had red hair. You couldn't tell on TV; all TVs were black and white then.

On the show, Godfrey sat at a long desk sipping Lipton tea from a teacup and talking to his famous guests. He had singers and dancers on. His sponsor was Lipton Tea. Alkonie asked nobody in particular if they thought that the Lipton Tea people were also anti-Semites. My family all drank Sweet-Touch-Nee tea that came in the red and gold tin. It was kosher. The refrigerator people Frigidaire, the Pillsbury Cake Company and Chesterfield cigarettes were also Godfrey's sponsors.

Godfrey was always smiling and laughing and playing his ukulele. The public loved him because he was like a friendly next-door-neighbor. He looked like a nice man. He never said anything bad about Jews on television. Why would he hate Jewish people? He broke my heart. I couldn't understand why anyone would hate us. But even someone famous like Arthur Godfrey hated us? We weren't bad people. We never hurt anyone. My mother couldn't tell me why. I asked, "Why don't they like us Mommy? What did Jewish people do wrong?" Trying to minimize the hurt for me, my mother said, "At least they aren't trying to kill us. Not everybody likes us; so, they don't like us. We aren't going to that hotel anyway. Who can afford such things? In Russia, they wanted to kill us because we are Jews. Here, people are free to say and do what they want, even if we don't like what they say, and even if what they say is mean. This is a wonderful country."

It was the 1950s, I was only seven years old, and I didn't know but at that time Americans didn't think it was unacceptable to have a sign that said, "no Jews". I never actually saw a sign like that, especially not in New York. But anti-Semitism was common in all parts of American society. You could discriminate against anyone you wanted to for any reason and Jews were unwanted. Jewish people couldn't buy homes in "better" neighborhoods even if they had the money. The "Aryans" from Darien didn't want us. Country clubs, where a lot of business was and is done, barred Jews from membership. Jews couldn't get into private colleges even if they had the grades and the price of tuition. There were jobs that were closed to Jewish people. But as my mother said, at least nobody was trying to convert us or kill us.

After two months in Florida, my mother and I went home. This time we took the train north. We didn't move to Florida because despite the lovely warm climate I didn't stop coughing.

In Florida, one of my mother's cousins, I think it was her cousin Bubble, told her about a children's clinic at the Columbia Presbyterian Hospital up in Harlem. It is on 168th Street and Broadway in upper Manhattan.

So, my mother schlepped me all the way downtown, and then up to northern Manhattan on the subway. We walked to the Freeman Street station of the El and walked all the way up the stairs. It cost a nickel for my mother. When the train came, we took window seats and watched as the Bronx went by. We could see the hustle and bustle of Southern Boulevard until the train went down into the tunnel barreling under the East River to Manhattan where it became a subway. The subway stations were dark, dirty and usually crowded and sometimes smelly, but always interesting in a mysterious way. You never knew what you were going to see. There is an entire world under the streets of Manhattan on the subway station platforms. People yelling at one another through the haste of the crowds, mothers shouting at their kids to move along and not get lost. There are all sorts of stores and shops and peddlers selling stuff, from newspapers and candy to men's ties and women's blouses, umbrellas on rainy days. There are panhandlers and performers of all kinds, each with their hand out for coins. Usually I loved to look at all of this but that day I was scared because I didn't know what to expect.

I thought that Columbia Presbyterian Hospital was scary. I didn't like being in a hospital. I didn't know what they were going to do to me there, and I didn't like the antiseptic smell either. After making us wait a very long time, they told my mother that she needed an appointment. My mother told them that she was sorry she didn't know that but we had come all the way there from the other side of the Bronx, and that she had taken me out of school to come. So, they agreed to fit us into the schedule for that day.

Finally, they called us and took me into a room where they asked my mother all sorts of questions. They poked and prodded me and took my temperature. They looked down my throat, into my ears and up my nose. Then they sent me for a chest x-ray. I didn't really know what an x-ray was. It sounded scary and looked even worse. I never saw anything like that machine before except on television. I didn't stop being afraid just because the x-ray lady in her white lab coat said it wouldn't hurt. They wouldn't let my mother in with me. It was only a few minutes but I was frightened there all alone but didn't say anything. I didn't cry. I just did what they said. My mother told me it was OK. I shouldn't be scared they were there to help us. The lady told me that machine could take a picture of the inside of my chest like a camera. It was cold but didn't hurt. They examined me some more and did all sorts of tests. When they were finished, they ushered us into see a doctor.

Finally, this doctor told my mother that I had allergies and that was what was making me cough. He explained allergies to my mother as best as he could. In 1951, the unfamiliar word "allergies" hadn't as yet become part of the American vernacular. I don't know that my mother understood what he was saying any better than I did. We both understood that he was saying that if I was allergic to something then that was what was making me cough. He wrote down all the things that he thought I was allergic to and told my mother what to do about it and how to do it. He told her that if she did what he said I would get a lot better and probably stop coughing.

That doctor told my mother that I was allergic to chocolate and nuts and shouldn't eat them anymore. He also said that I was allergic to feathers and that I couldn't sleep on feather pillows or with my down quilt and neither could anyone who slept in the same room with me. Bea and I slept in the same room, Bea's down quilt and pillows had to go too. My mother didn't tell the doctor, she told me afterwards that it was a lot of money to buy new bedding for me and Bea but they would have to do it.

The doctor also said that I was allergic to cats and dust. Well my mother kept the house very clean so the dust wasn't a problem. The doctor had told my mother that I shouldn't go near cats. He said that I shouldn't even go to someone's house that had a cat. We didn't have a cat because my mother didn't believe in having animals in the house; but my friend Karen had a cat. My mother told me that I wouldn't be able to go to play at Karen's house anymore but that she could play at our house. I said that I liked to play with Karen's cat. The cat's name was Kasha. Karen named the light brown cat kasha because when the cat was sleeping, she would curl up in a ball and look just like a bowl of kasha (buckwheat groats) cereal. I knew I was going to miss Kasha sitting in my lap.

My mother's bigger problem was that the doctor told her that I was allergic to milk. This doctor told my mother I couldn't have cow's milk or dairy products anymore. He said cow's milk was the main thing that was making me cough. My mother told the doctor that it can't be. How could milk make a child sick? She asked how a child can grow up healthy without drinking milk. My mother was very upset. She just couldn't believe it was possible. She didn't know what to do. What would she feed me if I couldn't have milk and shouldn't eat cheese?

I was what she deemed a skinny kid and a very bad eater before this. My mother would not take no for an answer when I said that I didn't want to eat. It was a constant battle between us. She would frequently do anything to get me to eat from nagging to bribery. She believed that hunger and malnutrition were the source of a lot of illness. Now this doctor was telling her that cow's milk was making me sick.

The doctor said that I wasn't allergic to other animal's milk and it wouldn't make me cough if I drank milk from a different animal, like goat's milk. Goat's milk was not sold in ordinary stores. The doctor told my mother about a farmer from New Jersey that sold goat's milk and that he came to the area near the hospital twice a week.

When I heard that I couldn't have milk, I was not unhappy. I hated milk. Before this, my mother almost had to force me to drink it. I never wanted to drink milk unless it was chocolate milk. So, my mother used to put Fox's u-bet chocolate syrup in my milk. I still really didn't want to drink it but it was more tolerable with the sweet chocolate but now I couldn't have chocolate because I was allergic to that too. Frequently my glass of milk would accidentally somehow spill. Sometimes when two days had gone by without my drinking any milk my mother would follow me around the house with a glass of milk and a spoon trying to hand feed me. I hated being nudged so much, even more than the milk. My mother's persistence would succeed in getting me to drink my milk so she didn't stop nagging me in this way. Other people in the family, like my uncle Abe, used to make fun of us. Uncle Abie said that she was feeding me like a baby. He told me, I should just drink my milk and be glad I had milk. He made me feel embarrassed and ashamed. So, when the doctor said that I couldn't drink milk anymore, I wasn't unhappy at all. But that was before I ever tasted goat's milk.

My mother used to schlep all the way to Harlem every week to get goat's milk for me. I think she finally gave up because it was a losing battle. She had to chase me around the house to get me to drink that too. Without the chocolate syrup, there was no way I was going to drink that stuff. I hated that milk more than regular cow's milk. I can still remember that taste in my mouth today. I stopped drinking any milk and I stopped coughing.　　　**ᗑ**

✎ *A Citizen Now* ✎

𝔉ranklin Delano Roosevelt was the first president to give his message to the public on the radio. FDR used to talk to the country on his radio broadcasts that he liked to call his "fireside chats." He usually started with, "Good evening, friends." Like the rest of the country, Frieda and Sam never missed any of these chats. They sat "watching" the radio, hanging on to his every word. FDR told the people about what was happening in the country, and what he was doing to resolve their problems. Their President told them that they had nothing to fear but fear itself. My parents, with their ears glued to his voice, believed him. They knew President Roosevelt would do what he could to make things better, and Roosevelt made good on most of his New Deal promises. He instituted Social Security and all sorts of programs that made life better for the average man.

In this country, when World War II was raging in Europe, most people were on the side of the Allies. But even so, most Americans were isolationists who wanted this country to remain neutral. They were against going to war to save Europe, and wanted the United States to stay out of it. After World War I, they had had enough of war.

Not everyone in America was an isolationist. Many people thought that we would end up in the war eventually, or we would end up speaking German. The Jews who knew about what was going on in Europe tried to convince FDR to do something to help. Afraid of an anti-Semitic backlash, Roosevelt didn't do anything much to help the Jews. My parents didn't realize how little he had done, when he had the ability to do something about the Jews' plight. My parents, like most people, didn't realize that the "great" FDR, the champion of "the little guy," wasn't perfect. They didn't realize that the President and the State Department did not bother to stop Hitler's nightmarish attempt to annihilate the Jews of the world when they could have helped. In those years, my parents couldn't imagine that Roosevelt wasn't doing all he could to save the Jewish people of Europe.

At the end of FDR's second term in office, he decided to break with the tradition set by George Washington limiting the Presidency to two terms, and run for an unprecedented third term. This was not a popular position, but the much-loved FDR won anyway. He ran against the Republican candidate, Indiana businessman Wendell Willkie.

In New York City, there were FDR re-election campaign volunteers on every corner urging people to register to vote so they could vote for FDR. Sam was already a citizen and a registered voter. At his brother Abe's urging, Sam, Max and Lena had become American citizens as soon as they were legally allowed to. Sam had voted for Roosevelt in the previous two presidential elections. With religious zeal, Sam never missed any political election. Frieda couldn't vote. Even though she was very proud of America, and considered herself an American since she first came to this country, she had never actually become a citizen until she met some of Roosevelt's campaign volunteers.

At a Roosevelt reelection campaign rally, one woman, a campaign volunteer, urged Frieda to become a citizen so she would be able to vote. She convinced Frieda that she could study and learn what she needed to know to pass the citizenship test. The kind woman gave Frieda a wonderful little blue book called, "What Every Woman Should Know About Citizenship". It was written in English and Yiddish. Frieda took the book home and studied it. She became determined to become a citizen. She said everybody else here could become a citizen, and she would too; then she could vote like a real American.

[Photo:] Jewish women learning how to vote, Franklin D. Roosevelt Presidential campaign and Herbert H. Lehman Gubernatorial campaign, NYC (ca. 1936)
Photo courtesy of the NYC Public Library Photo Collection

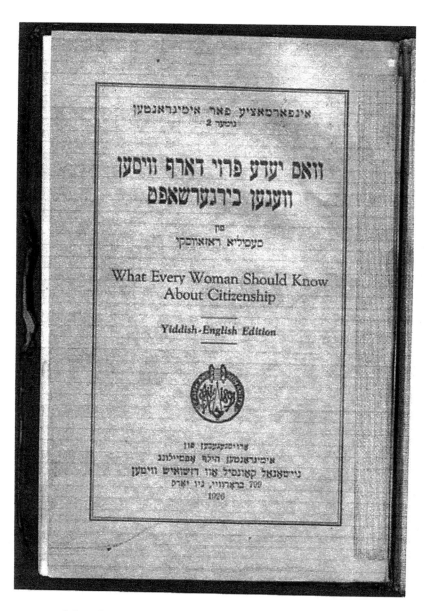

[Photo:] Frieda Mnuskin's copy of the little blue book on citizenship for Jewish women; "What Every Woman Should Know About Citizenship", printed in Yiddish and English (1926). Author: Cecilia Razovsky, Publisher - NY Depart. Of Immigrant Aid, National Council of Jewish Women
Photographer: Roslyn Rothstein

On Tuesday, November 5, 1940, Franklin D. Roosevelt, the Democratic incumbent, defeated Wendell Willkie. January 20, 1941 was Inauguration Day. Franklin D. Roosevelt put his hand on his family's bible as Chief Justice, Charles Evans Hughes swore him in for his third term as President if the United States. Henry Wallace was sworn in as Vice President. On that same day, January 20, 1941 my mother, Frieda Levine Mnuskin, formerly Fradal Valevelsky, very proudly became a United States citizen. She took the oath and said the pledge of allegiance to the flag, along with a room full of about fifty other new citizens and their families, and she meant it.

Four years later, on November 7, 1944, my mother had the supreme pleasure of voting for the Franklin D. Roosevelt/Harry Truman ticket. To use my father's words of delight, "They wiped the floor with Dewey and the Republicans." Frieda never missed voting in any election again in her life.

At the end of 1941, on December 7th, a peaceful Sunday, morning when our soldiers were relaxing, the Japanese bombed Pearl Harbor, and things changed. The next day, America entered the war against "The Axis Alliance" - Nazi Germany, Fascist Italy and the Imperial Japanese. The American soldiers of World War I, were called "Doughboys," but in World War II they were nicknamed GIs - short for "government issue."

Approximately 14 million men and women served in the U.S. Military during World War II; 550,000 of them were Jewish. Most of the Jewish GIs weren't thinking about Pearl Harbor as much as how to stop Adolph Hitler and his Nazis. My uncle Louie tried to re-enlist. They told him he was too old, and besides he had a family. My father, Sam, and his brother Abe were also both rejected by the Army. Sam was labeled 4F because he was colorblind, and also because he was deaf in one ear. Sam's left eardrum had been punctured when he was just a kid in Hlusk. Abie was rejected because he had a rheumatic heart, from having rheumatic fever when he was a boy at Atlantic Park. The army didn't want these three men, but the Navy did. They didn't enlist them as sailors, but they did put them to work in the war effort. My father, and uncles

Abe and Louie spent most of the war painting battle ships destined for combat in the Atlantic.

After the United States joined the war, the country rolled up its sleeves, and got to work in a way never seen before. At the beginning, Roosevelt said we would build 50,000 airplanes. Nobody believed him. This wasn't possible. The United States just didn't have the capacity to do this. But, by the end of the war, Americans had built over 300,000 airplanes and the shipyards had built 60,000 ships, including submarines. And unfortunately, we learned how to build atomic bombs.

The United States was lucky; even though there were German submarines off the coast of Long Island, and California feared a Japanese attack, the U.S. mainland was never bombed. But we did prepare for it. Basements and building lobbies were supposed to be shelters if we were attacked. People volunteered to be air raid wardens during the air raid drills. Signs were put up showing people where the shelters were. When they heard the sirens on the street corner blast, they had to find shelter somewhere indoors. Everyone was supposed to turn off all the lights and stay indoors until the sirens sounded again.

The sound of Tommy Dorsey's band playing and Frank Sinatra singing love songs, helped the country forget about the sound of sirens with - "All the Things You Are", "As Time Goes By", and "Let's Get Away from It All" -

> Let's Get Away from It All
> *Let's take a boat to Bermuda*
> *Let's take a plane to Saint Paul.*
> *Let's take a kayak to Quincy or Nyack,*
> Let's get away from it all.

Long before D-Day and the Normandy Invasion, getting things was no longer a problem because there wasn't any money;

now it was a problem because of the shortages. On behalf of the war effort, the government was sending everything to our soldiers in Europe and the Pacific. There was a shortage of almost everything you could think of from food and clothing, to gasoline.

The Japanese had taken the rubber plantations, so the first thing that the government started rationing other than food was rubber. They started asking people to collect scrap rubber like old tires, old garden hoses, rubber shoes, old raincoats and galoshes. The government wanted to turn these things into new tires for the army jeeps. Macy's Department Store canceled their annual Thanksgiving Day parades from 1942 to 1944, and gave their 650 pounds of rubber balloons to the scrap rubber drive. The shortages weren't as bad in the United States as they were in Europe, but it was hard. The national motto was: "Use It Up, Wear It Out, Make It Do, or Do Without."

Benny Goodman and his band were heard on the radio playing the funny, not really funny, World War II song about the shortages, "Yes, We Have No Bananas".

The shortages and rationing caused long lines when stores did have something to sell. If you saw a line somewhere, you just got on it, because for sure they were selling something you needed, because most things were in such short supply that people needed everything. People just got on line, and waited, and waited, and hoped that whatever was being sold at the front of the line wasn't all gone when they got their turn. If you finally got to the beginning of the line and nothing was left, your complaint to the storekeeper, would always be answered with, "There's a war on, you know!"

One time, when Mrs. Jacobson, our neighbor from the 2nd floor, was downtown, she saw a bunch of people waiting on line, and, of course, she joined the queue. She waited and waited her turn; it was a long line. When she finally got near the front, she saw the line was going into a church, and the people seemed to be coming out empty handed. She asked the lady on line in front of her what they were selling in there. The woman said, "They aren't selling anything. They are giving away ashes. Today is Ash

Wednesday." So, Mrs. Jacobson being Jewish stopped waiting and left the line laughing.

Rationing wasn't the only thing that changed things during the war. Very poor women always worked, but most middle and higher income ladies, especially married women, did not. As the country's men joined the army and went to fight overseas, their middle-class wives and mothers left their cooking and sewing at home and went to work to help pay the bills. Over six million women, from all sorts of backgrounds, left their kitchens and went to work at industrial jobs. They did the jobs that men usually did. They worked in factories, as gas station attendants, in steel mills, lumber yards, and foundries - anywhere they could get jobs. Most importantly, they worked in defense plants, building the ammunition that was needed by the soldiers at the front. The government did what they could to encourage women to go to work to help in the war effort. The 1942 song "Rosie The Riveter", written by Redd Evans and John Jacob Loeb, gave rise to the iconic nickname "Rosie the Riveter" for all the women who did the rigorous work of men.

"Rosie The Riveter"
    by Redd Evans and John Jacob Loeb

All the day long,
    Whether rain or shine,
    She's a part of the assembly line.
    She's making history,
    Working for victory,
    Rosie the Riveter
    Keeps a sharp lookout for sabotage,
    Sitting up there on the fuselage
    That little girl ....

My mother, Frieda, kept talking about going back to work. But Sam wouldn't hear of it. My father believed, like lots of men of his time, that it was his job as the man of the house to bring in the paycheck, and if he couldn't do that, he was no man. And he believed that it was a woman's job to stay home and take care of the house and kids. Sam didn't say that because he knew that argument wouldn't influence his wife. She would not have stayed home for that reason. He kept saying that children need their mother. Sam believed that too. I wasn't born yet; the children he was talking about were my then seven-year-old sister Bea and my nine-year-old brother Marty. Betty Friedan didn't kick off the social movement for women's liberation with her book, "The Feminine Mystique," until 1963. The book announced to the world how things should be different for women and men, if the world was fair. But in 1942, like lots of women, Frieda was ambiguous about what, twenty years later, came to be known as women's liberation. There were things Frieda agreed with, and other things that she didn't agree with at all. Frieda had started working when she was twelve years old, and saw no reason for women to be held back in the workplace. Frieda felt she could do whatever any man could do. She used to say that we just have to convince them that women can do it. We just need a chance. "And you can't succeed if you don't try."

Unlike most American women, who weren't supposed to know how to fix things, Frieda could fix almost anything. It was mainly because she believed she could, and was completely unafraid to try. My mother used to say that you just open the thing up and look inside to see what makes it work. Then you fix what is broken. My father could fix things too, but somehow, men were expected to know how to fix things. Both of them came from shtetlach. The very rugged existence of shtetl life required self-reliance, expecting people to fix their own things themselves.

There was actually little that Frieda thought she, or any woman, couldn't do. Then again, Frieda agreed with her husband and thought it was better for the children if their mothers could stay home and watch them. She said, "I love my children, but being a mother is boring work. But mothers should be home. It isn't good for the children when their mothers go off to work. Who will watch them? Who will take care of them? And the older they get, the more they need to be watched. A baby sitter? A nanny is not like the mother. When Bea and I became mothers, our mother frequently gave us the strict instruction to watch our kids ourselves, saying, "Whose eyes are better than a mother's eyes?"

Even though when Frieda worked she was just a factory worker, she appreciated working. She really liked having the extra money, and she also loved the freedom and independence that came from being out in the world, and not home behind the stove all day. But that didn't stop her from doing all the cooking and house cleaning, even when she did go out to work. Frieda always cooked for my father and us, even when she worked and he didn't. In his life, my father never even cut a sandwich in half. He wasn't any different from his father or his grandfathers. Things were that way since before anyone knew why. Before Sam was married, his mother, Miasha, cooked for him and the family. After my parents were married, my mother did all the cooking. If my mother didn't cook, my father didn't eat. In my mother's mind, it could and should be different. In my father's mind, he thought it demeaning for a man to do housework or take care of the children.

Frieda used to complain that, when their children were small, Sam never "helped her". Their gender based, antiquated shtetl ideas on the division of labor, and all ideas relating to the roles of men and women, were hard for both of my parents to change. Frieda thought that Sam could and should help. But they both thought in terms of it really being Frieda's job to be the *balabusta* (homemaker), and being the bread winner was Sam's responsibility. It never occurred to either of them that taking care of the children and the home and earning a living should be joint responsibilities. Although, ambiguous about the roles of women's lives, my mother was absolutely not ambiguous about their sexual freedoms. A very modest woman, she thought that it was important for people to be married before having sex. Frieda believed that pre-marital sex was bad for women, and their resulting children. She thought that children born out of wedlock weren't good for anybody, and that children needed a mother and a father. Like Bubby Miasha, Frieda also said, "Men don't buy cows when they get the milk for free." She never thought that one day women would think in terms of not needing men for an income, or to give their children their father's name.

During World War II, Frieda decided that she was going to go back to work. She didn't have to listen to her own inner voice, or her husband's arguments against it, because she knew that, like most grandmothers, Bubba Miasha would lovingly take care of Bea and Marty, as well as Frieda did herself. Trusting Miasha to watch the children, she got a job working in a leather-goods factory, making belts for military uniforms. She liked working at that factory, even though the work was very hard. The factory conditions weren't as harsh as they had been when she had first come to America, but it was still hard work. But Frieda liked being out in the world with people, rather than spending all of her time with just the family and neighbors. Frieda and her coworkers in the leather factory worked non-stop from the time they got there until they left at the end of the day. They took a short time off for lunch, and except for taking a smoker's break, that was about it. So, lots of the workers smoked, because it was considered a legitimate reason to take a break. Otherwise, you couldn't just stop working, and go stand around to relax. It just wasn't done – you would be lookeddown on as a no-good loafer. So, Frieda took her breaks by smoking cigarettes like everyone else. She liked to smoke Lucky Strike cigarettes – Luckys for short.

Frieda stopped working after she got pregnant with me, and her belly got big. Her last day at the factory, a bunch of the workers were standing in the hall, taking a break and smoking. They were talking about all the strange beliefs and superstitions people had about pregnancy, and birthmarks in particular. As my mother was walking away to go back to her sewing machine, one of the men threw a piece of leather at her, and purposely hit her on her behind. He had the odd shtetl notion that the baby would have a birthmark, like that piece of leather. He said, "Let's see what kind of mark your kid has on his behind, when he is born." I truly don't have any birthmarks anywhere on my body, except for one brown patch on my *tush*.

My parents were not too well off. They had an eleven-year-old boy and a nine-year-old little girl; they didn't need another baby. As an adult, I once told my sister Bea, I realized that my birth was probably not a happy surprise, and that some of the nicest people were probably accidents. She said that all three of us were. Our parents were never in a position to have any of us, but here we are. Actually, my old-fashioned father was very happy about my birth. It made my mother stop working and go back to the kitchen to take care of the children.   ⍥

Statistics — Just Numbers

My father's formal education was started in cheder (hAy' der n. - Jewish children's school) when he was about three years old. He did very well in his Jewish education, but only had an elementary school education in English, and modern secular studies. Once the family came to America, he had to go to work. He wasn't able to go to school anymore, except at night. In night school, he learned a little arithmetic, and to read and write in English. He was always sorry, that he didn't go any further. The most important thing to both of my parents, but especially my father, was that their children have an education. They wanted us to have better lives than they had, and to be more than factory workers. My parents believed that the key to that dream was a college education. They fanatically hammered that idea into us, and would have done anything necessary, for the three of us to go to college.

We all did go to college. Marty graduated from Baruch City College in 1955. He majored in statistics and got a good job after graduation with a very good salary of $65 a week. When Marty, the first one in the family to go to college, was graduating, everyone was very proud of him, especially my parents. But the one person who was the proudest of him, her first grandson, was Bubby Miasha. "So *nu*, what have you been studying all these years? What will you do with yourself now that you are finished with college, and you are an educated man?" our bubby asked him in her broken English. Not knowing how to describe statistics, or the career of a statistician, Marty told her, in terms that Bubby Miasha could understand, that he was studying numbers. Bubby Miasha, obviously very disappointed and upset, yelled at him in almost pure English, "Numbers! Numbers! A bookie! You had to go to college to be a bookie?"

Marty grew up to be a handsome young man with a Brylcreem soaked curly top that, as the radio commercial claimed, "A little dab'll do ya." He was charming and friendly, and always the life of the party. A lot of girls wanted him, but one of Bea's best friends, Sandy Feldhendler, got him. Bea and Sandy had been friends since they were in the seventh grade. Sandy's father, Milton, and my father had been friends since they were young men in their Bronx neighborhood. Sandy had been Marty's first date when they were teenagers, and then they both went out with other people. They started dating again when they were in college. Sandy went to Hunter College and became a schoolteacher. Marty and Sandy had a June wedding on June 23, 1956. They have three children and six grandchildren.

[Photo:] Marty & Sandy's wedding, June 23, 1956
left to right: Sam, Bea, Morty, Sandy, Marty, Rozzie and Frieda

[Photo:] Celia and Milton Feldhendler,
Sandy Feldhendler's parents the Bronx, (ca. 1933)

Bea also went to City College and became a schoolteacher. While in college, she had a blind date with this boy named Morty Kalin. My mother always said that Morty looked like the actor Gene Kelly. I think my mother just loved the very likeable Morty. Morty was always counting things. After the kids' TV show Sesame Street became popular, Bea nicknamed Morty "The Count" after "The Count" who was also always counting things on that show. And Morty became an accountant. I don't remember who introduced Bea and Morty, but they have been inseparable ever since. They were married on September 8, 1956, two months after Marty and Sandy's wedding. Morty's wonderful parents Anna and Alex, and even his aunt Lily and uncle Harry became part of our family. I can't imagine not having Morty as my brother and Sandy as another sister.

[Photo:]   Anna & Alex Kalin – Passover Seder, our house, 1958

[Photo:] Bea & Morty's wedding, Sept. 8, 1956

In October of 1960, Marty and Sandy had Bruce, the first grandchild. Six months later, Bea and Morty had a little girl, named Lesli. Seven months after that, Marty and Sandy had another baby, Lisa. With all these grandchildren around, we all started calling my parents, Bubby and Zaidy. Lesli was three, when Bea and Morty had another baby, a boy named Evan. Marty and Sandy bought a house in Westchester and gave birth to Eliott. They didn't stay in Westchester long. In 1970, Marty got a job he couldn't refuse in Denver. He, Sandy, and their three kids, moved west to Colorado.

Their children are all grown now, and they have six grandchildren. Bea and Morty bought a house and moved to Rockland County. They enjoy that house, and they have been living there ever since. Bea and Morty are also grandparents now and have two grandchildren.

When Lesli was an honor student in high school, she raised a baby chick from an egg that she had incubated as a science project. She named the chick E.G.G. The chicken went home with Lesli, and E.G.G. lived with the Kalins as a family pet. My mother said that E.G.G. looked just like Kuriza, the pet chicken she had when she was a little girl in Europe.   ◯

❧ *Back to Manhattan* ❧

*I*n 1970, Sam retired because his knees were worn out and unwilling to cooperate with him. He had arthritis and couldn't work anymore. He was 64 years old. After World War II, my father left the painting business, and had become a hard wood floor finisher. He spent most of his life crawling around on new wooden floors with a shellac or stain brush in his hand. Now the pain in his knees made it hard for him to even walk, let alone crawl around on all four, staining and varnishing floors. My parents had to move from their third floor, walk-up apartment because my father couldn't walk up and down those stairs anymore. They had lived in the apartment near Burnside Avenue for many years. It wasn't paradise, but they were used to it. It was home. When my father retired, my parents moved from the Bronx to the Upper West Side of Manhattan. There, they found an apartment they could afford, in
a building with an elevator. And the Upper West Side is not as hilly as their Burnside Avenue neighborhood where they lived in the Bronx. In Manhattan, it was much easier for my father to get around.

Moving to Manhattan was a very hard move for my parents. But it wasn't just the physical moving that was hard for them. Frieda and Sam had each lived in New York City since they were kids and had gotten off the boat at Ellis Island. But for most of their adult lives, they lived in the Bronx. The Bronx is not Manhattan. Most of the Bronx is much quieter than, and not as crowded as Manhattan. Frieda went into culture shock. Now she couldn't stand the noise, the dirt and crowds, the tumult of Manhattan. She wanted to move back to the quieter Bronx. They didn't move back, they eventually got used to the energy of New York, and learned to love it. My parents had some of the best years of their lives there.   ଔ

ೞ *The First Tuesday, After the First Monday in November* ೞ

My parents, frequently used to schlep on the train from the Bronx, and later Manhattan, to visit us up in Westchester, especially if one of my two kids was sick. My kids adored my parents. Their bubby and zaidy were always there for them, with shopping bags full of tasty food, hugs, kisses and stories. After a few months of living in Manhattan, their bubby and zaidy became too busy to come to Westchester very often. Frieda had found that they had lectures and inexpensive kosher lunches at the Jewish senior citizens' center in their neighborhood. At first, my father was insulted at the idea of being old enough to go to anything having to do with senior citizens, and absolutely refused to go. He said he had plenty of time before he was going to go to a place for old people. He was too young. In my mother's typical way, she said that she was going, and, if he didn't want to join her, he could sit home alone. As usual, that threat worked, and Sam reluctantly went with her.

Since the time I was born, I thought my father's name was Sam. Everybody, the whole family, always called him Sam. He used to receive mail that was addressed to Sam Mnuskin. My mother, his sister, Aunt Lena, his brothers, Abie and Max, and even Bubby Miasha, when she was alive, called him Sam. The whole family called him Sam. My cousins all called him Uncle Sam. They all thought the name being the same as "Uncle Sam", the American icon, was very funny. It wasn't until my father retired, that I realized that his real name was not really Sam, but was Solomon.

When my parents started going to the senior center, my father started introducing himself as Sol. It was then, that I heard the story about his name being changed to Sam for his initials - Solomon Alex Mnuskin. He didn't like being called Sam, but he accepted it, and Sam stuck for almost fifty years. Moving to Manhattan and a new life in retirement, he took the opportunity to recapture the use of his real preferred name - Solomon.

This new man, Sol, found out, that at the senior center, he was really needed. He and my mother were able to help people who were much older than they were. And they both became very involved with the West Side Senior Center. They were elected officers of the center and were on many committees. When the center moved to another location, Frieda was elected the first President and two years later, Sol was elected Vice President at the new center. My mother, Frieda, was always outspoken and courageous in what she felt was right, and in her own way, very eloquent. Even at 90, if you showed her a mike, she could still do twenty minutes impromptu. Sol, an officer of the center, worked very hard, but did not like to speak publicly himself. He always pushed his wife, Frieda, to go talk. Sol was very proud of her, as she was of him.

After they moved to Manhattan, my parents also became very involved with their synagogue, Congregation Shaare Zedek on West 93rd Street. It is around the corner from where they lived. My father started going to the morning minyan every day. He never had time to do that when he was working, because he used to leave the house at five in the morning to go to work.

My father, Sol, now started his days by getting up early to make the morning *minyan,* and after that he went to the Senior Center. He got to the center before most other people because he supervised all aspects of the preparation of the lunches made in the center's kitchen. He was their volunteer, unpaid, but official *moshgiach* (mosh gE' ock). A *moshgiach* is the necessary inspector that ensures that a restaurant or public kitchen is kosher, and strictly adheres to the many, and complicated Jewish dietary laws. Sol also arranged for a bus pick-up for shut-ins, so they could get to the center. It enabled disabled shut-ins to leave their homes, go to the center where they had a hot lunch and an enjoyable day with other people. Sol rode that bus every Thursday to make sure that everyone on the bus was OK. He continued doing this even when he was walking with a cane and in a great deal of arthritic pain himself. Sol stopped going on the bus for shut-ins when he became very ill and wheelchair bound.

Until then, both Frieda and Sol also spent a lot of time raising money for UJA- Federation. UJA supported and helped fund all of the activities that they were involved with. Their beloved senior center wouldn't exist without UJA. So, you knew where they were every "Super Sunday" - UJA's annual fundraiser. My parents spent one Sunday on the telephone each winter when UJA has their annual phonathon, calling people to ask for donations. Not many people could say "no" to my parents begging, them to help UJA.

As far back as I can remember, the first Tuesday after the first Monday in November, - Election Day, was almost like a holy day in our house. My parents cherished their right to vote. Frieda and Sol always knew who all of the candidates were and the importance of all of the issues. My mother would wait for my father to come home from work to go vote, and then they would go together. When I was little, they took me too. One of them would take me into the voting booth with them and show me how to vote. They would let me pull the lever to open the curtain and register their vote. My parents insisted that I learn the importance voting.

Franklin D. Roosevelt, and especially Eleanor, were my parents' heroes, even long after the Roosevelts had died. My parents were lifelong Democrats. People talk about the voters who vote a straight party line; that was my parents, and with few exceptions me too. My father, to use the cliché, would literally have voted for the Democrat running for office even if they put a dead man on the ticket. My father always said that it wasn't the candidate that was important, but the party. You should have heard him when the first time I was eligible to vote, I very idealistically voted for John V. Lindsey, a Republican, for mayor of New York City. And then I did something even more awful in my father's mind; I convinced my mother to vote for Lindsey, too. My father fumed. I think he finally forgave me when Lindsey changed parties, and became a Democrat.

So, it wasn't a big surprise when both Frieda and Sol became involved with New York City politics. It was a natural outgrowth of their work with the senior Center, because politicians were always campaigning there, and asking for help with their elections. Seniors are not only eligible voters, but when motivated, actually go out to vote. My parents became particularly involved with the politics and issues that affect seniors, but also worked to promote other worthwhile social issues, even if the causes they believed in didn't affect them personally at all.

They were both tireless in their efforts to support the causes they believed in, like universal health care and affordable housing. Campaigning for health insurance for everyone was an ongoing thing. They both fought for this, even though they didn't need it for themselves. They had health insurance through my father's union and Medicare, but they knew what it was like before health insurance existed. My father used to say, "This is a very rich country. Healthcare should be done the same way we have the police and fire departments when we need them. We should have doctors and hospitals like that too. Sol used to say, "Health care should be free like libraries, roads and schools - why not health care? They have this in other countries. Congressmen and their families have free health insurance, with dental too yet. Why shouldn't everybody?"

My father wrote to his Congresswoman, Bella Abzug, in support of a national health insurance bill and she wrote back to him. Thirty years later we still have millions of people who don't have health insurance, but it's not called politics for nothing.

BELLA S. ABZUG
20th District, New York

COMMITTEES:
GOVERNMENT OPERATIONS
PUBLIC WORKS

Congress of the United States
House of Representatives
Washington, D.C. 20515

October 15, 1975

WASHINGTON OFFICE:
1507 Longworth Office Building
Washington, D.C. 20515
202-225-5635

DISTRICT OFFICES:
152-7th Avenue
New York, N.Y. 10001
212-620-6701

725 West 181st Street
New York, N.Y. 10033
212-840-0136

720 Columbus Avenue
New York, N.Y. 10025
212-850-1900

Mr. Solomon Mnuskin
176 West 94th St.,
New York, N.Y. 10025

Dear Mr. Mnuskin:

Thank you for your letter urging me to support the National Health Insurance Bill, H.R. 21 and 22.

As you may know, I have been a long time proponent of National Health Insurance and of this bill. In 1971, I joined Senator Kennedy and Congressman Corman to co-sponsor the original Health Security Act. Again, in 1974, I became a co-sponsor of H.R. 22, the Griffiths-Corman Health Security Bill. I have repeatedly testified before the House Ways and Means Committee, in order to voice my support for a national system of health care.

At the moment, H.R. 22, of the 94th Congress, the Kennedy-Corman Bill, of which I am a co-sponsor, is pending in the Ways and Means Subcommittee on Health. Once again, I plan to testify before the Subcommittee when the bill comes up for public hearings on November 5th. I will stress the point that there must be public scrutiny, public accountability and public control over all aspects of health care.

Thank you for writing. You may rest assured that I will do all I can to insure the passage of some form of adequate national health insurance, the first step in the direction of quality health care for all Americans. Again, thank you for your interest and best wishes.

sincerely,

BELLA S. ABZUG
Member of Congress

BSA

THIS STATIONERY PRINTED ON PAPER MADE WITH RECYCLED FIBERS

[Letter:] Response from Congresswoman Bella Abzug to Solomon Mnuskin for his request to her to support universal health care (Oct. 15, 1975) author's own collection

My mother, Frieda recognized for her outspoken ability to tell it like it is, was invited to join the board of JASA, the Jewish Association of Services for the Aged. Frieda and Sol were sent as delegates representing JASA to Washington, DC, to campaign for reduced fares for seniors on public buses and subways. In Washington, they met their Congressman, Charlie Wrangle, and other officials. Frieda and Sol joined the group that went to the New York State capital in Albany to campaign for reduced fares for seniors. They felt proud of their efforts when the bill was finally passed, giving seniors the right to half price fares during non-peak hours on New York City's public buses and subways.

They worked hard for many other good causes too. My parents were always working for tenants' rights, even though this too was not an issue that affected them. Frieda was part of a group that went to support their wonderful State Senator, Leon Bogues in his fight for tenants' rights. The delegation met with him in his office in Albany. Leon Bogues' district was Harlem and Manhattan's Upper West Side, where my parents lived.

In 1976, Frieda and Sol worked to get Jerry Nadler elected to the New York State Assembly. They believed he was a good, honest man and on the right side of all of the issues that they fought for. Even though my parents were just neighborhood volunteers, both Scott Stringer and Jerry Nadler came to my parents' home on quite a few occasions. Frieda and Sol were very excited when Jerry Nadler won the election. My mother used to say, "Scott Stringer is such a nice and hardworking young man. He will go far." Today Scott Stringer is the NYC Comptroller, and Jerry Nadler is a very courageous and wonderful U.S. Congressman. My parents would be very proud of them both.

**[Photo:] Frieda Mnuskin meeting NY State Senator Leon Bogues
in his office, Albany, New York (ca. 1984)**

In 1978, under President Jimmy Carter, New York City was given a special grant by the Federal government. The City created a special policy board of advisors made up of representatives from local political districts. This board was going to advise the City on how to distribute the grant money. There was a special election to choose the board members. Frieda was asked to run for the position as the representative board member from her district. Campaigning all over her neighborhood, she, with her husband Sol and his cane at her side, went to every synagogue, church, and meeting place where they would let her speak.

This tiny woman, who was born in an almost medieval village in a house with a thatched roof, on the other side of the world, and with very little formal education, went all over the Upper West Side of Manhattan giving speeches and meeting people. She believed that the grant money should be spent for after school programs for the children. Frieda thought it would not only enrich the children's lives, but would also keep them safer in the afternoons, instead of them being on the streets. Plastering the Upper West Side with her campaign posters and giving out her campaign buttons, Frieda and Sol were tireless in their efforts to get her elected. My mother gave impassioned speeches, telling the voters what she thought should be done with the money wherever she could get people to listen to her.

It was quite a thrill to see my mother's political posters hanging in storefront windows all over the Upper West Side. It was a bigger thrill to see her name, Frieda Mnuskin, on a real New York City ballot, at the official New York City polls. Not living in their neighborhood, I couldn't vote for my mother, but I proudly went with my parents to see them vote. Frieda was elected and then re-elected for a second term. I hate to tell you, but the third time she ran, her opponent, a much better known woman in the area, won.

VOTE

for your local AREA POLICY BOARD or
the city-wide COMMUNITY ACTION BOARD.

NOVEMBER 30, 1983

Area Policy Boards will recommend the programs to receive Community Action
Funding by New York City's Community Development Agency.
You need not be a registered voter to vote but you must be at least 18 years of
age. You must have proof of residency and must provide signature verification.

Manhattan 7, 3 Candidates	Manhattan 7 At Large Candidates	Region 10 Candidates
Freida Mnuskin	Vicki Morris	Idalia Richards
Georgina Falu	Constancio Soto	Vincent Ruiz
Lydia E. Padilla	Carlos M. Prats	Charles J. Smith
Janet Tolbert	Joseph H. Moskowitz	Theodore Kazantzis
Jesus Allende		
Aurora Flores		
Lena Alexander		
Diane A. Correa		
Fernando Luis Alomar		
Ramona Intriago		

Polling Sites

P.S. 179 — 140 W. 102 St.

P.S. 163 — 165 W. 97th St.

P.S. 118 — 92nd St. Bet. Amsterdam
& Columbus Ave.

Nursing Home — 120 W. 106th St.

Phelps Houses — Community Room
Columbus Ave. Bet. 88th and 89th Sts.

For more information call
ELECTION HOTLINE: 219-0770

The City of New York

GET INVOLVED IN YOUR COMMUNITY!

[Political poster:] Area Policy Board Election Campaign – 1983
(Frieda Mnuskin listed 1st, far left column)

**[Photo:] Frieda's campaign button for the Area
Policy Board Election 1983 Campaign**
Photographer – Roslyn Rothstein

The summer of 1981 was both Sandy and Marty's and Bea and Morty's 25th wedding anniversary, and later that fall was my parents' 50th wedding anniversary. Our family had a lot to celebrate. The whole family came in from all over the country, and we had a party. It was held at El Avram, a kosher nightclub in Greenwich Village. We had a very good time, especially Morty. There was a belly dancer performing, and she chose Morty to dance with her. In his glory, Morty blushed all the way across the dance floor.

[Photo:] Solomon and Frieda Mnuskin (Zaidy & Bubby)
50th Wedding Anniversary, El Avram, Manhattan (1981)

JASA honored Frieda and Sol later that October with a 50th wedding anniversary celebration. It was a thank you for all of the work they had both done. The luncheon was held at their Senior Center. There was music played by an accordion player that had been hired especially for the occasion. At the dais were the top officials from JASA. They were there to honor Frieda and Sol Mnuskin. They gave speeches extolling all of my parents' hard work to better society, and especially their work for JASA and the Senior Center. Every table was filled with the members of the Center, most of them my parent's friends. It was truly very moving to have my parents honored in this way.

[Photo:] Frieda & Solomon on their 50th Wedding Anniversary - October 1981

In 1982, during Ronald Reagan's presidency, Reagan infuriated people by saying that ketchup could be considered as a vegetable in school lunch programs for children. Despite this, he was honored at a black-tie affair at the New York Hilton by the National Conference of Christians and Jews. They awarded him the annual Charles Evans Hughes Gold Medal for being a great humanitarian. New York Democrats were so outraged that they decided to hold an alternative luncheon honoring people they considered to be "real" great humanitarians. The New York City Coalition for a Fair Federal Budget held a Humanitarians' Award Luncheon in protest where they served cheese, ketchup and water. Frieda was chosen as one of the five people, they honored as great humanitarians.   ❧

embraced in the courtroom jury box, and   reuder is currently serving a jail sen-   Bradshaw, 76, was found d

Protesters mock Reagan award dinner ceremony

By RICK HAMPSON
Associated Press Writer

NEW YORK (AP) — Protesters organized a dinner of cheese and ketchup that mocked a black-tie affair and 10,000 demonstrators surrounded a hotel where President Reagan accepted a leadership award some religious leaders said he didn't deserve.

Tuesday night's protest, which police said was the biggest here since demonstrations outside the 1980 Democratic National Convention, was sparked by Reagan's visit to the New York Hilton in midtown Manhattan to receive the annual Charles Evans Hughes Gold Medal awarded by the National Conference of Christians and Jews.

The decision to award the medal to Reagan stirred dissension in the conference.

The award honors "courageous leadership in government, civic and humanitarian affairs." Irving Felt, president of the conference and of Madison Square Garden, said the award was non-political and cited the president's "uncompromising courage in dealing with inflation."

But Donald McEvoy, the organization's senior vice president for national program development, attended an alternative function to the NCCJ's $250-a-plate fund-raising dinner because he was,

AP Photo

An estimated 10,000 people joined protest against award given president.

"ashamed." He said he cared "for the victims of the administration's policies."

At a news conference in the morning, a group of Christian and Jewish leaders accused Reagan of cynical disregard for the poor and of being an "arch-supporter of the violation of human rights."

The Rev. Robert Kennedy, social action director for the Roman Catholic Diocese of Brooklyn, said calling Reagan's policies

humanitarian debases the "meaning of the English language."

At the alternative luncheon, held at Fordham University's Lincoln Center campus, Rabbi Arnold Wolf renounced the brotherhood award he got from the NCCJ 20 years ago, saying the award to Reagan had dishonored his own.

City planner Elinor Guggenheimer said she was returning her 1974 award, "which I thought I would treasure all my life.

"But I simply cannot think of one instance in which (Reagan) has been concerned with a single humanitarian thought or action," she said.

The menu was cheese, to symbolize surplus cheese the administration gave to the poor, and ketchup, because of a suggestion that ketchup was an appropriate vegetable for school lunches. The suggestion was later withdrawn by the administration.

Boston still has questions about black man's death

BOSTON (AP) — A blood spot on a commuter train and the driver's recollec

died, protesting his death and racism.
But Suffolk County District Attorney

ADJACENT TO N

Quality Care at A

Professional Dental Se

[Photo:] NY Daily News article with photo of 10,000 people protesting President Ronald Reagan being given an award for being a great humanitarian, written by Rick Hamson, Assoc. Press - 1982

❧ The Days of Awe ❧

My father's last couple of years was spent at home as an invalid. Despite the fact that my mother spent all of her time cooking for him, so that he would eat a thimble full of food, and nursed him constantly around the clock, in 1987 my father developed pneumonia and died.

He died the day after Rosh Hashanah, September 26, 1987, at the age of 81, thirty-five days short of his 82nd birthday. It was during the Days of Awe. It is believed that during the Days of Awe, the gates of heaven are open. During this very special time in the religious Jewish calendar, it is believed that it is easier to ascend to heaven. My father probably knew the Days of Awe were coming and waited till then to die.

To Jews, the Days of Awe are different from the rest of the year. The ten days starting with Rosh Hashanah, the Jewish New Year's Day, and ending with Yom Kippur are known as the Days of Awe, or the Days of Repentance. It is a Jewish belief that G_d has "books" that He inscribes with our names during the Days of Awe. These books hold the archives of our futures. Here it is written who will live and who will die, who will have a good life and who will not for the next year. During these sacred days, Jews contemplate their behavior, their sins during the past year, and try to repent. We beg G_d for forgiveness for our sins against him, for not being a good person, and for not fulfilling the 613 commandments in the Torah.

This repentance is between ourselves and G_d. Our sins against other people must be settled with them. We are supposed to ask the person we have offended for forgiveness, not G_d.

During the Days of Awe, time is taken to give charity and to do good deeds before Yom Kippur. The Jewish people believe that the "heavenly books" are sealed at sundown on Yom Kippur until the following year. This belief of G_d writing in books is the source of the way Jews wish each other a good new year during the Jewish High Holy days, with the greeting: "May you be inscribed and sealed for a good year" (*"L'shanah tovah tikatevv'taihatem"*). It is usually shortened to *L'shanah tovah* ("for a good year").

After the initial shock of losing her husband and constant companion of 56 years, Frieda resumed her political activities and started going to their beloved senior center. She became quite active again.

In 1990, after the Ellis Island Immigration Center had been closed for over 36 years, it was reconstructed and reopened as a national immigration museum. Bea and Morty arranged to have my parents' names, as well as Morty's parents Anna and Alex Kalin's, and Morty's Aunt Lily and Uncle Harry Weissman's names inscribed on the Ellis Island "American Immigrants' Wall of Honor".

Marty and Sandy took my mother there the following summer, when they came from Denver to visit New York. My mother was overwhelmed when they entered the Great Hall. She walked around, and almost immediately, recognized the bench where she and her sister Hasha sat over 70 years earlier. Frieda went and sat down, no longer the little girl Fradal, but a lifetime later a grandmother and great-grandmother. Marty took her picture.　　ⓒ঩

**[Photo:] Frieda Levine Mnuskin at Ellis Island, summer 1991
She is sitting on the same bench she sat on when she
first cameo Ellis Island as an immigrant little girl in 1921**

**[Photo:] Frieda Levine Mnuskin at Ellis Island –Frieda finding her
name on the Wall of Honor, with view of Manhattan
and the World Trade Center - summer1991**

❧ *It Could Be Kindness* ❧

When Frieda was about 94 years old, having trouble breathing, and needing constant oxygen, she was taken from the hospital to the Northern Manor Geriatric Center in Rockland County. Frieda couldn't remember as well as she had, but she never lost her sense of humor. While she was living at Northern Manor, we each went to see her at least once or twice a week, and usually took her out to eat at a nearby kosher restaurant. One day, while at the deli, my mother said she was going to the rest room. Knowing she got easily confused and might not be able to find her way, I offered to go with her. Still feeling her invincible self, she said, "Sit down Rozzie. I found America, I can find the bathroom."

The staff at Northern Manor loved this lady. They couldn't have treated my mother much better if she were their own mother. They knew her to be witty and charming. The staff also knew that she was still an iron-willed lady. Wheelchair bound, and despite her tiny size, she had a stubborn streak, and was still unwilling to put up with nonsense. Yes, she was feisty, and not willing to do whatever anyone said just because they said it, but she was also very grateful for everything they did for her. Most of the seniors there were impatient and demanding, but Frieda wasn't. She never failed to thank the people who helped her. When her difficulty breathing made it hard for her to speak, she thanked the staff by throwing kisses to them. The people who took care of her at Northern Manor were from varied cultural and racial backgrounds, but they all seemed to relate to this tiny little woman, with a Yiddish accent who was thanking them by throwing kisses.

One day, Bea asked our mother what she thought was the most important thing in life. She surprised us. Knowing our mother, we would have thought that she would have answered, the family and the *annicklakh* (Ain' nick lockh - the grandchildren), or education, or democracy and freedom. But she didn't say any of those things. Frieda said, "KINDNESS."

My mother saying this one very powerful word, rang in my mind, and in my heart and changed me. I would like to think that I am a kind and generous woman. I hope I have learned something from my parents. But, there are those people that one meets in life, that are not nice people. And there have been a couple of times since hearing my mother's words when I had good reasons to be very effectively mean, and anything but kind. Remembering my mother's words, almost like instructions, stopped me. It was very odd. Each time this has happened, a strange feeling came over me. It is a feeling of empowerment that replaces the hurt of being wronged. Being able to be kind, by not returning meanness when I was able to, made me feel good. My mother's lesson of kindness was a gift. Even with some of my mother's last words, her wisdom and power made things better.

Lately, as I think about how horrible people are to each other on a global level, I think of my mother's words of kindness, and what it could be like if our world's leaders learned her lesson. President Bill Clinton had talked about the prosperity of peace. It seems we could have that, if our leaders could stop the killing over nothing worth fighting for.

At the end, Frieda had congestive heart failure. As she would have said, "You shouldn't know from it!" It made her feel as if she was drowning. In the hospital emergency room, and with no one able to do anything much about it, she kept begging for help. Drowning in her own body, she kept desperately yelling out, "Help!

Help! Help me!" – just as someone does when they are drowning in an ocean of water.

We took her back to Northern Manor and called Hospice. One of the Northern Manor nurses, a very kind Catholic woman who didn't believe in the aid of Hospice, said it wasn't right to play G_d. I told her that we "play G_d." every time we try to save someone's life by giving them medicine or performing surgery to save their lives. If she thinks those things are the right things to do, then so is the kindness of Hospice. Hospice's staff made my mother feel better. Frieda stopped feeling as if she was drowning. And they taught our family how to allow my mother to die, by giving us the right words to say – all true. They taught us to tell my mother, that it was OK for her to leave us, that she had done her job, and that she and my father had made us the people we are. I made my mother laugh, and gave her some gratification when I said, "You even made us Democrats."

Thank G_d, for the kindness of the people from Hospice.

My mother died on the 18th of Adar, 5765 - March 29, 2005, at the age of 95. We should all die as my mother did – relatively healthy until the end, and surrounded by people she loved who adored her. ❧

৯০ *Our Legacy* ৫

Our legacy from this 95-year-old woman, who was born with the tragedy of anti-Semitism, war and bloodshed without rationale in her DNA, is her instruction to us to be kind at every turn, and at every level. We can, we must, learn to substitute kindness for retribution, for blind prejudice, for anger and, most important, for war. The poem below was inspired by my parents' words and their wisdom.

IT COULD BE KINDNESS

by Roslyn Mnuskin Rothstein

> It could have been a schoolhouse
> It could have been a highway
> It could have been a new way
> It could have been a talk down
> It could have been kindness
>
> Instead it was a cruel word
> Instead it was a murder
> Instead it was a bombing
> Without reason

Instead it was bloodshed
Always the bloodshed
Fighting without reason
Need another way

People are different
All very different
All want the same thing
Life without bloodshed
Life without fear
Life free of hate
A smile for the children

Billions of dollars
Millions of lives
All blown up in bombings
Shredded happiness and tears
For oil, copper, diamonds, power and gold

Power for whom?
Four hundred men
Singing and dancing
At the feet of the golden calf
Praying, praying just for more
Getting money, money, money
Blackwater ruling
Enron ruling
Exxon ruling
Corporate rulings
Bribery for votes
Anything for votes

People are people
Flesh and blood people
Not heartless corporations
Bleeding us dry

Four hundred men
Taking us into depravity
In their Mercedes chariots

They send us into insanity
To murder, to destroy
While the children starve
Dying on the mine fields
Orphans, from greed

Four hundred men
Tell us stories and lies
So, we will want to kill
Strangers of no harm
So they can make another buck
Another yen, a franc, a pound
Money, money, money
Killing just for money
For oil, copper, diamonds, power and gold

Killings without glory
Killings without reason
Dead in our blood-soaked rags
So four hundred men
Gain oil, copper, diamonds, power and gold

In their golden Lear jets
Filled with booze and delight
Flying high above us
Not seeing, not caring
How we live or die
The sick, the infirm
The injured, hungry children
The poor, the aged
Can all just rot?

In their golden Lear jets
They fly high above us
Not seeing, not caring
How we live or die
Four hundred men all seeking power
Money and power
Can all go to hell!

We don't need leaders
Taking us into depravity
Into insanity to murder and destroy
We don't need leaders taking us into hell

It must be a new way
It must be kindness
It must be a sit down
We can find a better way

It could be a schoolhouse
It could be a highway
It could be a new way
To the prosperity of peace
It should be children playing
It can be children playing
War an ancient nightmare
Reality must be peace!

಄಄಄

ഔ **The End** ൦

(This time, I really mean it!)

✍ *Family Tree* ☙

1833 - 2017

Solomon A. Mnuskin (Zaidy) & wife Frieda Levine (Bubby)
[aka. Zolmon Ellie Mnushkin (Zaidy) & Fradal Valevelsky (Bubby)]

**(1 son & 2 daughters, 4 grandsons, 3 granddaughters,
2 great grandsons, 6 great granddaughters)**

The Pale of Settlement - Belarus (White Russia), Russian Empire
Bubby's & Zaidy's families' ancestral home for many generations

BUBBY'S FAMILY

Drohitchin, Belarus - Bubby's birthplace (ancestral home of
paternal side of Bubby's family)

Hershel Tzyvi Reifuss (doctor) 1833-1915 **& w. Frayda** 1835-1907
(Bubby's pat. great grandparents)
Son – escaped the Tzar's army – Halifax, Nova Scotia, Canada
    Rachmiel Reifuss
    Alkonie Reifuss & w. Rachel - Halifax
        Michael (adopted)
   2 daughters
   (frat twins) - Miniver & Dave Reifuss & w. Rose- Halifax
       Shelby & h. (Sabra) – (Israel)
        2 daughters
      Marvin & w. – (Montreal)
        2 stepdaughters
  Bobba Reifuss & h. – David Aron Kaplan - Drohitchin
     Gedalia & w. Perel Piasetsky (daughter of Shmuel Yudel Piasetsky
             - the Elder of Drohitchin)
       Aaron - NYC
   Sarah
   Esther
   Chaim
   Yudel

<u>Rivkah Reifuss</u> & h.- <u>Zelig Valevelsky</u> (Bubby's pat. grandparents)
   Maitta - & h. – Drohitchin
      7 children
    Aaron & w. - Drohitchin
    Zolmon - & w. - Drohitchin

6 children (daughter Sonia in Israel)
Yenta & h. – Drohitchin
stepdaughter
Broucha - stepdaughter - Springfield, MA.

Beryl Yosski Valevelsky (Barney Levine) & 1st w. **Chaiya Bailya**
(Frieda & Hasha's **parents** – Chaiya Bailya – b. in Pinsk 1898 – 1920 d.
Drohitchin)

Hasha Valevelsky /Anna Levine 1905-1935 & h. Nathan -
Brooklyn)
Clara & h. Alan Putzer (Queens, N.Y.)
Howard & w. Paula
Adam & w. Spencer
Dana
Debra
Hunia (hun′ ia) – Drohitchin 1907 – 1920 Drohitchin
Fradal Valevelsky /Frieda Levine Mnuskin (Bubby)
1909 -2005 (named for great grandmother Frayda Reifuss)

****

Barney Levine & 2nd w. Disha Dorsky (Dora) - no children –
Brooklyn, NY (Frieda & Hasha's father & stepmother)

****

BUBBY'S FAMILY

Drohitchin, Belarus - Bubby's birthplace (ancestral home of
pat. side of Bubby's family)

ZAIDY'S FAMILY

Babruysk, Belarus - Zaidy's birthplace (mat. ancestral home/
pat. ancestral home was Hlusk)
Shima & h. Elitche Lubanoff - Kfar Tabor, Israel
10 children
girl – infant – died Hlusk
Mikhel Mnushkin (Michael Mnuskin) & 1st w. - **Sima Razel**
(Zaidy's parents)
Elka & h. Dovid Spielkoff– (Russia)
Rosa
Shura
Fanya

Laya (Lena) & husband Louie Levine
    Sylvia Rose – d. - Florida
        Carole & h. Steve
            Wendy & h. Aaron
            Noa
            Erica & h. Joshua
                Sookie Madelyn
                Eden Zoe
      Mae & h. Marvin - Florida
        Tyler & w. Leah
        Miles
        Heidi – d.
            Logan
            Morgan
Faygle & h. Reuben (Bronx, New York)
    Sima Razel
Zolmon Ellie Mnushkin/Solomon A. Mnuskin aka "**Sam**"
(Zaidy) 1905 – 1987 & w. Fradal Valevelsky/Frieda
Levine (Bubby) 1909 - 2005 - NY (married Oct. 31, 1931)
      Martin & w. Sandy   - Denver, Colorado
        Bruce & w. Jackie – Toronto, Canada
            Ryan
            Erin
        Lisa & h. Steve - Denver, Colorado
            Alexis & h. Yoni (Alexis named
                for Zaidy)
            Bridgett
        Eliott & w. Jenny - California
            Celia
            Elizabeth
      Bea & h. **Morton** - Rockland County, NY
        Lesli – d.
            Danielle
            Solomon (Solomon named for
                Zaidy)
        Evan & w. Donna
      Roslyn ("Rozzie") - d. - Westchester County, NY
        Roger
        Sonnie Elahna & h. Michael

Mikhel Mnushkin (Michael Mnuskin) & 2nd w. **Miasha** 1881 -1954
    Bronx, NY (married Babruysk, 1906)
      boy - infant - Babruysk
        Avraham Mnushkin /Abe Mnuskin & w. Dottie – Florida

Michelle & h. Henry
Melissa & h. Jae
Alexandra
Aidan
Stephanie & h. Scott
Alex
Samantha
Emily
Lynn – d.
Marc & w. Mary
Michael
Dana & h. Christopher
Alexa
Mason
Brenda & h. Jeffrey
Jessie & w. Linda
Paulette & h. Barry
Rachel & h.
Alanna
boy - infant - Babruysk
Muttel (Max) & w. Pauline - Bronx
Ronnie – (stepson)
Jerry – (stepson)
Michael

ഔ *Bibliography* ൙

Aish.com - www.aish.com
American Jewish Archives, Cincinnati, OH 45220 - www.americanjewisharchives.org
American Jewish Historical Society: www.ajhs.org
Ask Moses.com - www.askmoses.com
Ask the Rabbi - www.Chabad.org
Belarus Museum Towns: Pinsk - - www.belarusnow.net/pinsk_belarus_museum_town.html
Belarussian State University of Transport, Gomel, Belarus
B'nai B'rith, Klutznick National Jewish Museum - www.bnaibrith.org
British National Maritime Museum, Romney Road, Greenwich, London, England – www.nmm.ac.uk/
British National Maritime Museum, Romney Road, Greenwich, England
Bronx Historical Society, 3309 Bainbridge Ave., Bronx, NY
Bronx County Clerk's Office, 851 Grand Concourse, Bronx, NY
Brooklyn Historical Society, Brooklyn, NY
Armed Forces Museum, Moscow, Russia http://www.armymuseum.ru/kaz1_e.html*The Cossackdom - The History Of Cossacks,* Colonel W.V.Chereshneff, 1952
CIA World Factbookhttps://www.cia.gov/library/publications/the-world-factbook
Compton's Encyclopedia
Cossacks, Kiev - www.cossacks.kiev.ua/history.html
Cunard Steam Ship Society – www.cunardsteamshipsociety.com
Digital History.com- www.digitalhistory.uh.edu/ The Jazz Age – The American 1920s – Prohibition
Dinur Center for Research in Jewish History of the Hebrew University of Jerusalem, Israel
Ellis Island Museum, Ellis Island, New York City
Ellis Island - www.ellisisland.org/genealogy/ellis_island_history.asp
Encyclopedia Americana
Encyclopedia Britannica
Encylopaedia Judaica
Encyclopedia of Ukraine - www.encyclopediaofukraine.com/Cossacks.htm
Everyday Yiddish-English-Yiddish Dictionary - www.translationdirectory.com/dictionaries/dictionary004_a.htm
Finf Hundert Yor Yiddish Lebn – Drohiczhn"; "500 years of Jewish life - *Drohiczyn* (the Drohichyn Yizkor book) written by the survivors of Drohitchin, Edited by: Dov Warshawsky, Book Committee Drohitchin, Pub. Drohitchin Book Committee, Chicago 1958
Ford, Nancy Gentile, 2001 Americans All!: Foreign-born Soldiers in World War I Texas, pub.- Texas A&M University Press www.worldwar1.com/dbc/ngf.htm
Ford, Nancy Gentile, The Doughboy Center: article - *How America Trained Her Immigrant Army*
Gersh, Harry, *When A Jew Celebrates,* pub. Behrman House, NY, 1971

Hammond International Atlas

Harry S. Truman Presidential Library & Museum, Independence, MO
– Trumanlibrary.org

Hebrew University of Jerusalem, Library & Archive

Holocaust Museum & Study Center, Spring Valley, NY

Home of President Franklin D. Roosevelt, (Presidential Library & Museum)
- Hyde Park, NY

Israeli Ministry of Immigration Absorption, Israel - www.moia.gov.il/Moia_en

Jewish Encyclopedia

Jewishgen.org - www.jewishgen.org

Jewish Museum, Fifth Ave., NYC Jewish Museum, Fifth Ave., NYC -
- www.thejewishmuseum.org/ Jewish Museum of Maryland: www.jhsm.org

Jewish National and University Library – National Library of Israel -
http://jnul.huji.ac.il

Jewish Virtual Library - www.jewishvirtuallibrary.org

Jewish War Veterans of the United States of America - www.jwv.org

Jewish web index.com - www. jewishwebindex.com

Judah L. Magnes Museum: www.magnes.org

Judaism 101 - www.jewfaq.org

Kenney, Kim, americanhistory.suite101.com/article.cfm/prohibition,
Prohibition in the 1920s, The 18th Amendment Made Alcohol Illegal, Jan 2009

Kurth, Peter, *The Lost World of Nicholas and Alexandra Czar*, 1995, New York,
pub. Little, Brown Kushner, Jeremy, Knox, Katharine, Frank Cass, *Refugees In
An Age Of Genocide,* - 1999, Gr Britain,pub.

Library of Congress Photography collection

Lillian and Albert Small Jewish Museum:www.jhsgw.org

Memorial Book of the Community of Babruysk, and its Surroundings
    (Babruysk, Belarus), 1967, written by former residents of
    Babruysk in Israel and USA, Pub. Babruysk Yizkor Book
    Committee,Tel-Aviv, Translation from: Babruysk; sefer zikaron
    le-kehilat Babruysk u-veneteha, Edited by: Y. Slutski, -
       www.jewishgen.org/yizkor/ Babruysk /bysktoc1.html

Merseyside Maritime Museum - Liverpool, England

Museum of Art and History, Brussels, Belgium

Museum of the City of New York, Fifth Ave., NYC

Museum of Jewish Heritage-A Living Memorial to the Holocaust:
www.mjhnyc.org / Edmond J. Safra Plaza, NYC

Museum of the History of Polish Jews –
www.sztetl.org.pl/en/cms/news/1144,yad-vashem

Museum of Southern Jewish Experience: www.msje.org

National Arts Museum of the Republic Belarus, Minsk, Belarus

National Geographic - nationalgeographic.com/travel/Belarus

National Museum of American Jewish Military History, Wash, D.C.

National Museum of American Jewish History: www.nmajh.org

National Conference on Soviet Jewry (NCSJ), Washington, D.C.

National Library of Belarus, Minsk, Belarus
    www.belarus.by/en/about-belarus/architecture/national-library

National Museum of Culture and History of Belarus, Minsk, Belarus
National Park Service, US Depart. of the Interior, Wash. DC –
    www.nps.gov/hofr/index.htm
National Museum of American Jewish Military History, Wash, D.C.
New York Public Library, Lionel Pincus and Princess Firyal
    Map Division - 42nd St., NYC
New York Public Library, Miriam & Ira D. Wallach Division of Art,
    Prints and Photographs, Photography Collection, NYC
New York Public Library Center, Kingsbridge Road, Bronx, NY
New York Public Library - www.nypl.org Ocean-Liners.com -
    www.ocean-liners.com/ships/imperator.asp
Public Library of Antwerp, Antwerp, Belgium
Red Star Line Museum, Antwerp, Belgium -
    www.redstarline.be
Reeves, Pamela, *Ellis Island – Gateway to the American Dream*, pub.
    Michael Friedman Pub Group, NY, 1991
Rosten, Leo, *The Joys of Yiddish,* pub. McGraw-Hill, New York,1968
Central Armed Forces Museum, Moscow, Russia - www.cmaf.ru/
Samtur, Stephen M. and Jackson, Martin A., *The Bronx Lost, Found,*
    and Remembered 1935-1975, pub. ;Back in the Bronx Magazine, NY,
Schmemann, Serge, *Echos of A Native Land – Two Centuries of a*
    Russian Village, pub. Alfred A. Knopf, New York, 1997
Southhampton Library, Southhampton England -www.southampton.gov.uk
Southern Jewish Historical Society: www.jewishsouth.org
State Historical Museum, Moscow, Russia - www.shm.ru/
Stephen Roth Institute for the Study of Contemporary Anti-Semitism
    and Racism, Annual Report 2005, Belarus
Thomer.com - www.thomer.com/Yiddish
U.S. National Archives, Wash. DC - http://www.archives.gov/United
    States Embassy, Minsk, Belarus
United States Holocaust Memorial Museum, SW Wash., D.C.
    www.ushmm.org.
U.S. Military Records -Gov. Military Records.com
United States National Veteran's Administration
U.S. presidential-libraries - archives.gov/presidential-libraries.html Virtual
Guide to Belarus - www.belarusguide.com/main/index.html
White House Archives -   -
www.whitehousc.gov/about/presidents/lyndonbjohnson
World Atlas
The World Fact Book - www.cia.gov/library/publications/the-world
Yiddish Dictionary Online - www.yiddishdictionaryonline.com
Yiddish Dictionary Online - www.yiddishdictionaryonline.com
YIVO Institute for Jewish Research, NYC - www.yivoinstitute.org

Author, Roslyn Mnuskin Rothstein

Made in the USA
Lexington, KY
22 May 2017